Welcome to DNA DISCOVERIES

If you're curious about the stories locked within your genes you've come to the right place. This *DNA Discoveries* guide has been created to help you learn more about using DNA to discover your roots and explore your family story.

Read on to find out how DNA can help you solve family mysteries, finding unknown parents and grandparents. Learn how DNA can unlock family puzzles and help you break through family history research roadblocks. As Ancestry's Brad Argent tells us (page 8) everyone's family history is exciting if you look hard enough, each packed full of incredible stories, and DNA is the key to bringing your family's past to life.

With articles, step-by-step guides, and top tips, the ***DNA Discoveries*** guide is here to help on every stage of your DNA learning journey.

The guide will help you:

- Decide which test is best for you
- Understand what each of the DNA testing companies offers
- Learn about the science behind the tests
- Make sense of your DNA match list
- Explore your ethnicity estimates
- Start a DNA project and so much more

The majority of the guide covers autosomal DNA testing; that's the mainstream tests which many people start with. But there's coverage of Y-DNA and mtDNA tests too.

You're about to gain a wealth of knowledge about genetic genealogy, but this guide is just the beginning! Sign up for our newsletter (at **bit.ly/free-dna-course**) to register for our FREE bitesize DNA course and keep your learning going!

Helen

Helen Tovey
EDITOR
DNA Discoveries
& Family Tree
helen.t@family-tree.co.uk

Family Tree
Helping you discover your family story

Just starting your family history?

Find advice to get started at www.family-tree.co.uk/getting-started

Keep in touch with us!

enquiries@family-tree.co.uk

www.family-tree.co.uk

www.family-tree.co.uk/newsletter-sign-up

facebook.com/familytreemaguk

@familytreeplus.bsky.social

@familytreemagazine

www.youtube.com/@familytreeplus

DNA Discoveries is published by Warners Group Publications plc, publishers of ***Family Tree***, and printed by Warners (Midlands) plc, The Maltings, West Street, Bourne, Lincolnshire PE10 9PH, UK. Newstrade distribution by Warners (Midlands) plc.

ISSN 9781910525517

DNA DISCOVERIES

THE ULTIMATE FAMILY HISTORY GUIDE

CONTENTS

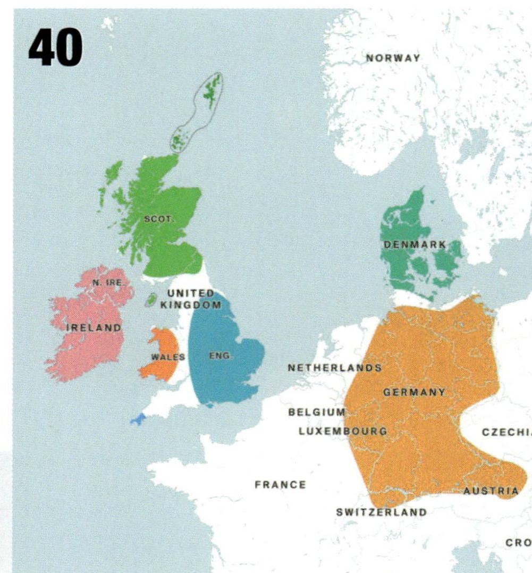

SIGN UP FOR YOUR FREE DNA COURSE SEE PAGE 34

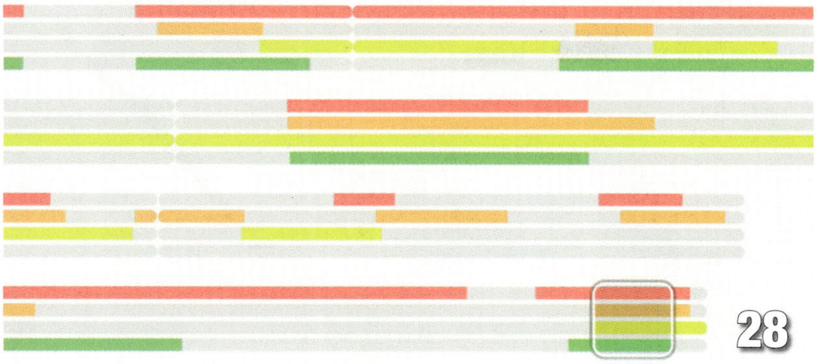

ON THE COVER

Why take a DNA test?

Taking a DNA ancestry test can transform our understanding of the past, helping you to smash brick walls, solve your family history mysteries and find long-lost relations. Read on, to learn 10 extremely useful reasons for taking a DNA test to improve your understanding of your roots.

1 Explore your genetic ancestry – to find clues the papertrail can't provide

Take your family history research to a new level, using DNA testing to complement your paper-based findings and help you to find living relatives. DNA can help you solve age-old family history puzzles in a way which traditional documents never could.

2 Break through a brick wall

Family tree brick walls which were unsolvable before the advent of DNA testing are now being solved with the help of DNA results. By finding living relatives who share your DNA, a brick wall such as a family member or ancestor with unknown parents could be solved.

3 Connect with your kin

An autosomal DNA test can be taken by both males and females, placing your details into a matching database to connect you with genetic cousins. As the generations go on, it's easy to lose touch with more distant branches. How many of us know all of our third cousins? These third cousins (with whom you share great-great-grandparents) will very likely show up in your DNA match list, as long as they have taken a DNA test with the same company. From a family history perspective, these new-found relatives may have documents and photos relating to your family tree, allowing you to help each other with your research.

4 DNA testing is simple

Taking a DNA test couldn't be simpler. Most family history tests require just a cheek swab or a sample of saliva, which you submit to the testing company, and then sit back and excitedly wait for the results (which are usually available in not a great deal more than a month or so).

How many of us know all of our third cousins? These third cousins will very likely show up in your DNA match list

5 Test now and help future researchers

The more family historians who take a DNA test, the higher the chances of everyone finding matches for their tree. The databases become larger with each person who tests, and so, even if you don't immediately solve your family history mystery, there's always the chance someone new to DNA testing will be connected to you in the future – with great results. Your DNA and your family history research may also be a great help to someone else.

6 Make sure you're on the right track

Whether you're new to tracing your ancestors, or have been building your family tree for many years, a DNA test is the perfect way to be sure that your research is rock solid and you're tracing the correct ancestors. It's all too possible for errors to creep into your family history research, whether this is on account of you accidentally confusing two people by the same name (DNA will enable you to shine a light on this issue) or whether there are unexpected parentage events.

7 Research your surname

The advances in Y-DNA testing and the growth of DNA surname projects can allow you to learn more about both your direct paternal line genetic inheritance and the origins of your surname and other surnames.

8 See your place on the world tree of humanity

If you take a Y-DNA test or an mt-DNA test with FamilyTreeDNA, for instance, you will learn your haplogroups for your direct paternal and maternal lines (note that only males can take a Y-DNA test, as females do not have a Y chromosome). Learning your haplogroup(s) will allow you to discover more about your deep ancestry and migratory history back over tens of thousands of years.

9 Follow the trail of migrant ancestors

A DNA test is a great way to see when and where your ancestors migrated over the centuries, providing information which traditional paper-based sources often can't. For example, if your ancestor migrated from the British Isles many centuries ago, there will be few records showing where they came from – whereas a DNA match may help provide a location to search for records for your ancestor.

10 DNA test affordability

DNA testing is now much more affordable than in previous years. Modern DNA tests can provide you with more information and details about your ancestry than ever before, so now is the perfect time to take the plunge and begin your DNA family history adventure.

Why do you want to take a DNA test?

Thinking about the reasons why you want to take a DNA test can be very useful in advance of testing. They can help you establish which sort of test is best for you (autosomal, Y-DNA or mt-DNA). Your time reflecting will help you work out your DNA goals too – which will help you focus your research when you get your DNA test results back. Turn to pages 88-91 for more about setting your DNA goals and deciding who to test.

An exciting journey into our past

Family Tree DNA expert Karen Evans recently spoke to Ancestry's Brad Argent, the co-presenter of ITV's *DNA Journey* to find out how he became involved in the primetime TV show, and why he believes DNA is the key to engaging more people in family history. Matt Hill reports

ITV's popular programme *DNA Journey* has a simple enough premise: a pair of celebrities both take a DNA test before their results are shared with them and the nation. But it's so much more than that, as the data reveals fascinating stories, unexpected heritage, and emotional connections to the past, and in doing so reveals just how powerful DNA can be.

Famous faces to have appeared on the show include Ant and Dec, Ricky Tomlinson and Sue Johnston, Oti and Motsi Mabuse, and Jamie Redknapp and Andrew Flintoff. Yet it is the DNA expert Brad Argent who is the star of the show, as he reveals the results and takes the celebrities on a journey back in time. So who is this Australian family history expert and how did he become a familiar face on our TV screens?

Brad reveals DNA test results to actors James Nesbitt and Sarah Parish in the fifth season of *DNA Journey* (© Voltage TV and ITV Studios)

Brad's own DNA journey

Brad's journey into the world of family history and DNA came via a banking career, and jobs in advertising and consulting, before he found his passion for genealogy and later combined this interest with an opportunity at Ancestry's new Australian office. 'I thought, you never get a job that's a hobby,' Brad says, 'but you've got to give it a shot, and it was just the right place at the right time.'

After holding various roles within the company, about eight years ago Brad was given the unusual brief: 'find out how to make television,' a mission he accepted and that ultimately led to the development of the ITV programme *DNA Journey*.

The innovative show became a passion project for Brad, combining his growing expertise in genealogy with the art of storytelling. He fondly recalls working with Ant and Dec on the first episode, first broadcast in 2019. 'What you see on telly is exactly who they are… they are just genuinely lovely people.'

Confirmation story? Or transformation story?

For Brad, the appeal of that first episode, and the subsequent work with other celebrities, is not only the opportunity to share personal, emotional stories, but to focus on the deeper discoveries DNA testing can reveal. Indeed, Brad believes this approach can be used to make our own family history more engaging to others. 'Think about your audience… who are they and what do they want to know?' He advises. 'And it falls into one of two categories: we either tell them a confirmation story – you thought you were this and here's the evidence to prove it – or a transformation story – you think you're Irish but you're actually Scottish.'

Rather than taking the traditional route and going back 'up' the family tree, *DNA Journey* has a more flexible, 'widescreen' approach, reflecting the far-reaching nature of DNA testing. 'We will jump to the left or the right if that's where the story takes us…' Brad says. This format reflects Brad's belief that family history is so much more than a collection of names and dates. As readers will no doubt agree, it's all about storytelling, social context, and the fascinating insights that can come from exploring seemingly ordinary lives.

'The juicy stories are there!'

Indeed, the happy problem Brad and the show's producers often face is working out which stories to include and which to leave out. 'We've never turned down anyone,' Brad tells us. 'We've had people on the show who didn't work for *Who Do You Think You Are?* because the stories weren't rich enough, or didn't fit within their universe, but that's the thing, there's always a story.'

'People say, my family history's a bit boring. What!? Maybe you need to look a little bit harder. Step to the left, step to the right. What did those great aunts and uncles get up to? What did their children get up to? The juicy stories are there!'

By combining the wealth of information that DNA testing

provides with the social context of our ancestors' lives, we can all uncover intriguing stories. It's a simple approach but one that we can often forget as we scan the information on the census records. As Brad says, family history should be 'storytelling rather than just fact gathering… Did they witness a coronation? Did they live through a war?'

Extraordinary stories revealed on *DNA Journey* include actor John Simm's discovery that the man he thought was his father was not his biological parent, 'It's spun my world… everything I thought I knew wasn't real,' he remarks during the emotional episode.

In Ant and Dec's two-part series, the inseparable duo find out they are distant cousins; in a later series comedian Tom Allen discovers he's related to presenter Gloria Hunniford; and actor Ricky Tomlinson is taken aback by his connection to pioneering American journalist Jane Cunningham who wrote about women's rights in the 19th century.

According to Brad, sharing these remarkable tales is often a case of drip-feeding the information and learning from the celebrity's reaction. 'Sometimes less is more,' he says. 'Start giving them little bits, and you literally see them lean in to the story as they want to know more.'

How to prepare for life-changing revelations

Of course, revealing stories can be an emotional experience, as John Simm's episode reveals. So how should researchers approach or prepare for this type of life-changing revelation? 'The first thing I do when looking at someone's results is check if they match expectations,' Brad says. 'Are there any matches that don't make sense? Sometimes it's very obvious when there's a sibling match and they said they don't have any siblings, or when there's a clear non-paternal event in the DNA.'

'If I find something unexpected, I look to see what the impact is – how recent was it? If it directly impacts someone who is still alive, like if a parent or grandparent is not who they thought, then that's significant. We usually contact the person and say, "Your results are back, and we've uncovered something we weren't expecting." Of course, we always tell them before they take the test that surprises are possible – but no one ever thinks it's going to happen to them'.

With the information confirmed Brad's team ensure the person has the support of a family member or advisor when discovering the information, and always ask whether they want to know more. 'We seek consent at every step… One fact could change their entire outlook, so we step them through it carefully,' he says. 'It's all about listening, giving space, and remembering the privilege you have when telling someone something they didn't know about themselves. You're creating a core memory for them, and that's an enormous responsibility.'

Which DNA tool does Brad recommend?

Brad's day job of working for Ancestry means he has a vast experience of the tools and information available via the ancestry.com website. So which tool would he recommend above all others?

British actors John Simm and Phil Glenister appeared in the fifth series of *DNA Journey*. The emotional episode saw John discover that the man he thought was his father was not his biological parent (© Voltage TV and ITV Studios)

'It's got to be the matches,' he explains. 'The ability for matches to help with brick walls. You know, I've broken through some of my own brick walls just by matching with cousins I've had in America that I had no idea existed, because why would my family go to America? But they did.'

'For me, that's the big unlock. Sure, it's an unlock from a family history point of view, I understand that. And I think intellectually, we all know we're related. But the ability to be able to show that scientifically through a genetic genealogy process, it makes the world a smaller place. And I think that's a good thing.'

Brad's career and dedication to genealogical storytelling have not only influenced his own life but have made family history more accessible and captivating for audiences around the world, no doubt convincing thousands of people to embark on their own DNA journey.

Video interview: Karen Evans | Written report: Matt Hill

Watch Karen's full interview with Brad at: www.youtube.com/@familytreeplus

How to approach unexpected DNA results

- Check for unexpected results before revealing anything
- Assess the impact (recent vs. distant family connections)
- Communicate with sensitivity, offering support resources
- Seek consent at every step, allowing people to process the news at their own pace
- Recognise the emotional weight of revealing life-changing information
- Follow up to provide ongoing support

What can each DNA company's tests do for you?

Understanding the unique strengths and features of each DNA testing company is essential for anyone looking to explore their family history through autosomal DNA testing. In this in-depth guide **Michelle Leonard** compares the four major autosomal DNA testing companies – Ancestry, 23andMe, MyHeritage, and FTDNA – on a feature-by-feature basis, giving you all you need to choose the right test

Ancestry's Ancestral Regions' provide percentage breakdowns, while 'Ancestral Journeys' pinpoint more granular locations and both can be studied via the 'Origins' section on the DNA summary page

ancestryDNA

Database Size:

This is a crucial consideration because the larger the database, the more matches you receive, increasing your chances of success in using DNA for family history purposes. Ancestry has by far the largest database of all the testing companies, with over 27 million testers, making it essential to test there to maximise your chances, especially if you have mysteries to solve.

Ethnicity Estimate:

Autosomal tests consist of two principal features: ethnicity estimates and DNA match lists. Ethnicity estimates provide percentage overviews of the global regions from where your ancestry originates. However, while they are the most well-known and advertised aspect of autosomal tests, it is the DNA match lists that are the most valuable for genealogy.

TIP! It's important not to take ethnicity estimates too literally and to remember that they will differ between companies because each has its own reference populations and algorithms

Companies also periodically update and refine their estimates (generally once a year at Ancestry), so they are prone to change over time as technology improves and reference sets grow.

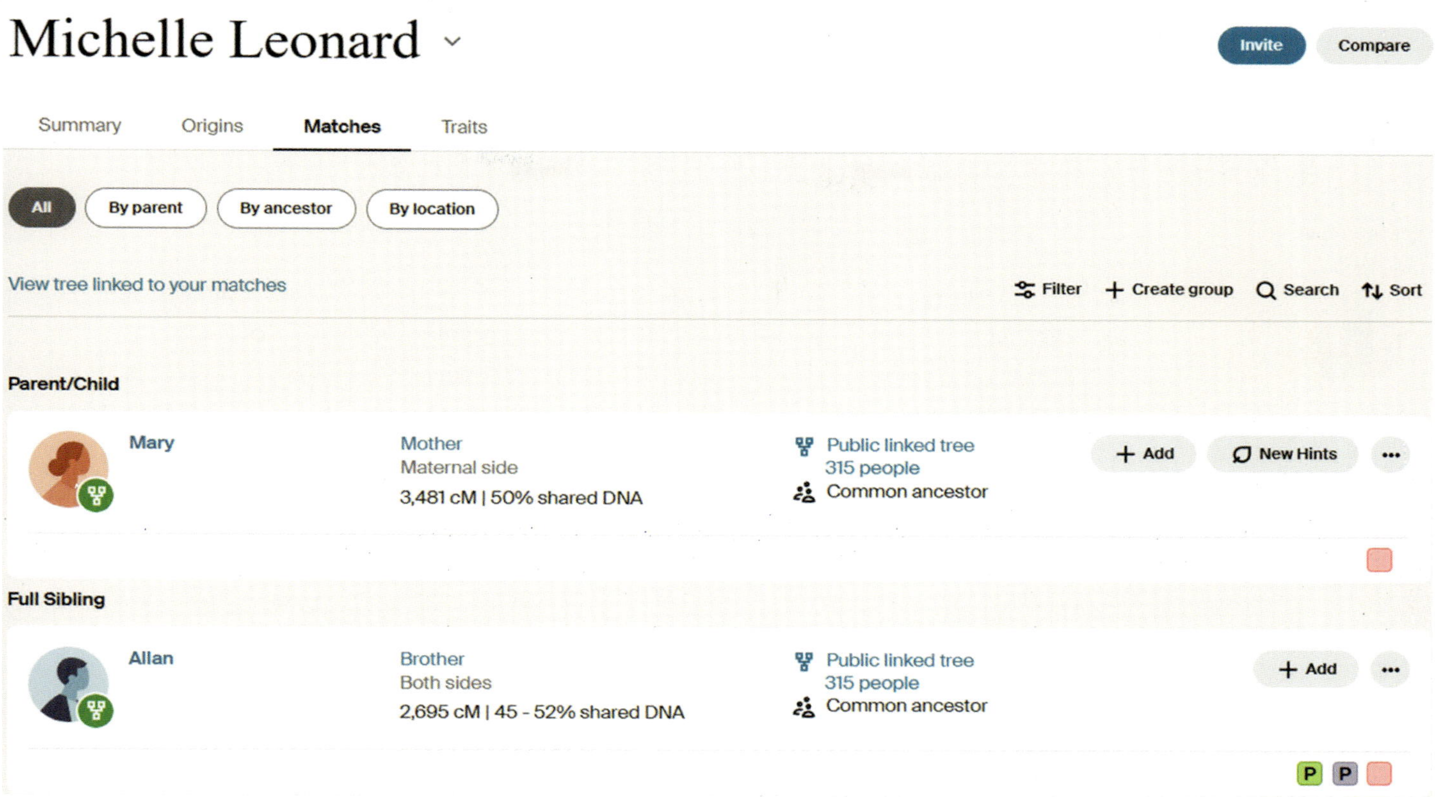

Make use of the filtering and searching options when studying your DNA matches; Michelle especially recommends using the 'Unviewed matches' filter to see your best new matches

Ancestry's ethnicity offering currently comprises over 2,600 global 'Ancestral Regions' and is bundled with their innovative 'Ancestral Journeys' (previously known as 'Genetic Communities'). The latter are identifiable by dotted line circles and pinpoint ancestry within a realistic genealogical timeframe of 50-300 years, unlike the broader 500-1000 provided by the ancestral region percentages. The 'Ancestral Journeys' are impressively accurate e.g. I have many matches with Ulster-based ancestors on their trees, so I've been placed in the 'Ulster' Ancestral Journey suggesting it's likely I also have Ulster ancestors. It even drills down to specific Ulster regions in the form of 'Central Ulster' and 'North Central Ulster' and I do indeed have ancestors from those areas.

DNA Match List:

This is by far the most important feature of a DNA test for genealogy purposes. It lists all other testers in the company's database with whom you share DNA, arranged from the closest to the most distant relatives. Ancestry's match list layout is clear and offers the best organisational tools across all the sites, with the option to cluster matches into colour-coded groups and the ability to link your DNA test to a family tree. The filtering and searching options are also very useful; you can filter by 'Common Ancestors,' 'Notes,' 'Trees,' 'Shared DNA,' 'Groups,' 'Journeys,' and I especially recommend using the 'Unviewed matches' filter to see your best new matches. Additionally, you can search by username, ancestral surname, and location. You can also add notes to each match to keep track of your research, and these notes are visible on the main match list and individual match pages.

Shared Matches:

The shared match list is a vital tool that often proves key to successfully identifying connections. Ancestry's standard shared match lists are extremely helpful. However, they only include matches who share over 20 cM with both the tester and the comparison match, and do not display how much DNA the comparison match and shared matches share with each other. Previously, to obtain that information, the comparison match would need to personally provide it or invite you to their results, but the launch of the Pro Tools subscription is a game-changer. A Pro Tools subscription includes access to the 'Enhanced Shared Matches' feature, which does display the amount of DNA the shared matches share with the comparison match. Note that with 'Enhanced Shared Matches,' you will see matches that match the test-taker down to Ancestry's threshold of 8 cM, but they still need to share 20 cM or more with the comparison match to be on the list. The ability to sort by those who share the most with the comparison match is also extremely helpful.

Trees:

Access to match trees and the ability to create your own shareable tree are important features. Ancestry is a leader in

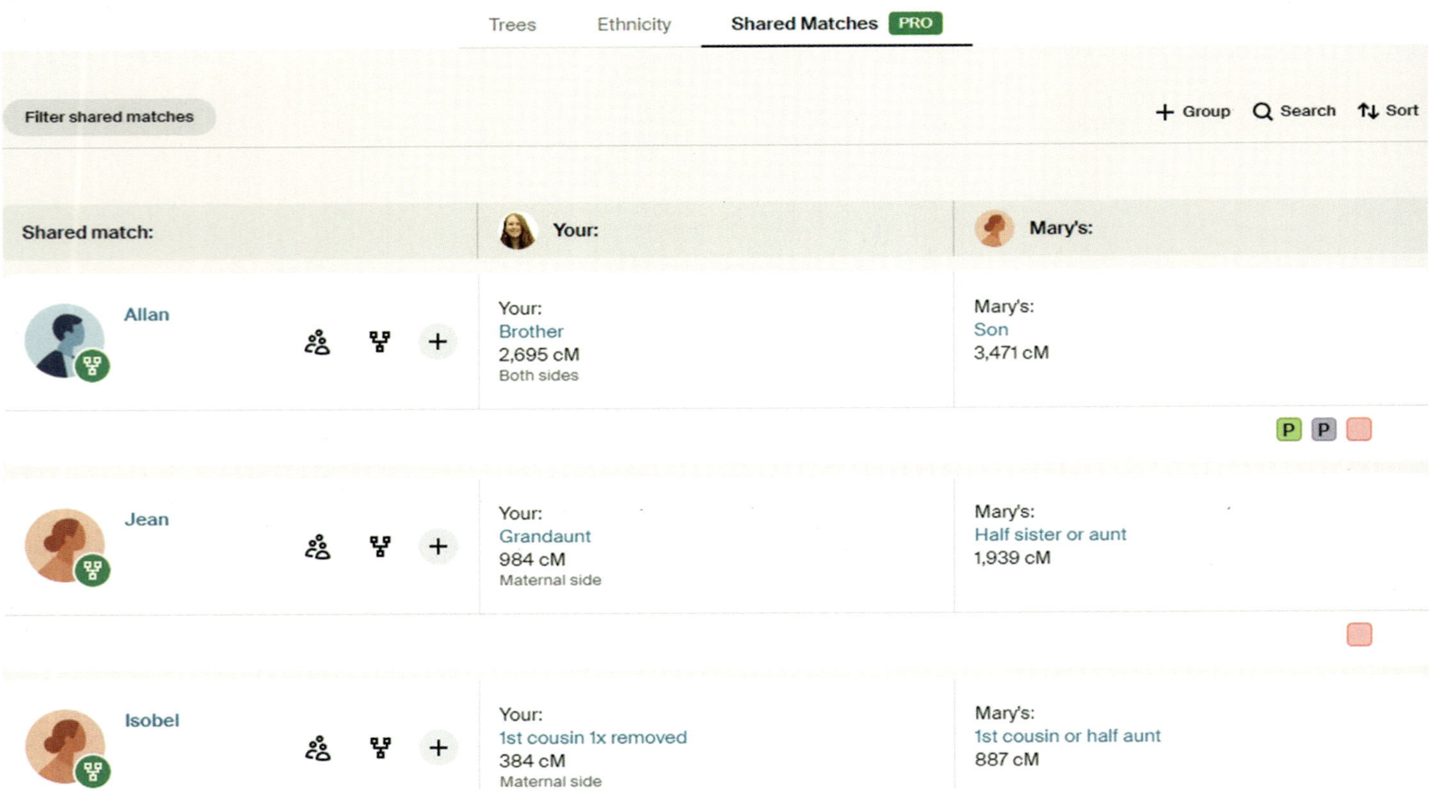

Ancestry's 'Enhanced Shared Matches' is a Pro Tools feature that displays the amount of DNA the shared matches share with the comparison match

terms of family tree provision and tree-building tools, which is a strong advantage for them. It is important to note that, while free accounts will be able to see a DNA match has a family tree and view its size, access to these trees requires an Ancestry membership. However, whether your matches create or attach trees to their results is an individual choice, so the number of trees available to work with will vary depending on your personal matches.

TIP! Make sure you link a tree to your results and ensure it is a useful tree with all your direct ancestors on it, as you can only link one tree

Chromosome Browser:

These are visual tools used to compare matches and display the chromosome locations of shared DNA segments. Ancestry does not provide a chromosome browser for privacy reasons. This lack of segment data is one of the few drawbacks of the site. If you want to use websites like DNA Painter, it is not possible to do so with Ancestry matches unless their results are uploaded to a platform that provides segment data, such as FTDNA, MyHeritage, or GEDmatch.

Raw Data Transfers:

Some major DNA testing companies allow free uploads of results from competitor companies, but Ancestry does not; therefore, you must test directly to be included in their database. However, you can download Ancestry raw data to upload elsewhere.

Additional DNA Tools:

Ancestry offer an array of additional tools and features, including 'SideView' (By Parent), 'ThruLines', 'Common Ancestor Hints', highlighted shared surnames and ancestor birthplaces for linked trees, predicted relationships, frequency of relationships probability charts (similar to DNA Painter's Shared cM Project tool), and the 'Edit Relationship' and 'Connect to Tree' organisational tools.

Additionally, the 'Compare with Matches' tool allows users to compare 'Regions,' 'Journeys,' and 'Traits' with up to ten matches at a time, and there's the option to invite others to view, collaborate, or manage DNA results.

Among these, SideView stands out as one of Ancestry's flagship features, uniquely capable of dividing both ethnicity inheritance and DNA matches into 'Parent 1' and 'Parent 2' categories without a parent needing to test. Another key tool is ThruLines, which leverages Ancestry's extensive tree database to suggest probable common ancestors. However, while ThruLines can provide valuable insights, it's crucial to thoroughly verify these connections before accepting them as fact. Finally, 'Matches By Cluster' is a new tool announced at RootsTech 2025 which will provide similar functionality to MyHeritage's AutoClusters.

Many of these features require either an Ancestry family history membership or AncestryDNAPlus membership.

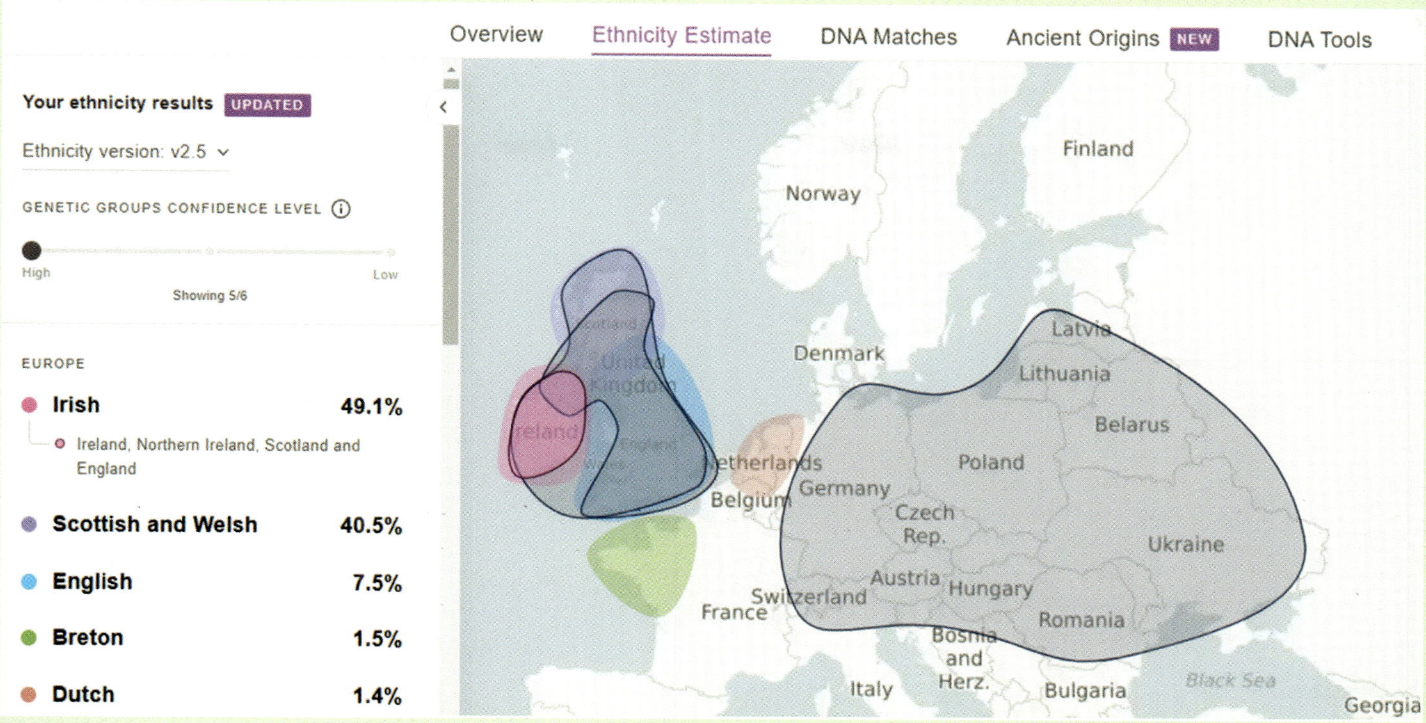

MyHeritage's ethnicity estimates encompass 79 top-level ethnicities and include the 'Genetic Groups' feature covering over 2,100 geographic regions

MyHeritage DNA

Database Size:
MyHeritage boasts a rapidly growing database with over 9.1 million DNA testers. They actively advertise in multiple languages, supporting 42 different languages on their website, and this contributes to their large and diverse European and international customer base. As a result, users can expect to find a broader range of matches within the MyHeritage database.

Ethnicity Estimate:
MyHeritage's ethnicity estimates encompass 79 top-level ethnicities and include the 'Genetic Groups' feature, which is comparable to Ancestry's 'Ancestral Journeys,' covering over 2,100 geographic regions. However, while 'Genetic Groups' offer a broad overview, they don't provide the same level of granularity as Ancestry's tool and may not be as useful for pinpointing very specific ancestral origins. A unique aspect of MyHeritage is their engaging video that introduces testers to their ethnicity estimate in a fun and interactive way.

DNA Match List:
MyHeritage's match list is impressively detailed, featuring excellent 'DNA Match Quality' information as well as a variety of useful filters and often including valuable details such as match age and country information. The platform also excels in organisational capabilities, offering 30 colour-coding labels and a notes facility to help manage and categorise matches effectively. However, it does fall short in search capabilities as it lacks the ability to search by ancestral location.

Shared Matches:
MyHeritage's shared match list is highly detailed, displaying every shared match, including low-level ones. Caution is advised with these low-level matches, however, as they are prone to anomalies, red herrings and false matching. The list not only shows the amount of DNA the test-taker shares with each shared match but also the amount shared between the comparison match and the shared matches. This comprehensive detail is comparable only to Ancestry's 'Enhanced Shared Matches' and 23andMe's 'Relatives In Common' lists. Additionally, it includes 'automated triangulated segment' icons and the 'Sort By' function enhances user experience by allowing the shared match list to be organised by the amount of DNA shared with the comparison match.

Trees:
MyHeritage, like Ancestry, has a significant advantage in tree-building capabilities, as it is also a market-leading traditional genealogy website with long-established tree-building tools. As a result, you will find more trees attached to DNA results on these two sites compared to others.

Chromosome Browser:
MyHeritage offer detailed segment data via one-to-one and one-to-many chromosome browsers, segment data tables and automated triangulated segments. The only downside is that X-chromosome DNA data is not included.

Raw Data Transfers:
MyHeritage accept transfers from Ancestry, FTDNA, and

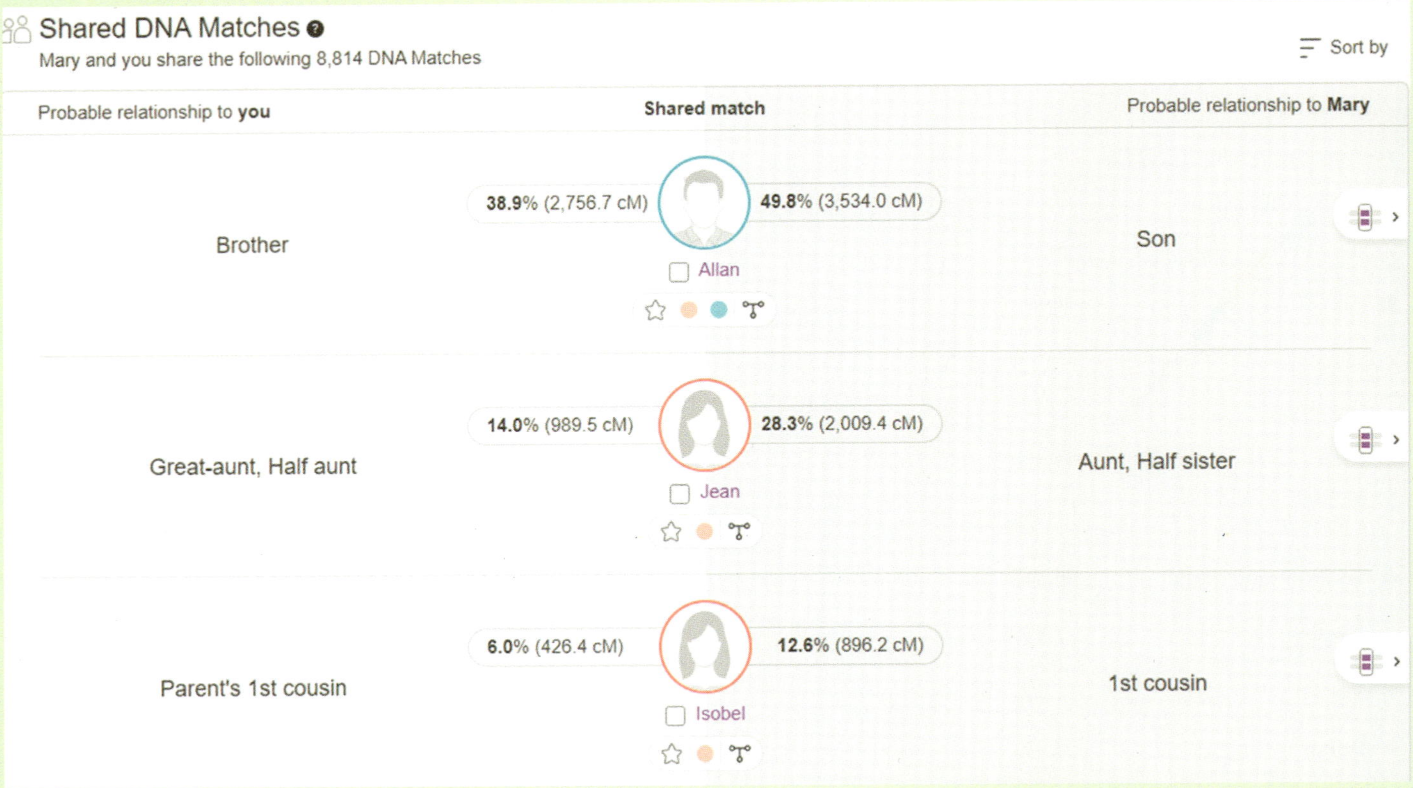

MyHeritage's shared match lists display the amount of DNA both the test-taker and the comparison match share with the shared matches

23andMe. Match lists are freely provided but a subscription or unlock fee (£35) is required for full access to shared matches, trees and other tools. Be aware, though, that if you test directly with MyHeritage, it's only possible to access these features via a subscription.

Additional DNA Tools: MyHeritage has a wide array of additional features such as 'Theory of Family Relativity' (like Ancestry's Common Ancestor Hints), Smart Matches, shared ancestral surnames and places, cM Explainer (probability tool) and the option to share DNA results with a collaborator. Additionally, MyHeritage offers an automated clustering tool, AutoClusters, which organises matches into shared match clusters within which the matches are likely to descend from the same common ancestral line. MyHeritage has also launched the entertaining Ancient Origins, which analyses your DNA to see which past populations you have descended from (such as Imperial Romans, Norse Vikings, Phoenicians, and Ancient Egyptians).

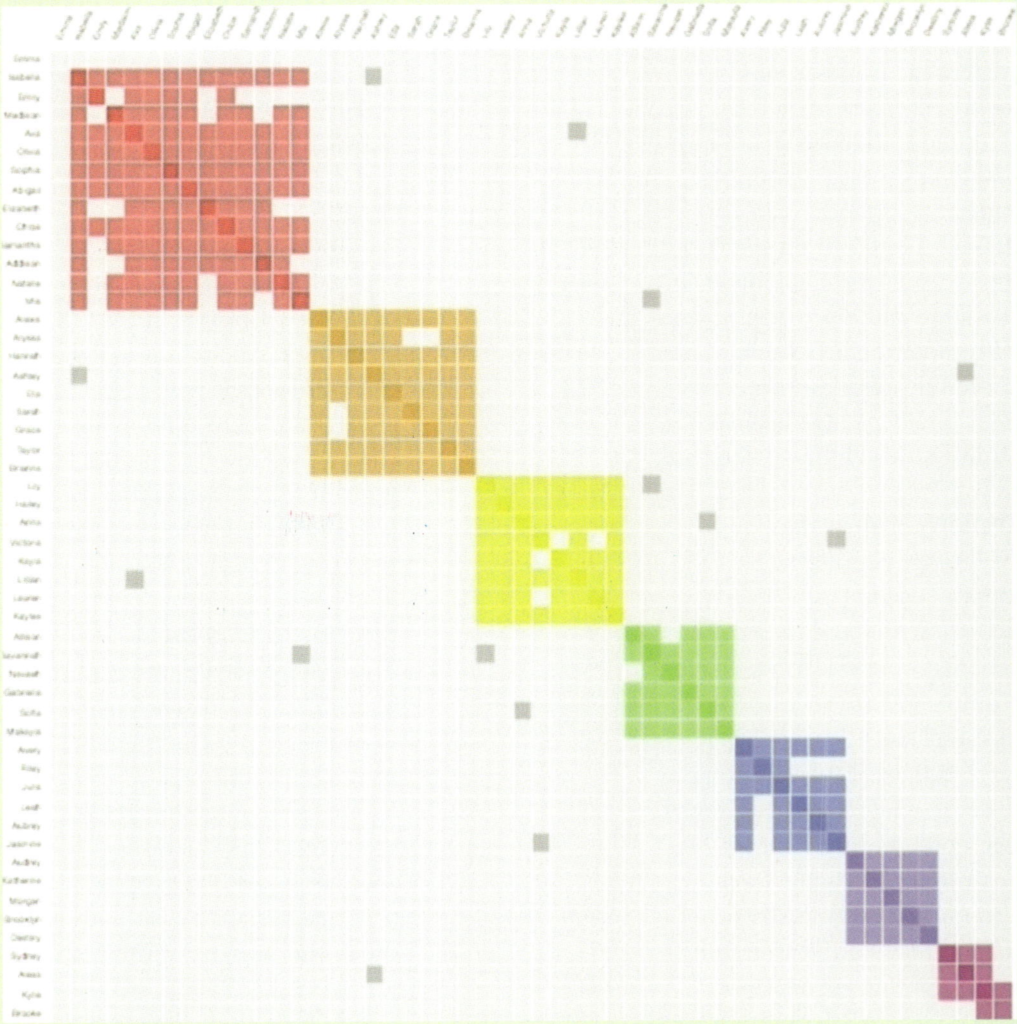

MyHeritage offers an automated clustering tool (developed in collaboration with Evert-Jan Blom)

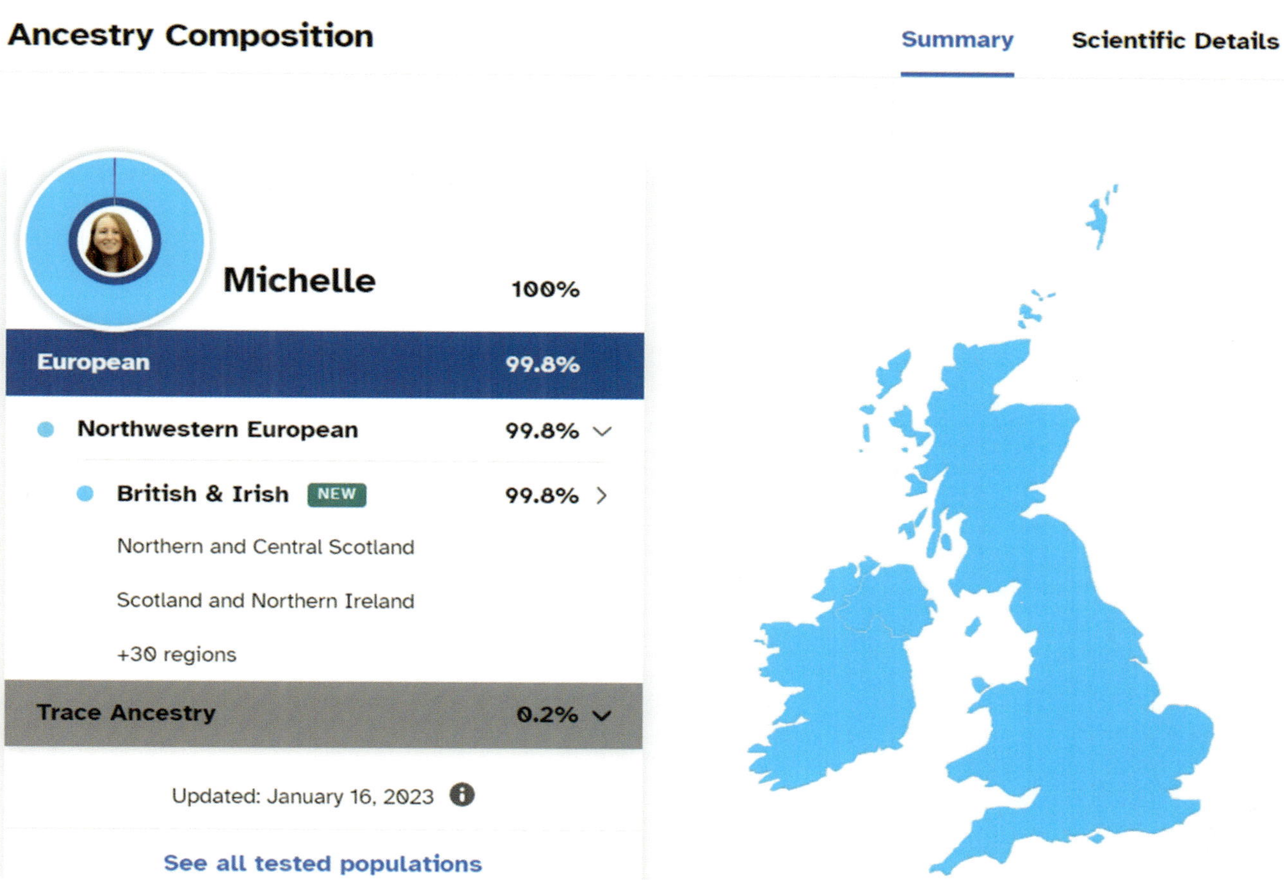

23andMe's Ancestry Composition provides ethnicity estimate information

23andMe®

Database Size:

23andMe's database, with over 15 million testers, is the second largest and should not be overlooked. However, it's important to note that many users test primarily for health insights, and some choose to opt out of the matching database.

Ethnicity Estimate:

23andMe's 'Ancestry Composition' provides a percentage-based breakdown using 47 regional populations. It also assigns 'genetic groups' and 'country matches' from a comprehensive list of over 2,000 possibilities. It also includes several unique features, such as the 'Ancestry Timeline,' which predicts the historical periods when your ancestors lived in particular regions. The 'Parental Inheritance' feature offers a detailed breakdown of the ethnicity percentages inherited from each parent, provided at least one has tested. Additionally, the 'Ancestry Composition Chromosome Painting' feature visually chromosome maps DNA segments by ethnicity, providing valuable insights for those with diverse backgrounds but may be less informative for individuals whose ancestry is concentrated in similar regions.

DNA Match List:

23andMe's DNA match list is capped at the closest 1,500 matches for standard users and 5,000 for 23andMe Plus subscribers. Despite this limitation, the layout is user-friendly, and the search and filtering capabilities are robust, allowing an unlimited number of filters to be applied simultaneously. Users can search by match name, ancestral surname, and location. For 23andMe Plus subscribers, 'Advanced Filters' include options like ancestry composition, haplogroup, and last active. The amount of shared DNA with matches is displayed as a percentage on both the main match list and individual match pages, rather than in centiMorgans (cMs). 23andMe does not currently provide cM values anywhere on the site. A notable feature on 23andMe is the ability to filter matches by parental side—'mother's side' or 'father's side'—if at least one parent has tested. Users can 'favourite' matches of interest, but this basic function does not offer the same level of organisational capability as the colour-coding features on Ancestry and MyHeritage.

Shared Matches:

23andMe's shared match list, known as 'Relatives In Common,' is very informative but has lost some functionality in recent times. It currently displays shared matches in percentage format down to around 0.2%

You have Relatives in Common

Each Relative in Common shares at least one small segment of DNA with Mary.

Relative in common	You	Mary
AL Allan	Brother (49.73)	Son (49.99)
AP Andrea	3rd Cousin, Once Removed (1.43)	2nd Cousin, Once Removed (2.20)
JP Jack	3rd Cousin (1.08)	3rd Cousin (1.68)
Elizabeth	3rd Cousin (0.93)	2nd Cousin (2.77)
Rusty	3rd Cousin, Once Removed (0.90)	2nd Cousin, Once Removed (1.46)
CT Cara	3rd Cousin (0.88)	3rd Cousin (1.42)

The shared match list on 23andMe is known as 'Relatives in Common' and displays how much DNA the tester shares with both the comparison match and shared matches in percentage format

(15 cM) shared meaning some lower-level matches are included, but the smallest matches have been excluded. It also provides the amount of DNA shared with both the tester and the comparison match. This means it offers a level of detail comparable to Ancestry's 'Enhanced Shared Matches' and MyHeritage's shared match list.

Trees:
23andMe does not currently support the creation of traditional shared family trees, which represents a significant drawback for the platform, as sharing family history information is vital to working out connections. While users can add external links to trees hosted on other sites and basic information such as grandparental birthplaces and ancestral surnames in the 'Family Background' section of their profile, these fields are often left incomplete. 23andMe offer an automated 'Family Tree' feature that attempts to predict genetic family trees and places matches into a manually editable tree but, while a step in the right direction, this falls short of providing a comprehensive solution to the tree-building limitation. The automated tree can be shared with up to five people, but it is generally best to share a link to a tree on another platform.

Chromosome Browser:
Until the credential-stuffing incident in October 2023, which led to a breach of 23andMe's database, the site offered the most detailed segment data and comprehensive one-to-one and one-to-many chromosome browsers among DNA testing sites. Unfortunately, these features have been disabled since that time, and there is currently no indication of when or if they will be reinstated.

Raw Data Transfers:
23andMe, like Ancestry, do not offer the facility to upload raw data from tests taken elsewhere so you must test direct, but they allow 23andMe raw data to be downloaded.

Additional DNA Tools:
23andMe offer several notable features, including maternal and paternal haplogroup designations and the Neanderthal Ancestry report, which is entertaining. Haplogroups trace the ancient origins of an individual's direct paternal and maternal lines. It's important to note that women will only receive a paternal haplogroup designation if a close male relative has also tested at 23andMe, as this is based on the Y-chromosome, which women do not inherit. However, these should not be confused with the standalone Y-DNA and mitochondrial DNA tests offered by FamilyTreeDNA, which, in addition to haplogroup designations, include access to matching databases.

Note: 23andMe has experienced difficulties since October 2023, as mentioned above, and news of the company continues to be reported in the mainstream press.

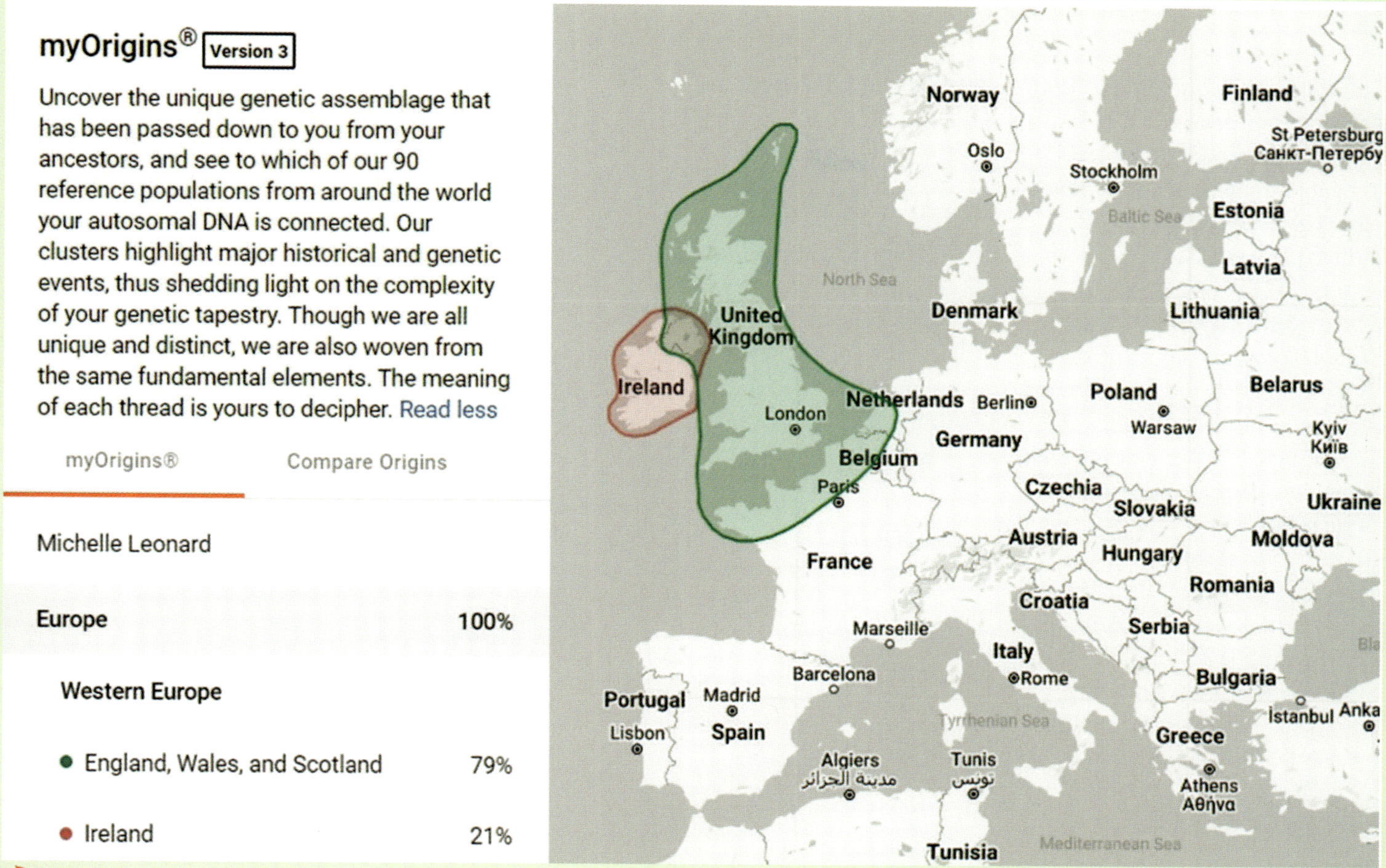

FTDNA's Ethnicity Estimates provide relatively broad information, for instance England, Wales and Scotland are reported on as a single percentage and not broken out

FamilyTreeDNA

Database Size:

FamilyTreeDNA (FTDNA) hosts the smallest autosomal DNA database among these four major providers with an estimated 1.6 million testers. This significantly smaller database size is a notable disadvantage for those considering testing with FTDNA.

Ethnicity Estimate: FTDNA's ethnicity estimates, offered through 'myOrigins' version 3, are derived from 90 reference populations, which are relatively broad (e.g. England, Wales, and Scotland are not broken out separately). Additionally, their 'AncientOrigins' feature provides percentage estimates for hunter-gatherer, Metal Age invader, and farmer populations. While the latter insights are interesting and enjoyable to explore, they should be approached with a light-hearted perspective and not taken too seriously.

DNA Match List:

FTDNA's match list is detailed and somewhat busy, as all pertinent details and features are consolidated onto a single page, unlike other sites that typically separate them into a main match list and individual match comparison pages. The platform offers several helpful filtering, sorting, and searching options, though it lacks the ability to search by location.

Shared Matches:

FTDNA's shared match list, 'In Common With,' functions similarly to Ancestry's standard shared match list, showing how much DNA the tester shares with both the comparison match and shared matches, but not how much DNA the comparison match and shared matches share with each other, although it is now possible to access this information via 'The Matrix' tool. However, unlike Ancestry, FTDNA does not impose a threshold, so all shared matches are displayed. Additionally, FTDNA offer a unique 'Not In Common With' list, which displays matches who do not share DNA with the comparison match. This can be used to help narrow down connections from a different angle.

Trees:

Until recently, FTDNA provided its own family tree builder tool, but this was retired and made read-only on 9th September 2024. To enhance user experience, FTDNA has strengthened its partnership with MyHeritage, allowing FTDNA testers to link their trees to MyHeritage for free to access advanced tree-building tools. Users can transfer their FTDNA trees to MyHeritage if they don't already have a tree on that platform. This integration offers improved tree features and leverages MyHeritage's robust tree-building capabilities alongside FTDNA's DNA testing focus. While there is a higher likelihood of finding matches with linked trees on FTDNA due to its focus on ancestral DNA testing, there are still fewer trees compared to dedicated traditional genealogy sites such as Ancestry and MyHeritage.

Chromosome Browser: FTDNA provide comprehensive DNA segment data via a combined one-to-one and one-to-many chromosome browser allowing users to compare up to seven matches simultaneously. The browser provides a visual chromosome view, detailed segment data tables, and includes X-chromosome data. This is a unique selling point for FTDNA, as it is currently the only major DNA testing site that provides X-DNA data.

Raw Data Transfers: FTDNA accepts raw data transfers from Ancestry, regardless of the test date, from 23andMe (V3, V4 and V5), and MyHeritage for results processed after 1st March 2019. Basic features, such as match lists and shared match lists, are available for free. However, access to additional features, including the chromosome browser and the 'myOrigins' ethnicity estimate, requires a small unlock fee of $19.

Additional DNA Tools: FTDNA offer a variety of additional tools to enhance DNA analysis. These include the 'Matrix' tool, which can compare up to 10 matches and displays the amount of DNA they share with each other, as well as the Advanced Matches tool, which allows users to search for matches who match them across multiple types of DNA tests, such as Y-DNA, mtDNA, and Family Finder. They also provide the 'Linked Relationships' tool, which, when used to link DNA matches to family trees, automatically populates maternal, paternal and both buckets to help organise matches by parental side.

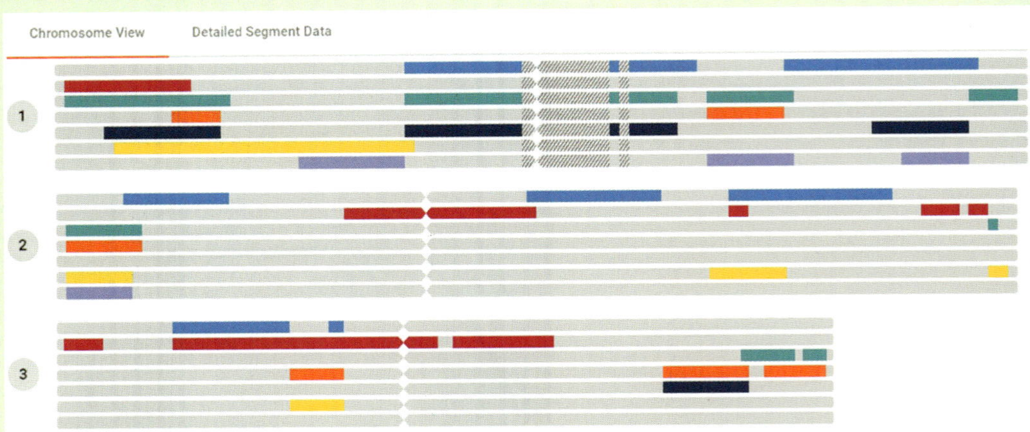

FTDNA's chromosome browser allows you to compare up to seven matches simultaneously (denoted by the seven colours in the example above). Note only 3 of the 23 chromosomes are displayed in this example

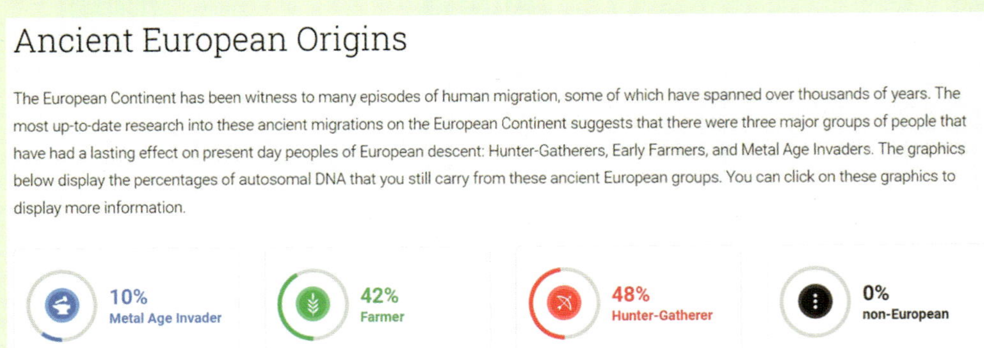

FTDNA's Ancient European Origins should be approached with a light-hearted outlook

Total cMs shared

	Veronica	Marion	David	Mary E	Ann	Michael	Agnes
Veronica		0 cM	0 cM	442 cM	659 cM	359 cM	244 cM
Marion	0 cM		33 cM	250 cM	258 cM	188 cM	0 cM
David	0 cM	33 cM		82 cM	46 cM	164 cM	0 cM
Mary E	442 cM	250 cM	82 cM		1034 cM	2739 cM	232 cM
Ann	659 cM	258 cM	46 cM	1034 cM		940 cM	157 cM
Michael	359 cM	188 cM	164 cM	2739 cM	940 cM		162 cM
Agnes	244 cM	0 cM	0 cM	232 cM	157 cM	162 cM	

FTDNA's 'Matrix' tool checks whether a group of matches match each other and provides the amount of DNA they share

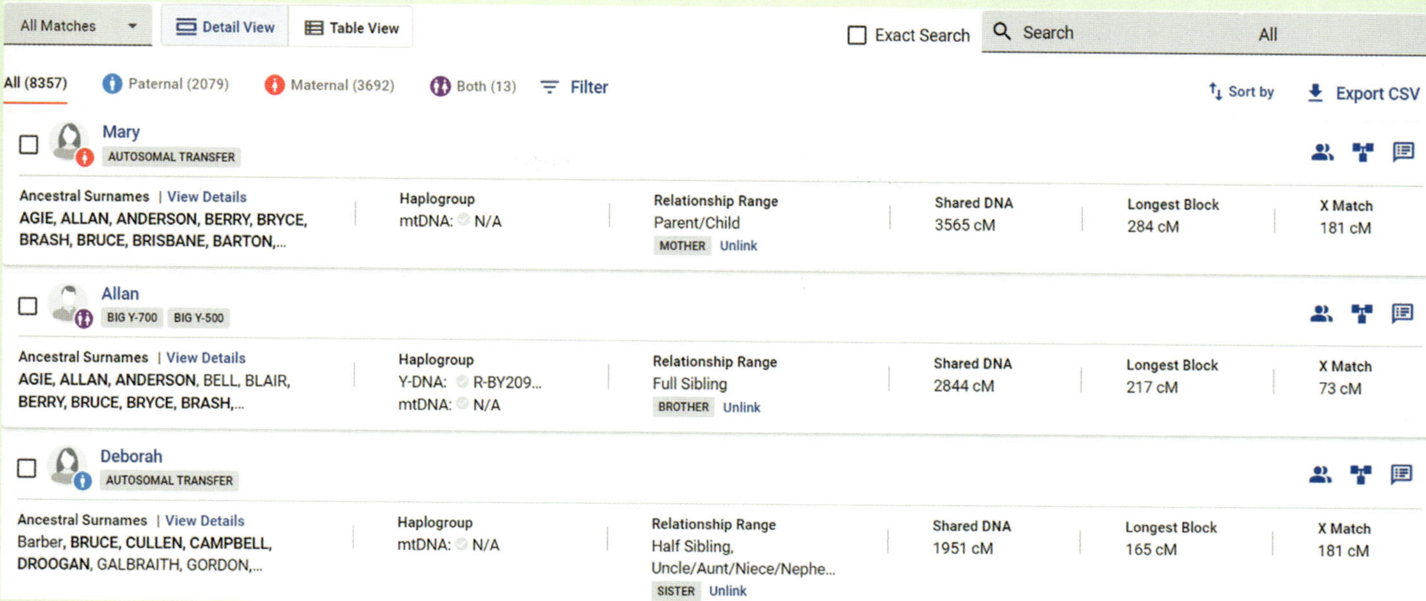

FTDNA's match list is very detailed as all features are consolidated onto a single page

Unique Selling Points:
FTDNA's most distinctive feature is that it is the only company to offer comprehensive Y-chromosome and mitochondrial DNA tests that include matching databases. Additionally, FTDNA supports over 12,000 volunteerled surname, haplogroup, and geographic projects, positioning the company at the forefront of genetic genealogy as a form of citizen science.

Additional considerations

Sample Collection Method:
Ancestry and 23andMe require a saliva sample for DNA testing, while MyHeritage and FTDNA use cheek swabs. Both methods are quick and simple; however, cheek swabs are often more convenient for elderly individuals or those who have difficulty producing saliva due to medical conditions.

Contacting Matches:
Ancestry, 23andMe, and MyHeritage all provide on-site messaging systems to facilitate contact with DNA matches. In contrast, FTDNA provides the email addresses of matches, allowing direct communication.

LivingDNA:
The fifth major DNA testing company, UK-based LivingDNA, offers detailed regional ethnicity breakdowns, Y-DNA and mtDNA haplogroup designations, and a matching database. However, its database is still relatively small, with around 300,000 users as of January 2021, and it lacks a family trees facility. Several new tools have been added in recent years, however, such as a chromosome browser and the 'Matchbox' colour-coding feature.

Conclusion:
My mantra for maximizing your chances of success in genetic genealogy is to 'fish in all the ponds'. This means participating in every available DNA database, as each one offers unique matches and features that can help you achieve your research goals. While each company has its own strengths and some limitations, all continue to innovate, providing new tools and resources to assist us on our DNA and family history journeys.

Further reading
Michelle Leonard is author of the *DNA Bootcamp Workbook* published by Family Tree (RRP £20; £12 for Family Tree subscribers and/or members of Family Tree Plus. **bit.ly/dna-wbook**) and co-author of *DNA: A Guide for Family Historians* published by Pen & Sword (RRP £16.99, see page 33 for more details of the revised edition and how to claim your exclusive 35% discount offer).

DNA unzipped

THE SCIENCE BEHIND YOUR DNA TEST

Knowing the science behind your DNA test can be very useful for understanding how to use your results. Dr Sophie Kay is here to help you master the foundation knowledge.

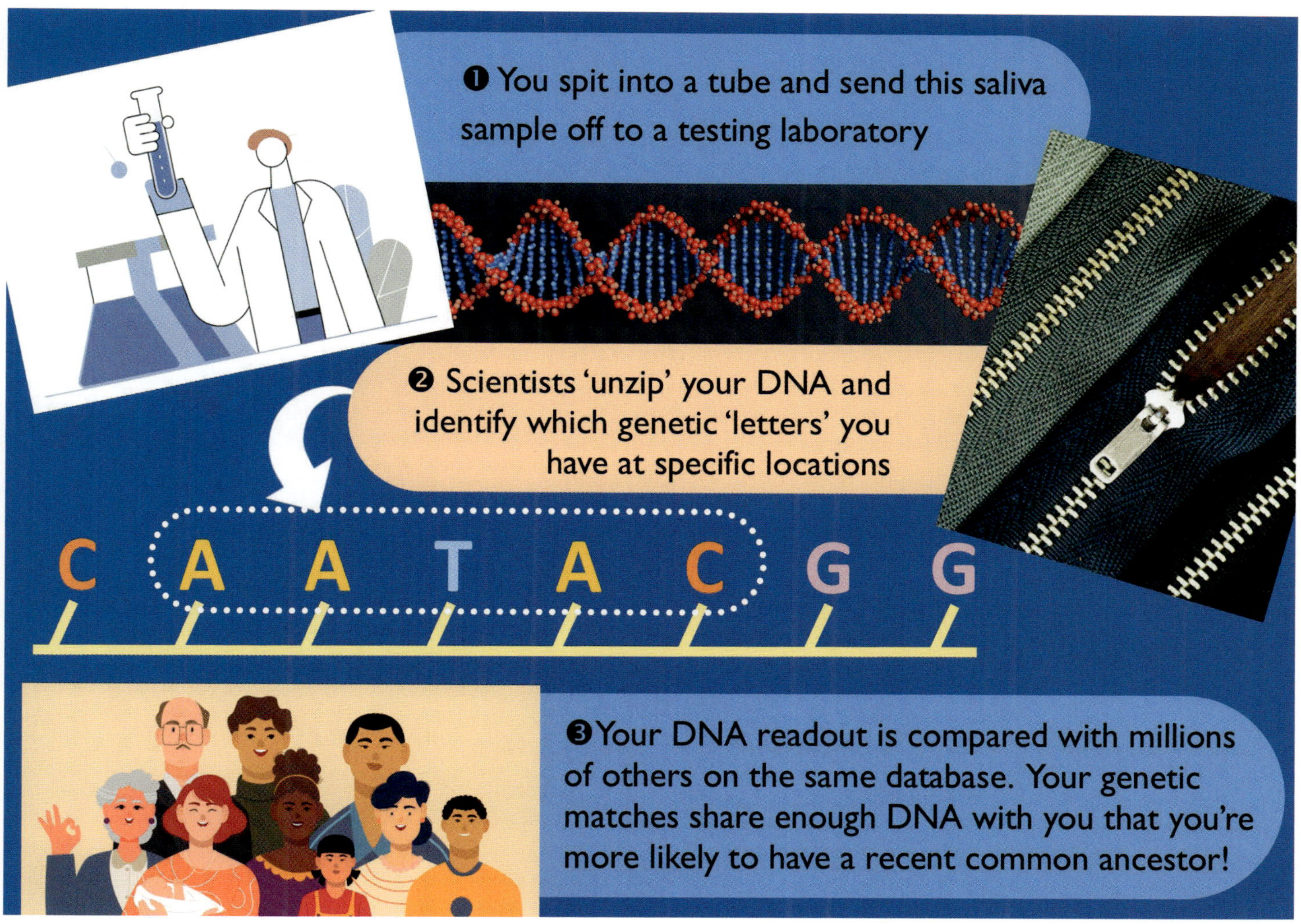

Figure 1: How does the DNA testing process work?

You buy a genetic test, spit into a tube until your mouth feels ridiculously dry, and then seal it up and send it off to the scientists for testing. To go from that to seeing a list of thousands of DNA matches – and using these in your family history research – might seem like a fantastical leap. So let's start with the marvellous molecule at the heart of all this: **DNA.**

- What exactly is it?
- How does it connect us to the other people on our match list?
- What implications does the science have for how we interpret our test results?

What is DNA?

I like to describe DNA as the 'recipe book of life', because it contains – amongst other things – a multitude of chemical instructions or recipes for combining ingredients in a specific order to make the substances your body needs to grow, repair itself, and function

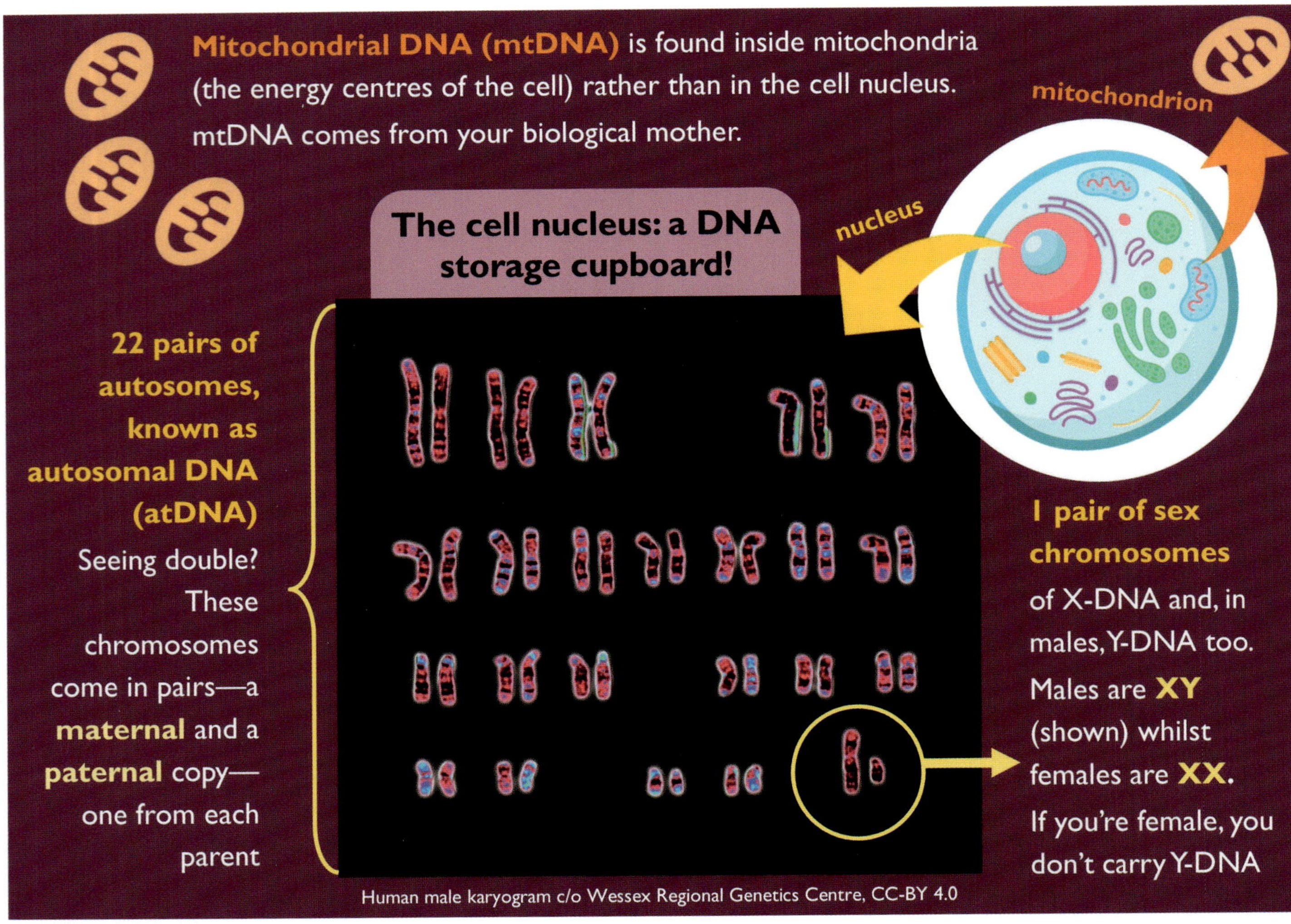

Figure 2: Where is the DNA stored in a cell, and what different types of DNA exist? Although we've shown a simplified version of sex determination here, in which males are XY and females are XX, not everyone falls into these categories: for instance, some intersex individuals may carry an additional sex chromosome (e.g. XXY) and it's also possible in rare cases for someone to be XX but have male reproductive development, typically when an X chromosome has picked up genetic material which usually lives on the Y chromosome.

day-to-day. DNA has a beautiful, spiral shape known as a 'double helix' (check this out in Figure 1) and if we unwound that spiral, we'd get a long, two-stranded structure rather like a zip.

Take a look at a zip now, if you can. Just as a zip has interlocking teeth joining its two halves together, DNA is also made up of two strands. One of these you can think of as the 'recipe strand', and the other is there to make the DNA molecule stable. If we 'unzipped' a length of DNA, pulled the two strands apart and zoomed in, we'd see a series of chemical groups sticking out along the length of each strand, rather like the teeth on a zip. These are known as 'bases' and although their official names are adenine, cytosine, guanine and thymine, we refer to them as 'A', 'C', 'G' and 'T' for short – "genetic letters"!

DNA sequencing is a process where scientists use special laboratory techniques to unwind and unzip your DNA, discovering which 'letters' are present at specific locations on particular strands of DNA.

Practically Speaking: This is why the file you can download from your testing company containing your genetic readout contains many pages of As, Cs, Gs and Ts.

When you close up a zip, the interlocking teeth on opposite strands fit together. The bases are a key part of this in a DNA molecule, because they come in complementary pairs: an A on one strand pairs with T on the opposite strand; likewise, C pairs with G. This is why we talk about DNA having 'base pairs'.

Practically Speaking: Close relatives are much more likely than unrelated individuals to match one another when we examine regions of DNA which typically show a lot of variability. This is why DNA testing is so useful for family history research!

If you were to take the all of the DNA from one egg or sperm cell, then it would contain over 3 billion base pairs (one copy of the 'genome', from either Dad or Mum). Most of the other cells in the human body contain two copies of the genome, so have twice this amount: over 6 billion base pairs (3 billion

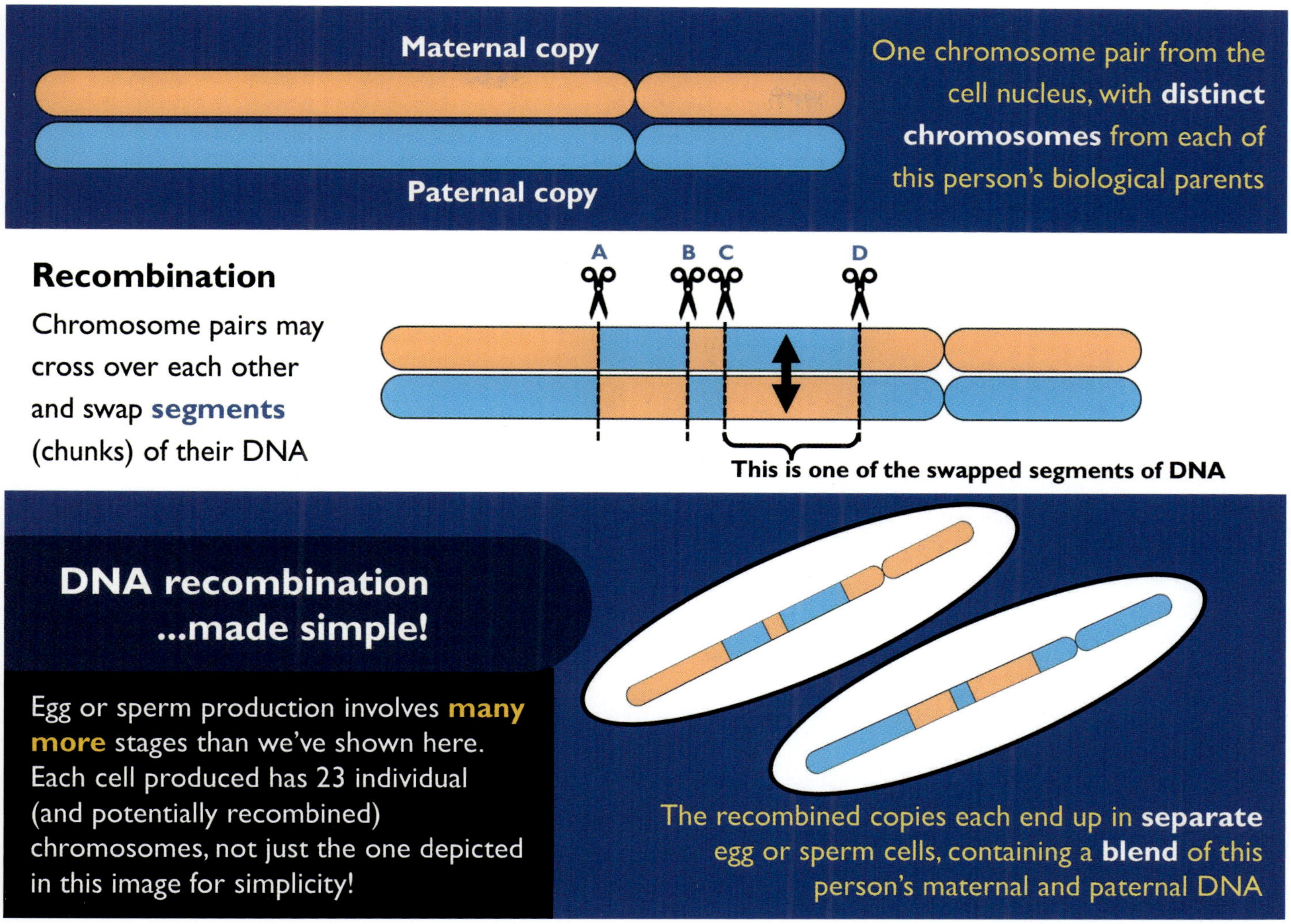

Figure 3: A simplified view of recombination, a process which occurs during egg or sperm production. Recombination may shuffle the DNA in each pair of chromosomes. Each egg or sperm only receives one of these shuffled chromosomes from each pair, passing on a blend of this person's maternal and paternal DNA to their children. Occasionally a chromosome may be passed on without any recombination having occurred.

coming from the egg and 3 billion from the sperm. When egg and sperm meet, they pool their genetic resources to create a baby carrying two copies of the genome – one maternal and one paternal). You can see these two copies lined up together in Figure 2.

If you unwound the DNA from a regular cell from your body and stretched it out end-to-end, it would be about 2 metres long – and yet most of the time, that DNA is so tightly packed that it fits into a nucleus 0.006mm in diameter. And you thought that your cupboards at home were full!

Which parts of our DNA are tested?

Any two people picked at random share about 99.6% or more of their DNA. This is because our DNA contains the recipes for building things common to all humans, such as skin, bones, internal organs, and the soup of chemical reactions happening every second inside our cells. As family historians, it's the final 0.4% of DNA which we're interested in, the part which makes us different from most other people.

When you take an autosomal DNA test with one of the major providers such as Ancestry, MyHeritage or 23andMe, they don't sequence all of your DNA. Instead they only look at specific locations inside those highly varying regions. If two people, on having their DNA sequenced, have the same bases as one another along a sufficient

To get started, you just need to know that in general, the more cM of DNA you share with another person, the closer the relationship

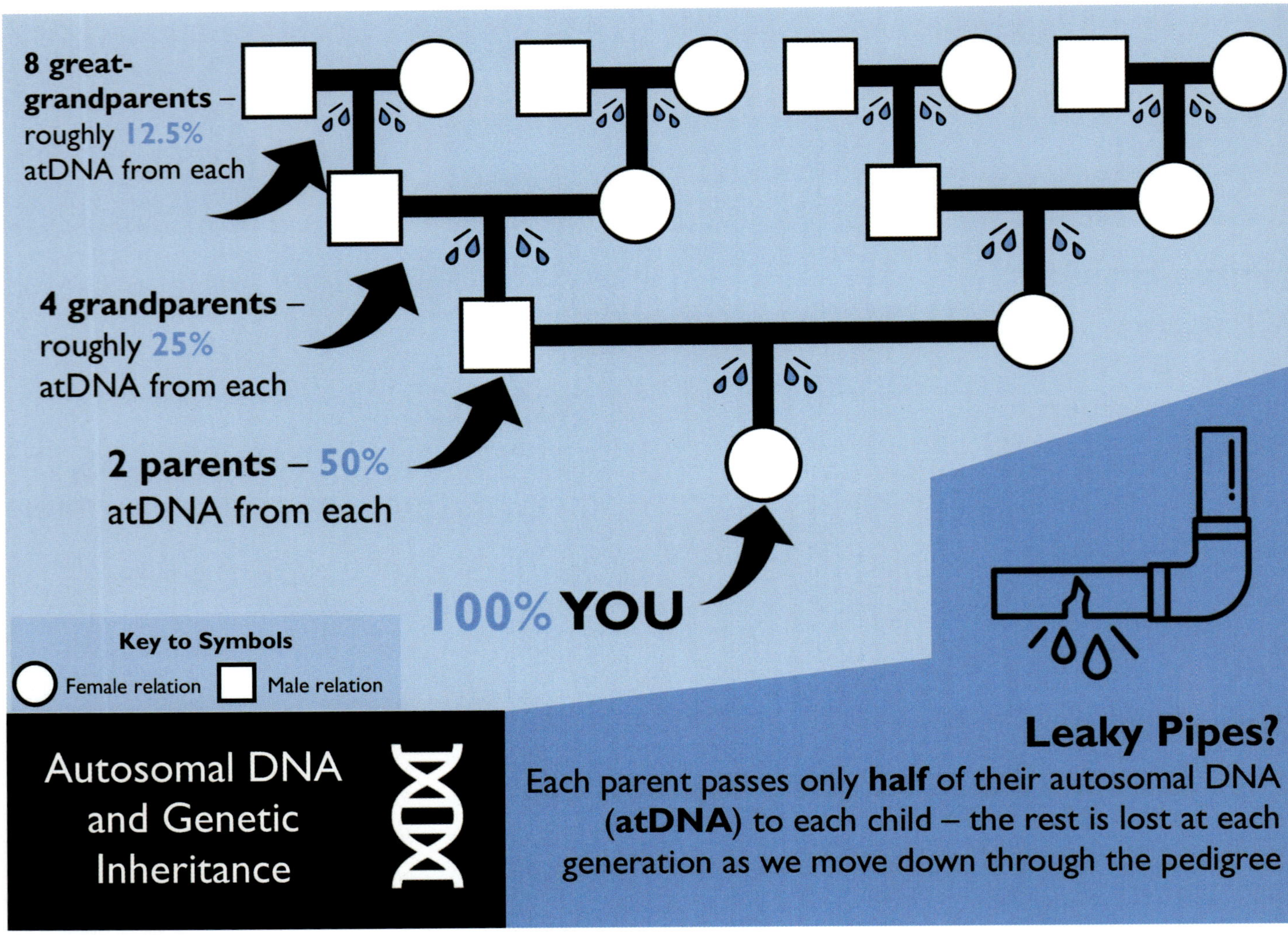

Figure 4: We don't inherit DNA from all of our more distant ancestors – autosomal DNA is usually best for studying the most recent 5-6 generations of our family tree.

portion of these regions, it's more likely that they have a common ancestor in the recent reaches of their family tree and they will be identified as a genetic match (though caution is needed, since some smaller matches can happen by chance between unrelated individuals).

Amounts of DNA are measured in centiMorgans (cM). To get started, you just need to know that in general, the more cM of DNA you share with another person, the closer the relationship. Be aware that this guideline doesn't always hold where there is complexity, such as endogamy (e.g. established intermarriage) or pedigree collapse (one or more ancestors appearing in your family tree multiple times) in your recent family history. To give you a sense of scale in non-complex scenarios, parents and children typically share around 3500cM DNA, siblings around 2600cM, and first cousins about 850cM. A length of DNA is known as a segment (seg) and your testing provider may tell you that you share so many cM of DNA with your genetic match, split across a certain number of segments.

The 23rd pair of chromosomes nestled in the nucleus are the sex chromosomes, which determine whether you are biologically male or female

Chromosomes and nuclear DNA

Now that we've looked at the basic structure of DNA and what sequencing achieves, let's open up that DNA store cupboard and consider the different types of DNA we might test.

Most cells in the human body have a central nucleus (Figure 2) where the majority of the DNA

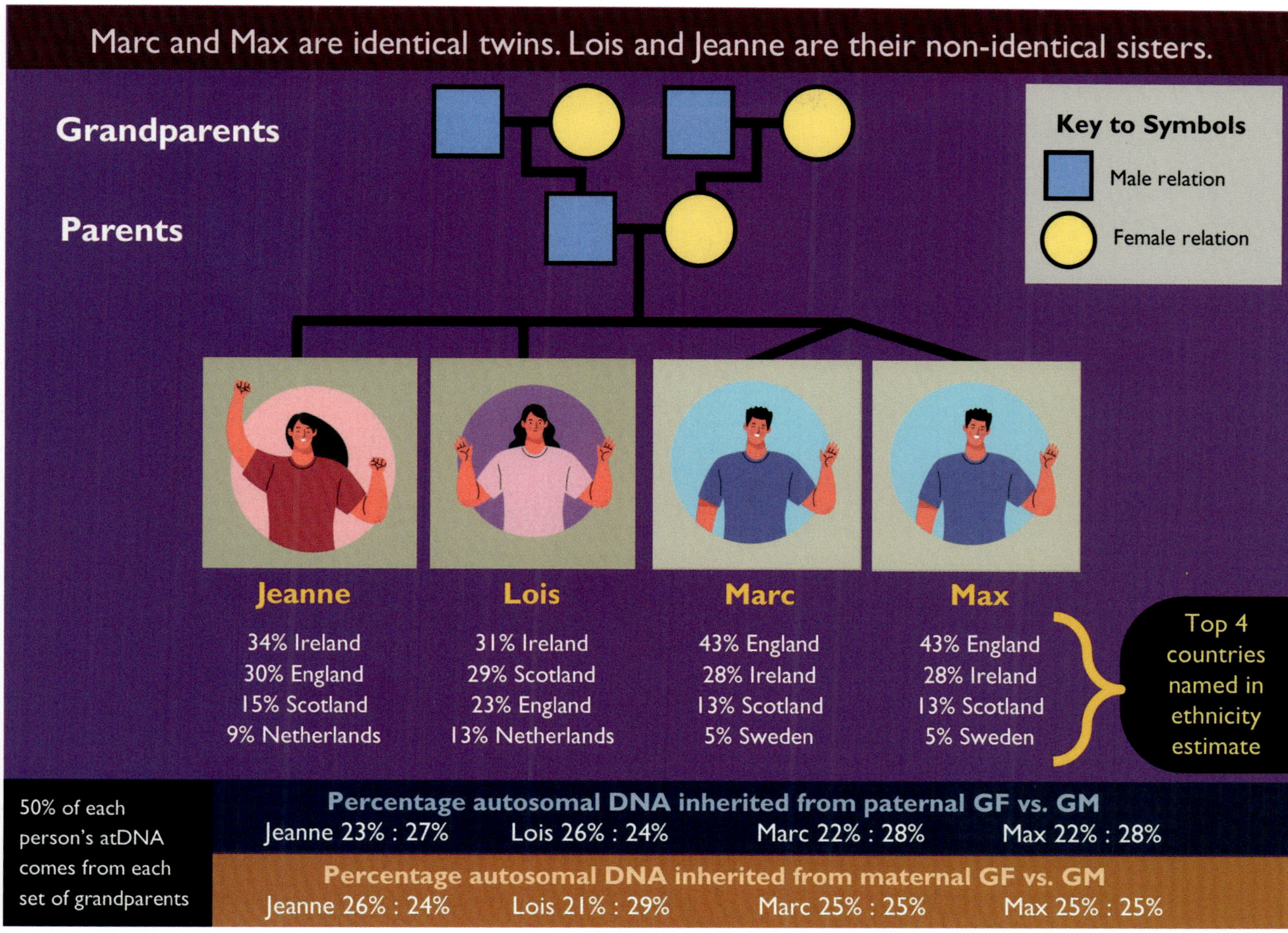

Figure 5: Four full siblings. Sisters Jeanne and Lois were 'single births' and are genetically distinct from their siblings. Marc and Max are identical twins, resulting from the same egg and sperm cell. Notice that Marc and Max, being genetically identical, get the same ethnicity results as one another. Their sisters have different results from them because they each inherited a different blend of DNA. Although everyone gets roughly a quarter (25%) of their atDNA from each grandparent, this might be slightly skewed between each pair of grandparents.

is stored – as 46 long threads of DNA called chromosomes, arranged in 23 pairs (yep, that's how the genetic testing company 23andMe got its name!).

The first 22 chromosome pairs are called the autosomes, or autosomal DNA (atDNA). This type of DNA is the focus of the most popular direct-to-consumer genetic tests at present (autosomal DNA tests) and you inherit it from both parents: one chromosome in each pair comes from your mother, and the other from your father.

The 23rd pair of chromosomes nestled in the nucleus are the sex chromosomes, which in most cases determine whether you are biologically male or female:

- Females have two X chromosomes (termed X-DNA), one from each parent;
- Males have an X chromosome (X-DNA again) from their mother and a Y chromosome (termed Y-DNA and passed father-to-son) from their father. Biological males can take a Y-DNA test.

Outside of the nucleus are small structures called mitochondria, which have their own separate DNA. This is mitochondrial DNA (mtDNA) and you inherit it from your biological mother. Both males and females can take an mtDNA test, but only mothers pass it on to their children. I'll focus on autosomal DNA for the rest of this article, but you can turn to page 67 to learn more about mtDNA and Y-DNA testing!

Practically Speaking: We can test autosomal DNA, Y-DNA and mtDNA – whilst X-DNA matching is included within some autosomal tests. The different inheritance patterns of each DNA type give us many avenues with which to explore our family tree, tackle genealogical research problems, and identify unknown ancestors.

Inheritance and your family tree

Think back to those chromosomes in the cell nucleus, arranged in pairs. We've seen that a healthy human has 23 pairs of chromosomes, formed by an egg cell and sperm cell fusing

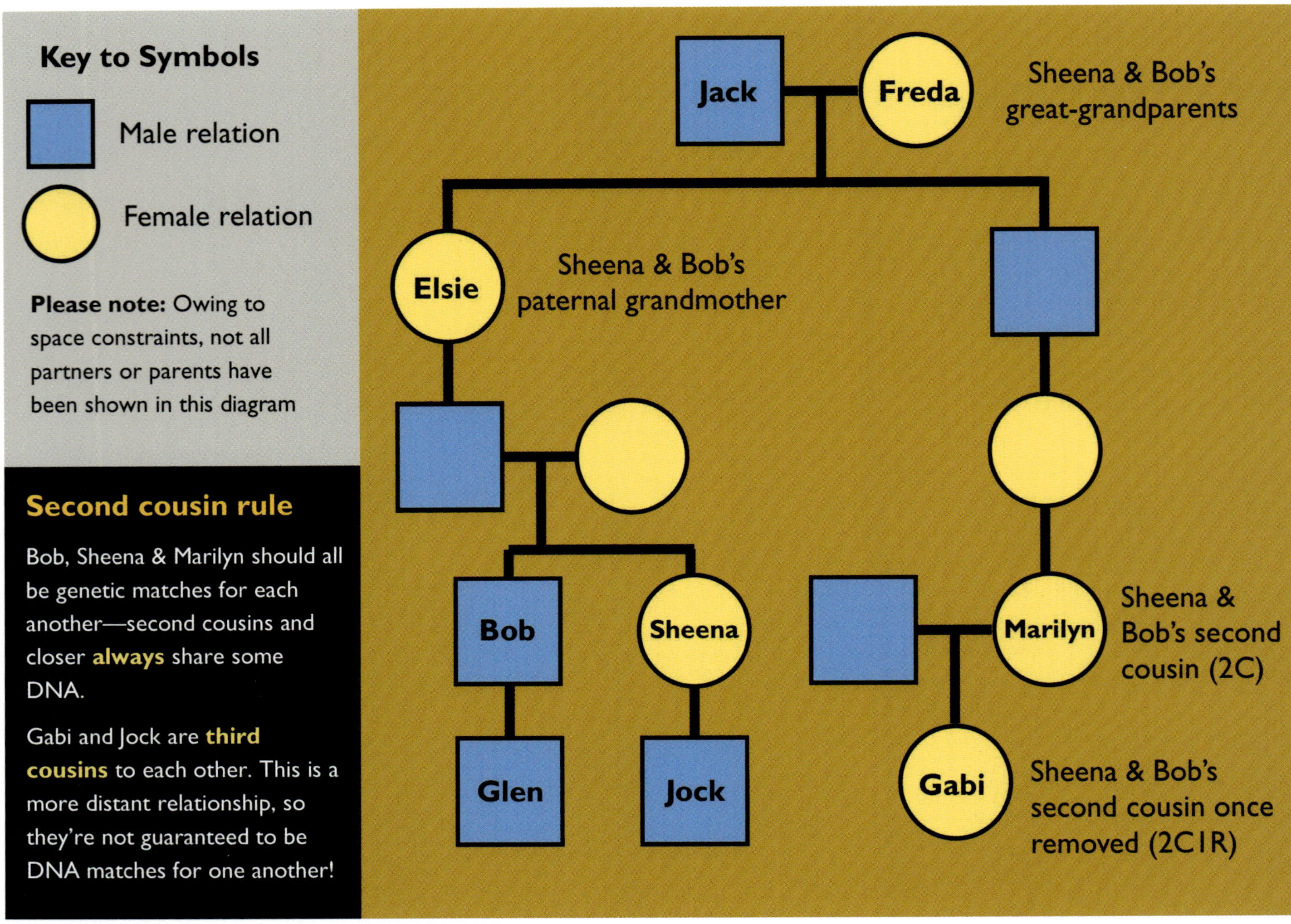

Figure 6: To the best of scientific knowledge at the present time, genuine second cousins or closer always share some some autosomal DNA when tested. More distant relationships than this are not guaranteed to be genetic matches – some may be, others may not.

together. Egg cells and sperm cells therefore contain a 'half amount' of DNA each – so you don't pass ALL of your DNA onto each of your biological children, only half of it.

But DNA is fond of variety! Egg and sperm production includes a shuffling step known as recombination (see Figure 3). In the recombination step the maternal and paternal copies in each chromosome pair come together, cross over one another and may swap chunks of their DNA. This creates two 'blended' copies of each chromosome pair, each containing a mixture of that person's maternal and paternal DNA.

After further cell divisions, each resulting egg or sperm receives a single chromosome from each pair, producing cells containing 23 unpaired chromosomes.

Your mother's egg cell which made you included a blend of DNA from each of your maternal grandparents, and likewise your father's sperm cell which made you included a blend of DNA from each of your paternal grandparents.

If you were to draw your family tree showing your recent direct ancestors, you can imagine the connecting lines as being like leaky pipes (see Figure 4). DNA pours down through the family tree from those ancestors to you, but half of the remaining DNA leaks out at every generation: those are the parts which you didn't inherit. Autosomal DNA is therefore best for studying the most recent 5-6 generations of your family tree: further back than this, matches will either be too weak to use as evidence, or you may have some ancestors whose DNA you simply didn't inherit. Great-great-great-grandparents typically sit on the fringes of what's reachable with atDNA.

> **Practically speaking:** You can't match a genealogical cousin on a part of your ancestor's DNA which you personally didn't inherit. If one of your forebears didn't inherit a particular part of the family DNA, then you as their descendant won't have it either.

The Sibling Shuffle – and what it means for match strengths

Non-identical siblings inherit distinct blends of DNA from their shared parents (compare the identical twins Marc and Max from Figure 5 with their non-identical sisters). If those siblings go on to have children of their own, the genetic differences between people in each line of descent continue to accumulate the further down the family tree you go.

As well as making you genetically different from your non-identical siblings, the genetic shuffling process may cause us to get stronger matches from some ancestral branches than others. On average, recombination produces 'blended' chromosomes which reflect a fairly even mixture of the person's maternal and paternal DNA, but it's not exact.

So although you inherit 50% of your autosomal DNA from your mother and 50% from your father, there may be a skew between each pair of grandparents in terms of how much of their DNA you received. Take your paternal grandparents, for example. You may have inherited 25% of your DNA from each of them, but it might be more like a 24-26 split, or a 30-20 split. Likewise, you'll have ancestors in earlier generations from whom you inherited more or less of your DNA and you may find yourself getting stronger or weaker genetic matches from particular branches of your family.

> **Practically Speaking:** Recombination produces genetic variation between siblings. Beyond the second cousin level, don't be surprised if your siblings have some DNA matches which you don't, or if you and your siblings receive different percentages in your ethnicity estimates.

Second cousins (2Cs) share a pair of great-grandparents, and at the present time there are no recorded cases of genuine 2Cs not being a DNA match.

Take Bob and Sheena from Figure 6. They are full siblings but are genetically distinct. Let's suppose that Bob has inherited 29% of his DNA from his paternal grandmother Elsie, whilst only 22% of Sheena's DNA comes from Elsie. If Bob and Sheena were to take autosomal DNA tests with the same provider, Bob may get stronger DNA matches from Elsie's branch of the family on average compared to Sheena, because he has inherited more of that DNA. By contrast, Sheena may find that she gets stronger matches than Bob on average for their paternal grandfather's side. Since Sheena's son Jock can only inherit Elsie's DNA via his mother, and Bob's son Glen can only inherit Elsie's DNA via his father, these differences might propagate to Jock and Glen and their descendants.

Leaky Pipes: who's a match?

Those leaky pipes of inheritance shed DNA at each generation of our family tree. Although we are always a genetic match to our closest relations, we can be genealogically related to more distant cousins without necessarily showing up as DNA matches.

Second cousins (2Cs) share a pair of great-grandparents, and at the present time there are no recorded cases of genuine 2Cs not being a DNA match. So in the family tree shown in Figure 4, Bob, Sheena and Marilyn should all match one another. As full siblings, we'd expect Bob and Sheena to share around 2600cM DNA, whereas Bob and Marilyn or Sheena and Marilyn, as 2Cs, might share around 230cM. These amounts might vary somewhat, depending on how the genetic inheritance has worked out at each generation down the tree from their shared great-grandparents, Jack and Freda.

Jock and Gabi are third cousins, one generation further down the family tree: some of Jack and Freda's DNA may have been lost from the lines of descent between Sheena and Jock, and Marilyn and Gabi. Although Jock and Gabi could be genetic matches for one another (perhaps sharing around 70cM), it's entirely possible that they might not show up as a genetic match, simply because their relationship is a more distant one. So if you take a DNA test and don't match all of your more distant cousins, this may be the reason why!

Taking time for the science is worth it!

As far as molecules go, DNA is versatile, beautiful and fascinating. By taking time to understand the science which underpins DNA inheritance, we can analyse and navigate our match list that much more readily. Whether you're evaluating the matches for a group of siblings, seeking out genetic matches from particular branches of your family tree, or wondering who to test for your next genealogical adventure, unzipping your DNA can bring a wealth of insights to help you make sense of the results in front of you – however many thousands of them there may be!

First steps

HOW TO FIND YOUR WAY AROUND YOUR DNA TEST RESULTS

Getting your DNA test results back is exciting, but taking that next step can sometimes seem a bit bewildering. To help you understand where to look and what you can do, DNA expert **Donna Rutherford** is here to help you navigate your DNA test results

Each testing company offers unique features to help you interpret your results, connect with relatives, and make sense of your genetic heritage. Note some tools and features mentioned in this guide may require a subscription or an additional upgrade, depending on the testing company.

AncestryDNA

Your AncestryDNA results are in! While it may seem overwhelming, a few key features will help you get started.

Your Origins

Ancestral Regions: see Figure 1.

- Click on the Origins tab to see your Ancestral Regions.
- The percentages represent the likely origins of your ancestors from approximately 500–1,000 years ago, based on your DNA.
- Keep in mind that these estimates are based on reference populations and can change as more data becomes available.

Ancestral Journeys: see Figure 2.

- Ancestry also provides 'Journeys,' which suggest possible migration patterns based on DNA connections.
- Unlike Ancestral Regions, Journeys are calculated differently and reflect more recent ancestry, typically within

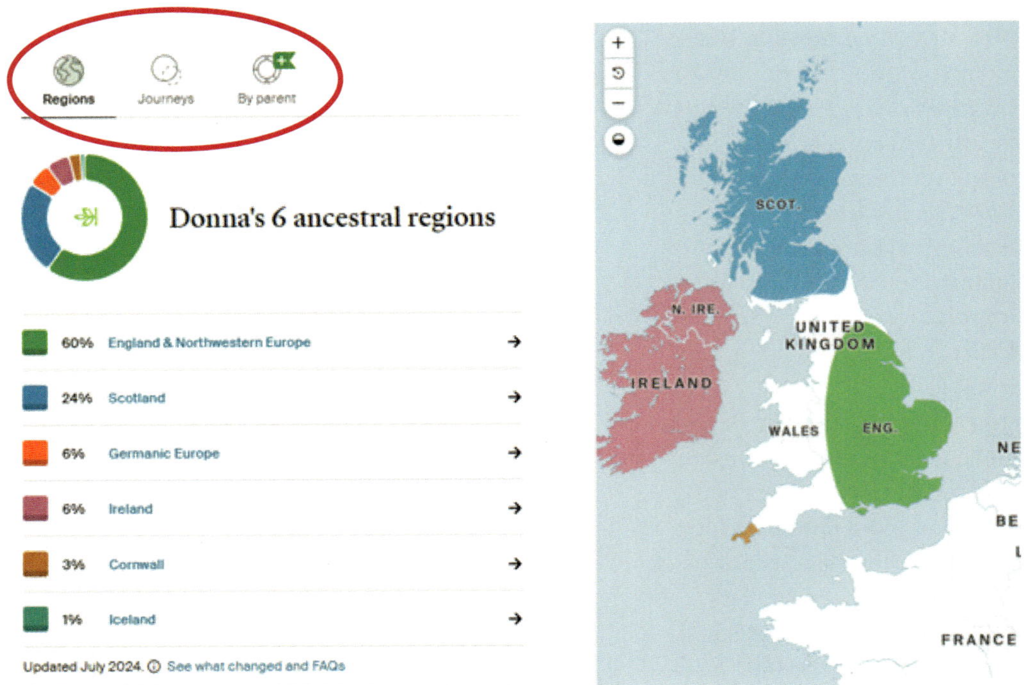

Figure 1

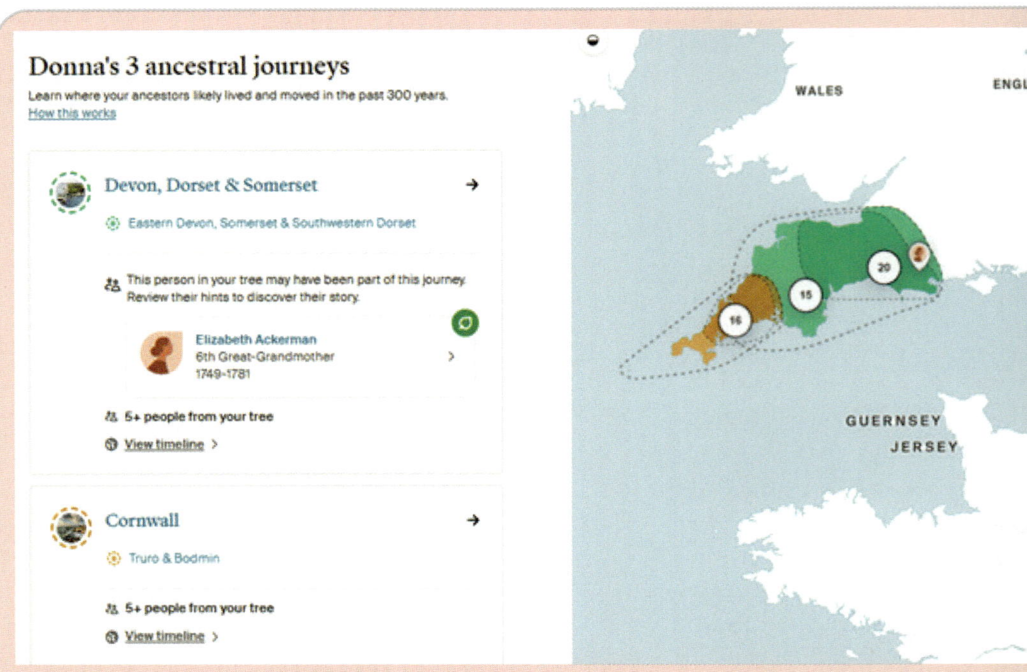

Figure 2

the last 100–300 years.

- Not everyone will receive a Journey, but as AncestryDNA updates its data, you may be assigned one in the future.

By Parent:
Ancestry's SideView technology splits your results into Parent 1 and Parent 2, which you can later re-label as Maternal or Paternal once identified (assignments vary by individual, for instance for some people your Parent 1 may turn out to be your maternal side, and for other people Parent 1 may turn out to be the paternal side).

Your DNA Matches

Go to the DNA Matches section to see your relatives: see Figure 3.

- Matches are grouped by relationship (e.g., close family, extended family).
- You can filter matches, add notes about each match, and view shared matches to spot family connections.

Learn more about a DNA match: see Figure 4.
Click a match to view their profile, including their tree, origins, and shared matches.

Your Thrulines

Locate your ThruLines: see Figure 5.

Next Steps with your Ancestry DNA results

- Link your Ancestry DNA kit results to a family tree on Ancestry for better insights. (Go to DNA > Your Results Summary > Link your tree).
- Contact close matches to collaborate (see page 82 for our guide to diplomacy when contacting DNA matches).
- Use the Shared Matches tool to group matches into clusters.

Figure 3

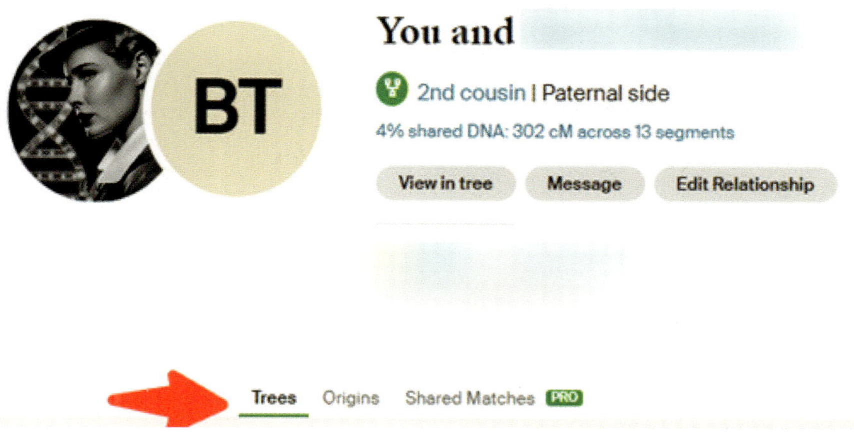

Figure 4

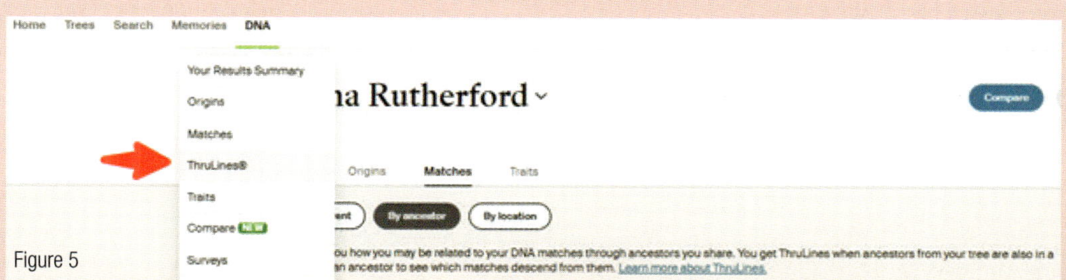

Figure 5

What are ThruLines?
ThruLines suggest possible common ancestors based on trees linked to DNA tests. The Ancestry algorithm explores the trees of your DNA matches, to build out and suggest ways in which you and your DNA matches may be related. It's a great way to identify relationships but always verify them!

Figure 6

FamilyTreeDNA (ftDNA)

FamilyTreeDNA offers powerful tools for exploring your DNA. Here's how to get started: see Figure 6.

MyOrigins

Click on myOrigins to view your ancestry breakdown. You can compare your origins with your matches on the Compare Origins tab: see Figure 7.

DNA Matches

Under Family Finder (refer again to Figure 6 to locate Family Finder Matches), you'll see your

DNA matches, organised by shared DNA.

Use filters and the relationship range to focus on close matches: see Figure 8.

Use the icons on the right to view 'in common with' matches and family trees, and to add notes. (NB 'in common with' is the term that FamilyTreeDNA uses for matches who share DNA with both you and the match).

Chromosome Browser

This tool lets you compare shared DNA segments with matches: see Figure 9.

Next Steps with your FamilyTreeDNA results

- Download your match list for further analysis.
- Use the In Common With tool to find shared matches for clustering.
- Explore the Family Finder Matrix tool to compare how matches match each other.
- Email matches directly using the address listed on their profile.
- Connect your ftDNA test to a family tree on MyHeritage.

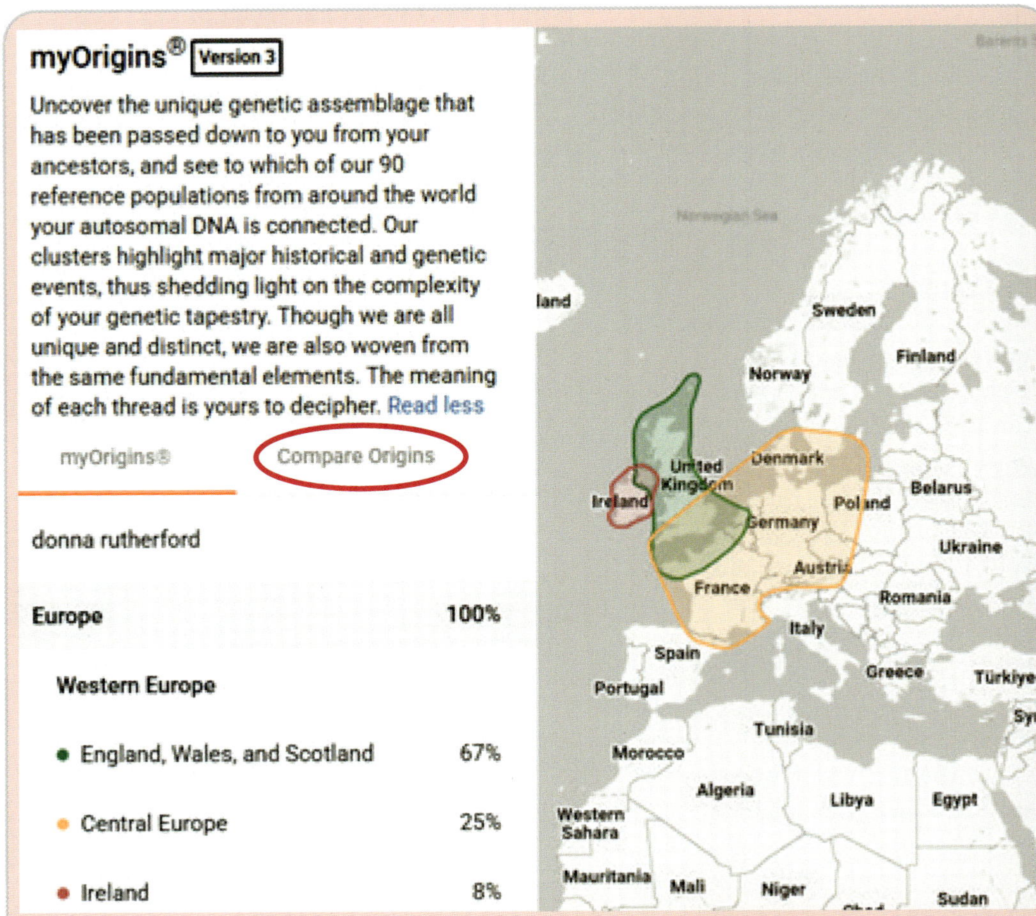

Figure 7

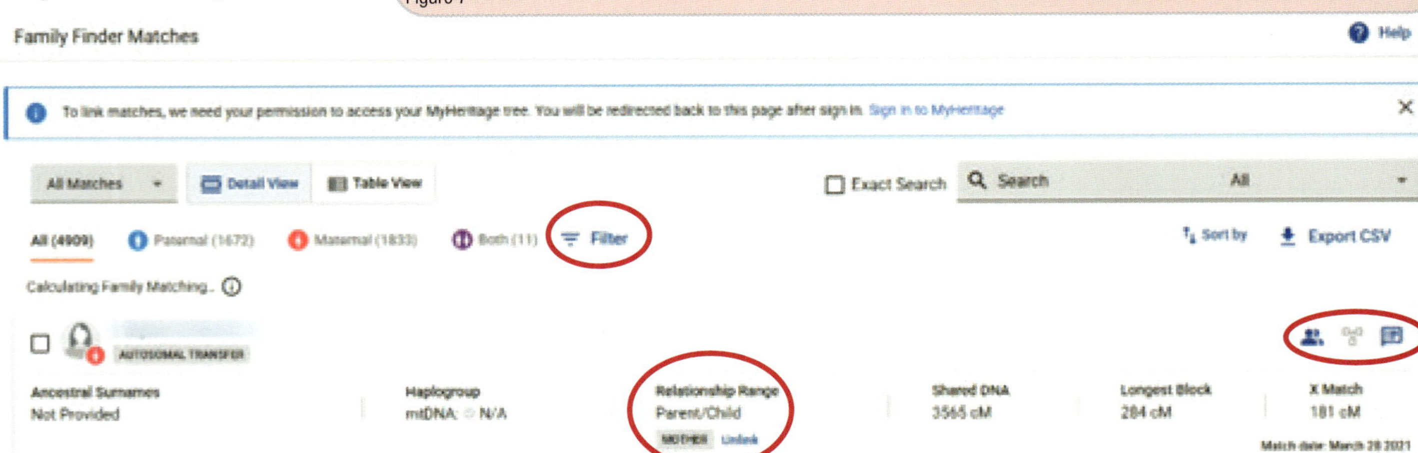

Figure 8

MyHeritage DNA

MyHeritage DNA is useful for connecting with relatives in Europe and other Commonwealth countries: see Figure 10.

Ethnicity Estimate

Click on Ethnicity Estimate to explore your ancestry.

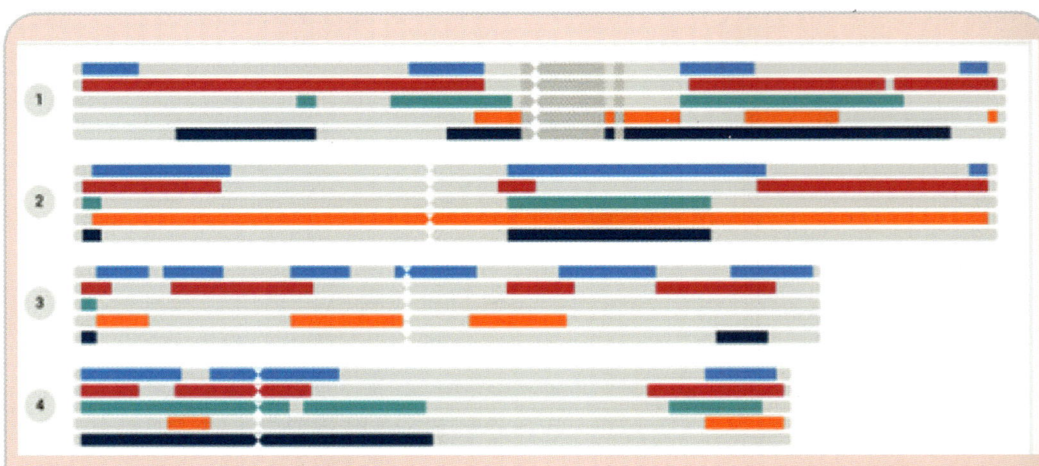

Figure 9

MyHeritage provides Genetic Groups, which refine your regional ancestry: see Figure 11.

DNA Matches

Your DNA Match list is ranked by shared DNA. Use filters to sort matches by relationship or country, or search for specific surnames within your matches: see Figure 12.

AutoClusters

This tool automatically groups your matches into shared ancestry clusters, helping you identify family lines.

AutoClusters are located in the DNA Tools menu, alongside other MyHeritage-specific features: see Figure 13.

Theory of Family Relativity

This hint tool works with the family trees of you and your matches to provide insights as to how you might be related. It's a powerful tool but each theory does need to be verified.

If a match has a theory it will be shown on the DNA match profile page.

Chromosome Browser

The Chromosome Browser tool helps compare DNA segments with the segments of your matches and is found in the DNA Tools menu: see Figures 13 and 14.

Next Steps with your MyHeritage DNA test results

- Contact close matches to collaborate with them.
- Use the Smart Matches tool to connect trees with DNA matches.
- Use the labels feature to cluster DNA matches manually.

23andMe

23andMe provides ancestry and genetic insights. Here's where to start.

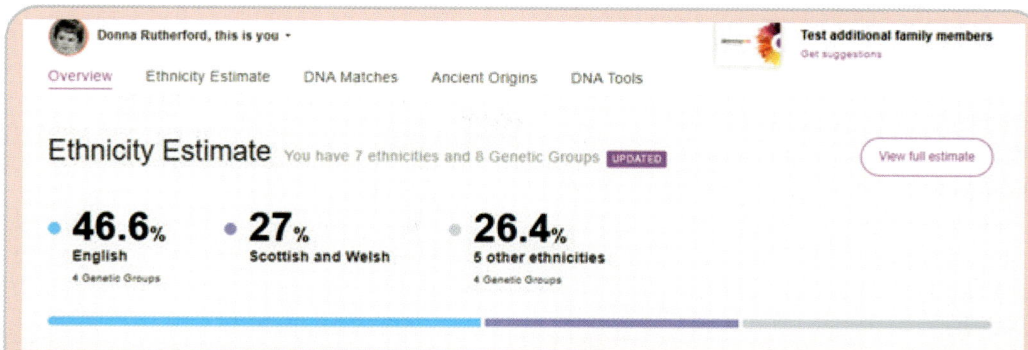

Figure 10

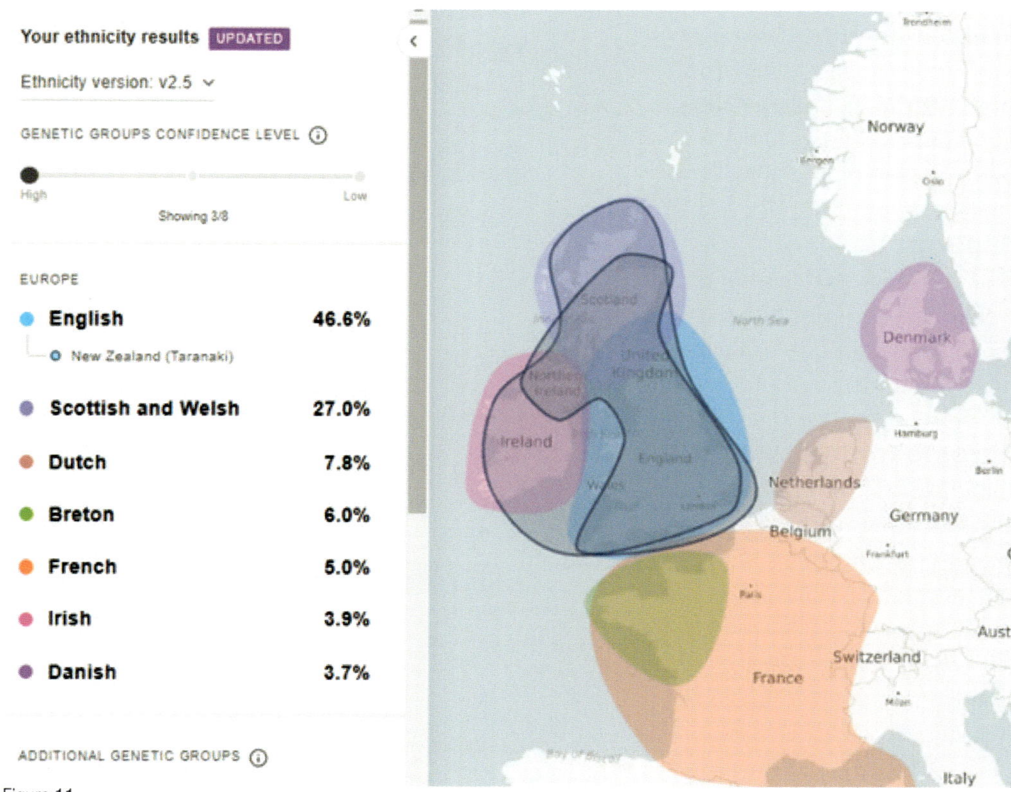

Figure 11

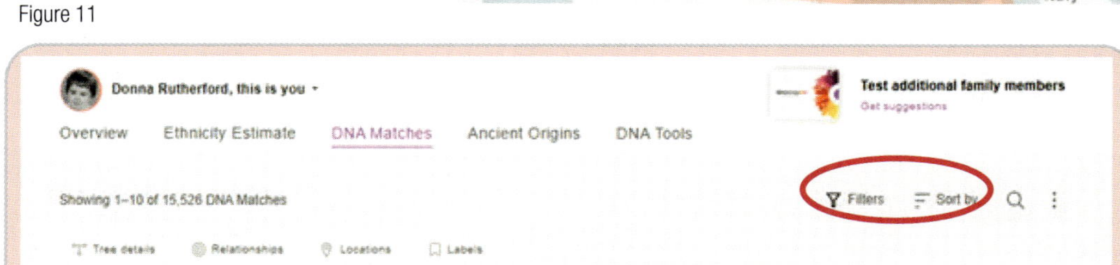

Figure 12

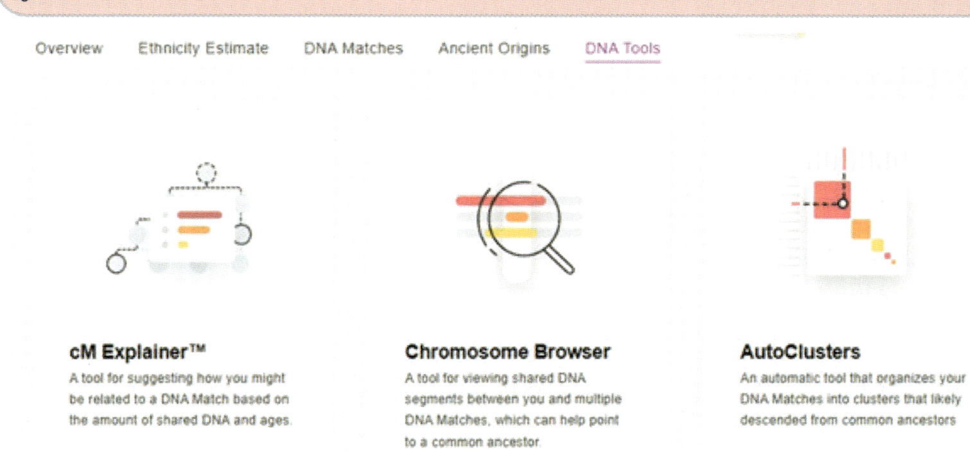

Figure 13

Ancestry Composition

Click on Ancestry Composition (see Figure 15) to view your ethnicity breakdown, which includes a chromosome-based map of ancestry origins: see Figure 16.

The Chromosome-based map is in the DNA Painting section (refer back to Figure 15).

DNA Relatives

Your DNA Relatives list ranks matches by shared DNA. You can see estimated relationships and compare shared DNA segments: see Figure 17.

Haplogroups

Find your maternal (and paternal, if male) haplogroups to trace ancient ancestry. The haplogroups are found under your profile.

Chromosome Browser

23andMe's Chromosome Browser allows you to compare shared DNA segments with matches to help identify common ancestors. However, this feature has been temporarily disabled as part of 23andMe's ongoing privacy measures.

Next Steps with your 23andMe test results

- Find shared matches at the bottom of each match page to identify relatives in common.
- Explore the Family Tree feature to see how matches may relate.
- Contact close matches for collaboration.

Final Thoughts

Now that you have a better understanding of how to navigate your DNA results, the next step is putting that knowledge into action. Connecting with DNA matches, exploring ethnicity insights, and using genetic tools will help you make meaningful discoveries about your ancestry. Turn to my guide, starting on page 36 to learn more about working with your DNA test results.

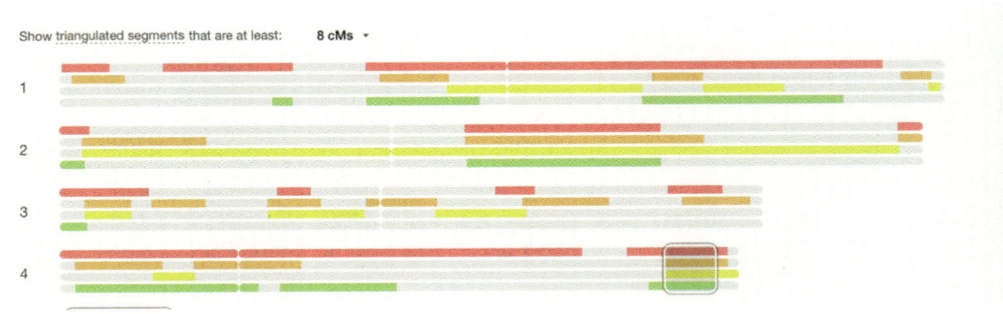

Figure 14

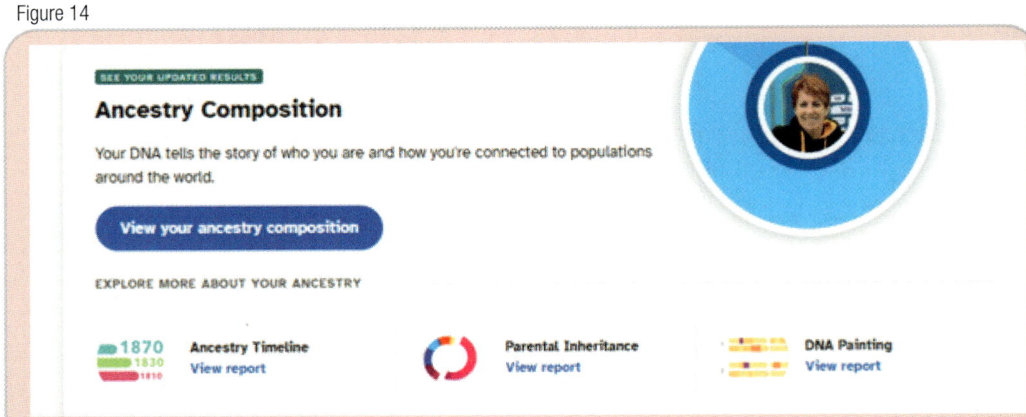

Figure 15

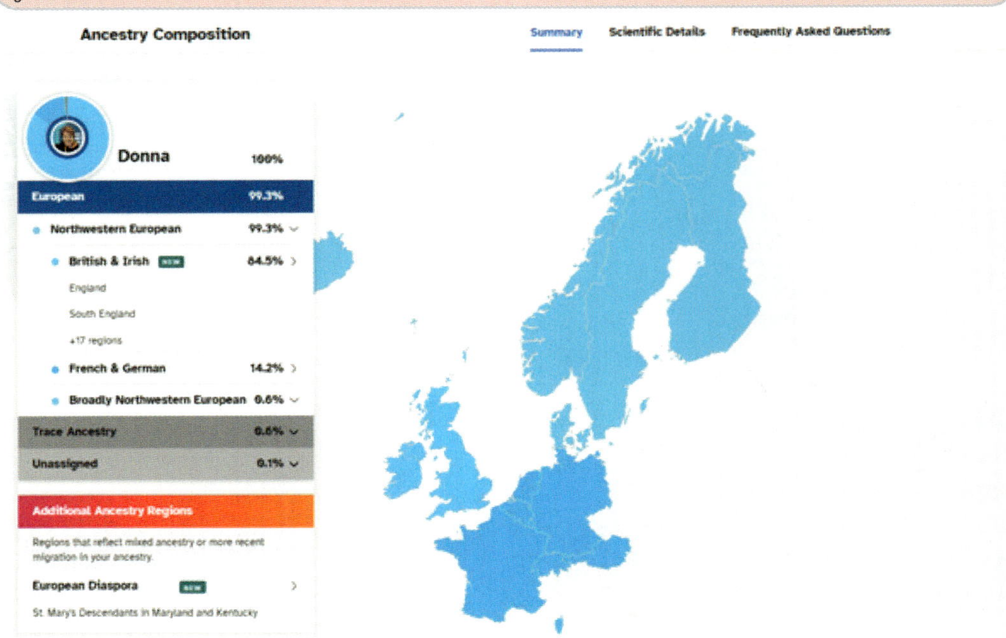

Figure 16

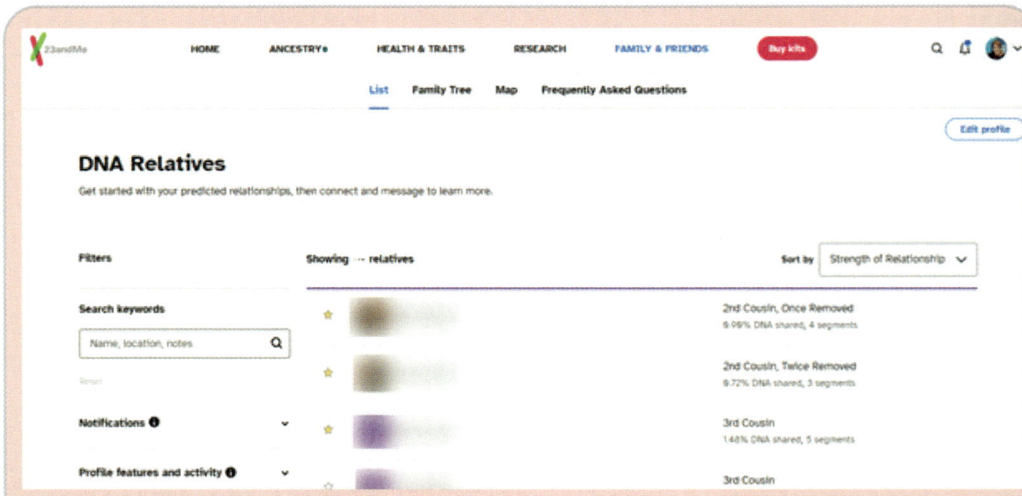

Figure 17

Learn with your FREE BITESIZE DNA COURSE

The DNA Discoveries guide to using DNA for family history is just the beginning. To help you get even more from your research, we've created a free five-week online course designed to enhance your learning, and give you hands-on experience. Through a series of emails and video guides, you'll gain useful insights and practical tips to make the most of your DNA test results. Sign up now to continue your journey!

If there's one thing the *DNA Discoveries* guide has shown you, it's that there's always more to discover when it comes to using DNA for family history. That's why we've developed an online mini-course to offer you another way to increase your understanding and gain practical skills for your DNA journey.

The free five-week course will take you through the essentials, helping you make sense of your test results and know what step to take next.

The course consists of email updates, packed with useful tips and links, and a five-part video course presented by *Family Tree*'s DNA advisor Karen Evans. Sign up and we'll deliver each part of the course to your in-box over the next five weeks, giving you the chance to learn in your own time.

Why take a DNA test? Exploring the three types

Before diving into your DNA results, it's essential to understand the different types of tests available and what they can reveal about your ancestry. The first part of the online course explores the three main types of DNA test used in family history research:

Autosomal DNA tests – the most common type, ideal for tracing relatives within the past 5 or so generations.

Y-DNA tests – used to explore the direct paternal line (only available to male testers).

Mitochondrial DNA (mtDNA) tests – passed down through the maternal line, helping trace deep ancestral origins.

Choosing the right test depends on your research goals, and this session will guide you through the benefits of each type.

How is DNA inherited? Understanding key concepts

DNA is often described as the blueprint of life, but how does it actually work in family history research? This module breaks down the science behind DNA inheritance in a clear and easy-to-follow way. You'll learn how DNA is passed down through generations, and what this means for your DNA match list.

How likely are you to match with relatives? Essential tools to help

One of the most exciting aspects of DNA testing is the potential to connect with living relatives. But how do you determine the strength of a DNA match, and what can it tell you about your shared ancestry?

This part of the course introduces essential tools that help you analyse your matches and estimate relationships.

Making sense of geographic origins and match lists

Many DNA tests provide an ethnicity estimate, offering a breakdown of your genetic origins by region. But how

ABOUT YOUR COURSE TUTOR

Karen Evans is Family Tree's DNA advisor and you can find her articles in the monthly magazine, covering reader case studies, and practical how-to guides. Karen also presents the DNA news slot in the popular DNA Club webinars, part of the Familyl Tree Plus online membership.

accurate are these results, and how should you interpret them? In this session, we'll explore how DNA companies determine your ethnic background, what influences the results, and why they can change over time as databases grow.

But ethnicity estimates are just one part of the puzzle. Your DNA match list is really the most valuable resource for genealogical research. We'll guide you through strategies for sorting and analysing matches, grouping them by shared ancestors, and using them to validate or expand your existing family tree.

No family tree? No worries! Tracing matches without a tree

A common challenge in genetic genealogy is encountering DNA matches who haven't built a family tree – or who have only minimal information available. But don't let that discourage you! This final session will equip you with strategies to work with DNA matches who don't have a tree, to help you piece together their ancestry nonetheless.

There's always more to learn ... That's why we've developed an online mini-course to offer you another way to gain practical skills for your DNA journey

You'll also learn how to record and organise your DNA research, ensuring that you keep track of findings, build strong case studies, and use your results effectively in future investigations.

Join the course and start your DNA journey today!

DNA testing has the power to break through brickwalls in family history research, connect you with long-lost relatives, and provide fascinating insights into your heritage. But to truly make the most of your results, it's essential to understand how to interpret and use them effectively.

This free mini-course is designed to give you the knowledge to do just that, and the confidence that you are starting your DNA journey on the right foot.

With reliable guidance, practical tips, and easy-to-follow explanations, you'll gain the skills needed to turn your DNA results into valuable discoveries.

Sign up today using the link below (or scan the QR code with your phone) and make sure you're not missing out.

DNA DISCOVERIES
FIVE-WEEK ONLINE COURSE

SIGN UP TO THE FREE ONLINE COURSE

Signing up to the course is simple, just visit the link below (or scan the QR code with your phone) and complete the short form. We'll then send you a welcome email and over the next five weeks you'll receive an email with useful links, advice, and the exclusive video guides.

You'll also begin receiving the hugely popular Family Tree newsletter which brings you weekly how-to guides, updates, offers and more.

JUST VISIT:

bit.ly/free-dna-course

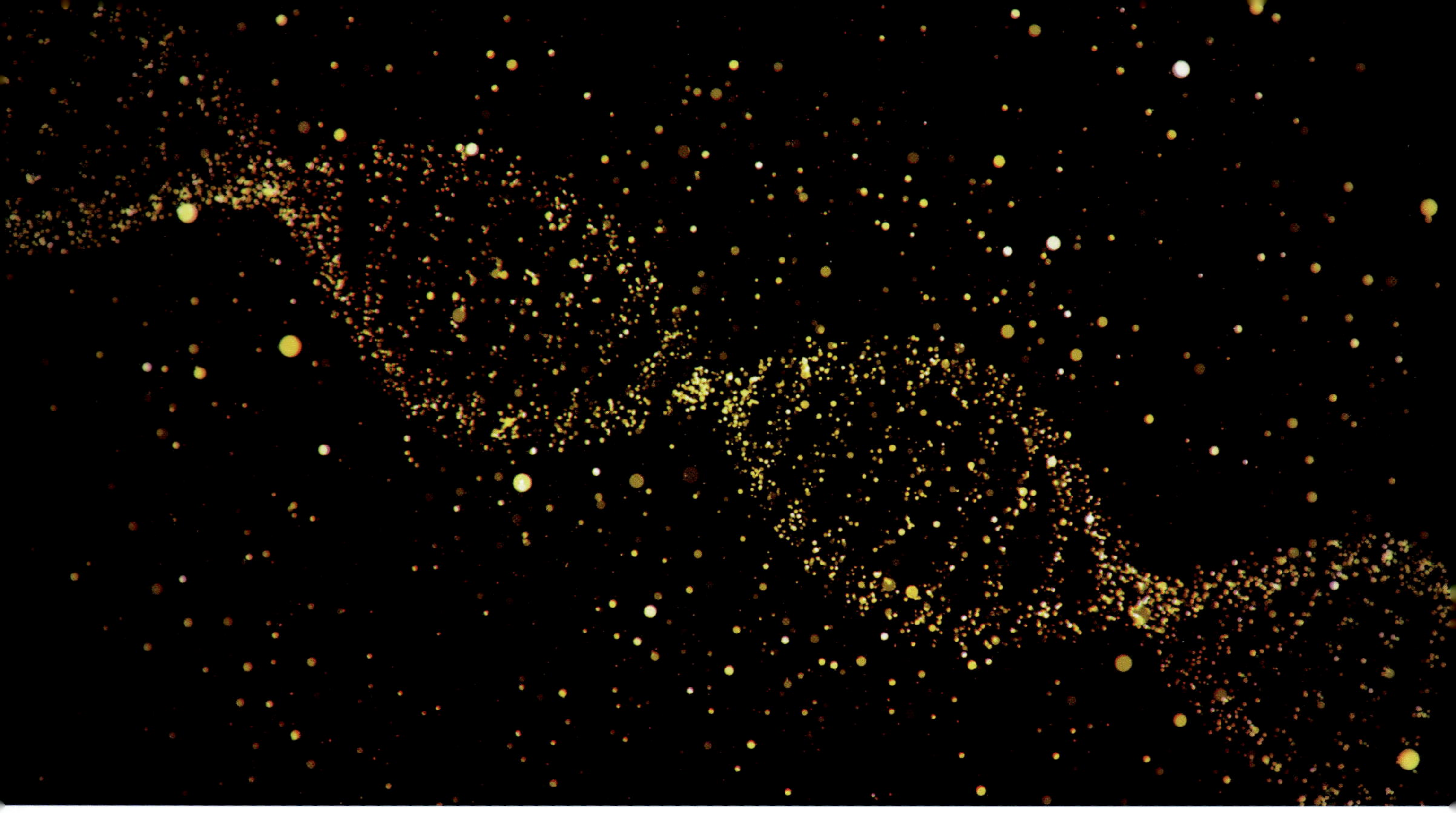

How to work with your DNA matches

HOW TO CREATE GROUPS & WHY THEY ARE USEFUL

Introducing – the Power of Clustering! **Donna Rutherford** is here to help you learn how to create groups of your DNA matches and to explain why this will help your DNA family history research.

What is clustering?

Clustering involves grouping DNA matches who are also related to each other (these matches are also known as shared matches).

These clusters typically represent a group that is related via a shared ancestor or ancestral line, making them invaluable for determining how a match fits into your family tree.

Note that the words 'cluster' and 'group' can be used interchangeably. They mean exactly the same thing.

Where to start with clustering?

A good starting point is a match who shares around 400 centimorgans (cM), likely representing a grandparent line. Alternatively, starting at 100 cM creates more refined clusters aligned to great-grandparent branches. (If you don't have any/many matches at these levels stated above, just choose your highest match (that is 30 cM or above) and start creating a cluster based on the matches that you share with them).

Once you have identified your first match to cluster, create a new colour-coded group (if using AncestryDNA, MyHeritage, or Living DNA) and assign your match's shared matches to the same group.

Several DNA testing companies offer built-in tools to help with clustering

Clustering tools across different DNA companies

We've mentioned the colour-coding clustering tools, so what are they and how do they work? Several DNA testing companies offer built-in tools to help with clustering:

- AncestryDNA allows you to manually group matches using a colour-coded system with up to 64 groups. Each group is represented by a coloured square and can include a letter, number, or emoji to help with organisation.

- MyHeritage provides AutoClusters, which automatically groups DNA matches into clusters based on shared connections. Their DNA Match Labels feature lets you also manually organise matches using 30 different coloured dots.
- Living DNA offers 32 coloured dots in their 'Matchbox' system, which allows you to create and track match groups.
- 23andMe and FamilyTreeDNA (ftDNA) do not offer built-in clustering tools, but clustering can be done using a spreadsheet.

How to Use Clustering on Different Platforms

Clustering on AncestryDNA

AncestryDNA offers a colour-coded grouping system to organise matches. You can create up to 64 groups, each with a coloured square, and a label that can contain letters, numbers, or emojis. In March 2025 Ancestry announced a new 'matches by cluster' visualisation tool coming soon

Read the Guide: Learn more about grouping and filtering your matches with the AncestryDNA guide: https://support.ancestry.co.uk/s/article/Grouping-and-Filtering-AncestryDNA-Matches

Clustering on MyHeritage

MyHeritage offers AutoClusters, which automatically groups DNA matches into a matrix of shared connections. The tool can be found under DNA Tools, and, when run, it generates a spreadsheet of clustered matches sent via email.

In addition to AutoClusters, MyHeritage provides DNA Match Labels with 30 different coloured dots for manual organisation.

Read the Guide: Learn more about creating groups on MyHeritage DNA: https://blog.myheritage.com/2021/11/introducing-labels-for-dna-matches-on-myheritage/

Clustering on Living DNA

Living DNA offers 32 coloured dots within its 'Matchbox' system to organise matches into groups.

Clustering with 23andMe and ftDNA

Since 23andMe and ftDNA do not offer built-in grouping tools, spreadsheets can be used instead.

A simple approach is to use a spreadsheet. See the example below. A spreadsheet provides flexibility in tracking matches, especially for platforms without colour-coded labels.

If you don't like spreadsheets you can create a table on a Word document or even pen and paper!

No coloured grouping tools? A solution

23andMe and FamilyTreeDNA don't provide colour-coding tools to help you group your DNA matches. There is a simple workaround however, using a spreadsheet.

Create a new group on AncestryDNA

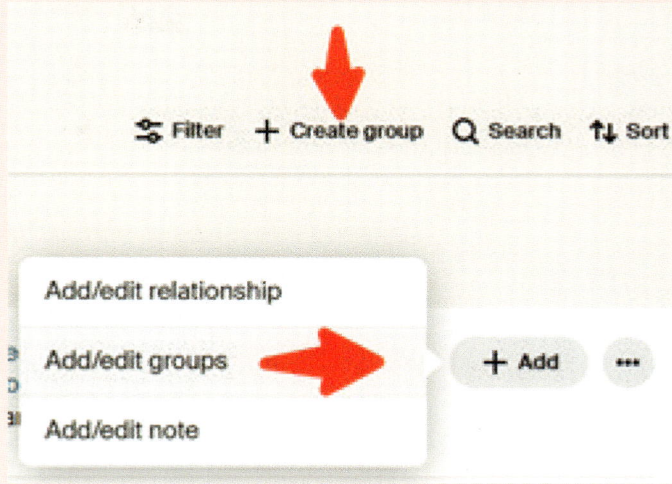

1. Click the 'Create group' button on the main match list or a match page.

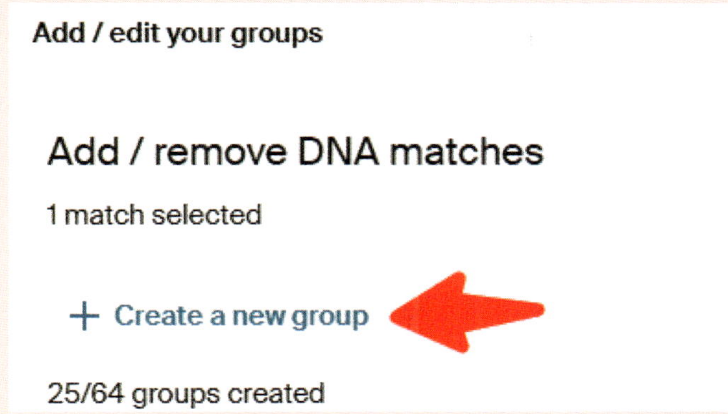

2. A fly-out menu will show the number of groups available and a '+ Create a new group' button.

3. Assign a name, a first character (letter, number, or emoji), and a colour to the group.

4. Your main match list will display group assignments for each match. Over time, groups can be refined to represent verified family branches, such as great-great-grandparent lines.

Create a label on MyHeritage DNA

1. Click on 'Create label' from the main match list or a match page.

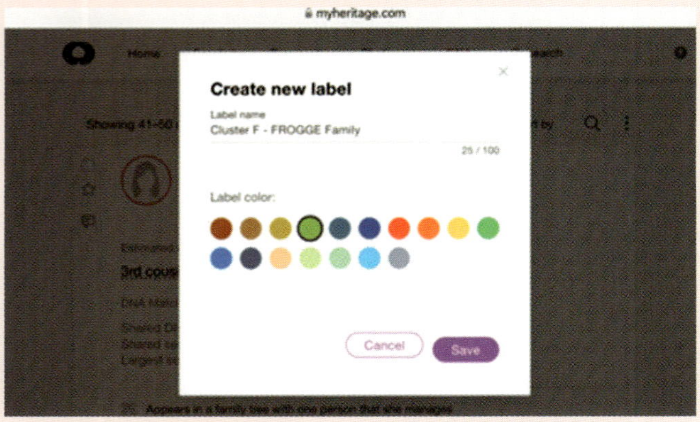

2. Choose a coloured dot and enter a name for the group.

3. Matches will display their assigned labels on the left side of the main match list. Labels can be edited or deleted at anytime to align with your clustering strategy.

How to cluster on Living DNA

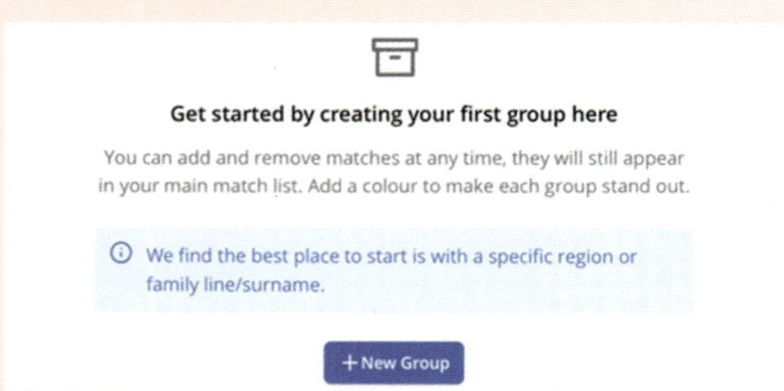

1. Navigate to the Matchbox menu within Family Matching.

2. Assign coloured dots to matches to help categorise shared ancestry.

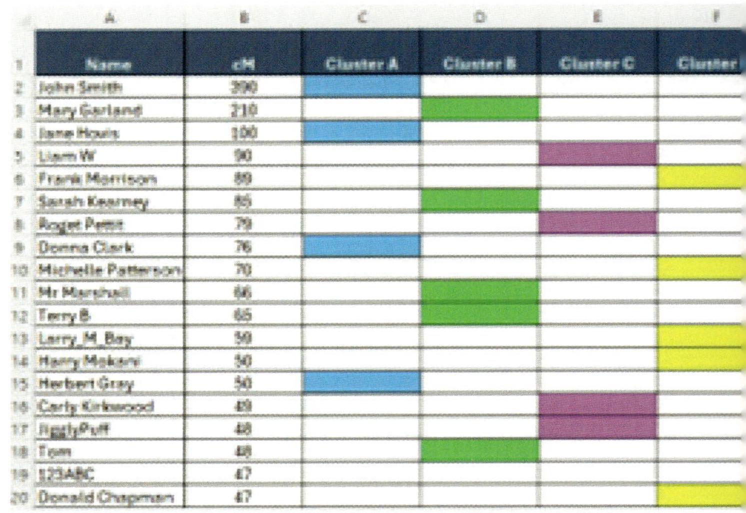

Name	cM	Cluster A	Cluster B	Cluster C	Cluster
John Smith	390				
Mary Garland	210				
Jane Houis	100				
Liam W	90				
Frank Morrison	89				
Sarah Kearney	85				
Roger Pettit	79				
Donna Clark	76				
Michelle Patterson	70				
Mr Marshall	66				
Terry B	65				
Larry_M_Bay	59				
Harry Makani	50				
Herbert Gray	50				
Carly Kirkwood	49				
[illegible]Puff	48				
Tom	48				
123ABC	47				
Donald Chapman	47				

How to fill in your spreadsheet to create clusters

1. List each DNA match alongside their shared cM amount.
2. Use coloured cells in columns to represent clustering groups. Colour a cell for the match in a column representing the new group.
3. Identify shared matches and assign them to the same colour-coded group.
4. Continue this process, working down your match list to about 30 cM, by which point matches may be too distant or unreliable for confident clustering.

Why clustering is useful?

Clustering your DNA matches can help identify common ancestors, whether you have a documented family tree, or are researching brick-walls such as unknown parentage

By grouping matches, you can determine which branch of your family tree a match belongs to and narrow down relationships.

If you are working with unknown parentage, clustering helps you identify whether a group must fit into an unknown or known ancestral line, guiding your research toward potential connections.

Once clusters are established, you can compare surnames, locations, and family trees to pinpoint shared ancestry. Many genealogists use a private, unsearchable tree (often called a 'quick & dirty' tree) to build out connections and link clusters through genealogy.

This structured approach transforms an overwhelming DNA match list into a powerful research tool.

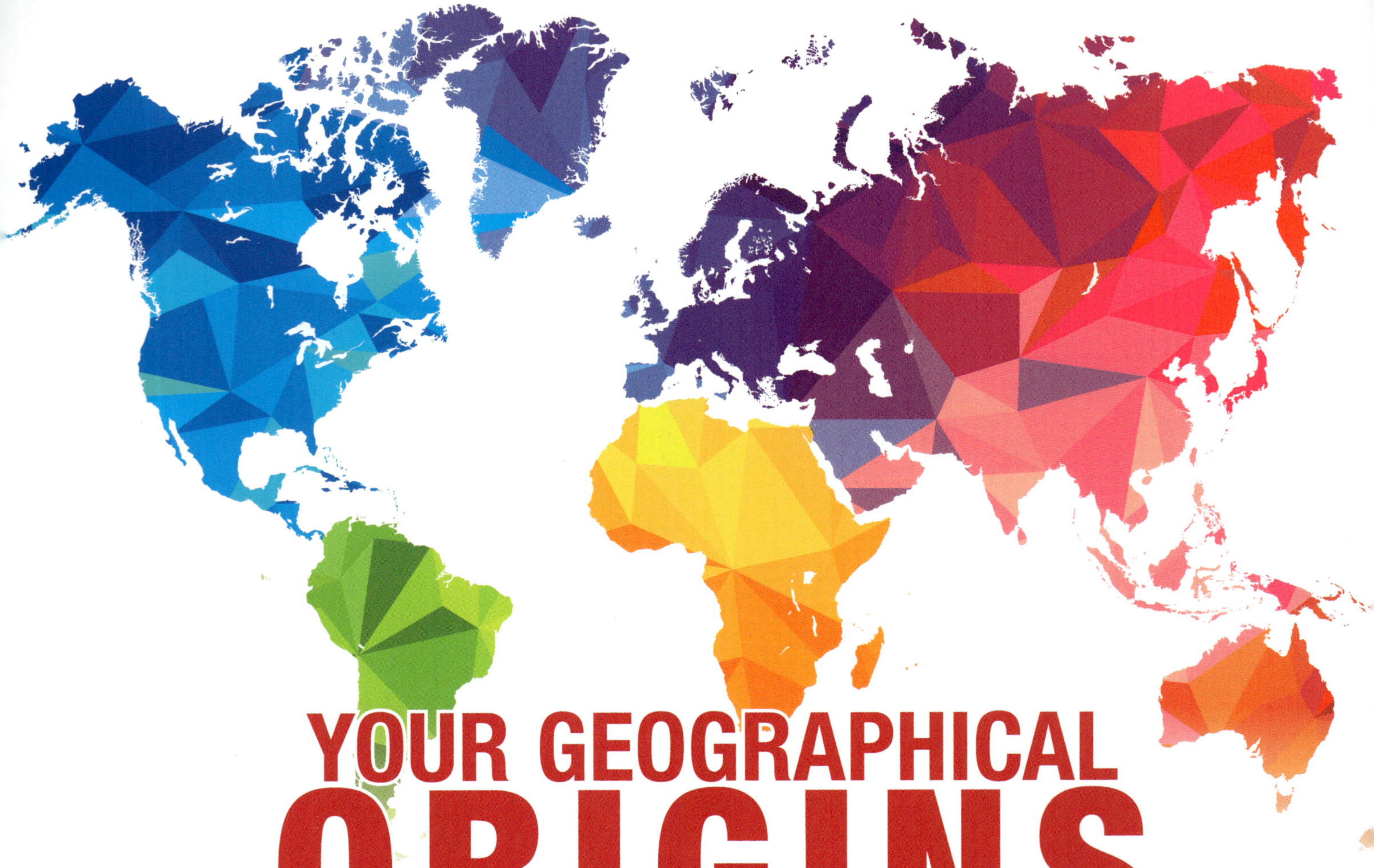

YOUR GEOGRAPHICAL ORIGINS *explained*

Information about geographical origins is one of the most immediate and perhaps obviously appealing aspects of getting your DNA test results back. But how are your percentages calculated? Why do they vary? And what do they really tell you? Find the answers to these questions and make better sense of this intriguing aspect of your DNA report

Those fascinating colourful maps showing your ancestral origins are probably the first place we investigate when we get our DNA test results back. While on the one hand it can seem super simple, stating the percentages you have for your places, based on your DNA test results; you may wonder what do these percentages actually mean. And how the figures and locations were arrived at. Let's take a look.

What do your DNA geographic origin percentages mean?

Your DNA geographic origins, often called your 'ethnicity estimate' (or, more formally your 'admixture'), provide broad-brush information about your genetic inheritance stating where your ancestors once came from.

For the past few years ethnicity estimates have been useful for providing accurate information at the continental level. For instance, while the continent will very likely remain the same, when the DNA testing company you tested with issues an ethnicity estimate update, you will notice that your precise percentages for each country stated may change. With more recent developments, more precise location-based information is becoming available too.

How are your DNA percentages calculated?

Your DNA ethnicity estimate percentages are calculated by comparing your DNA sample with a reference panel.

Take, for instance, Ancestry's

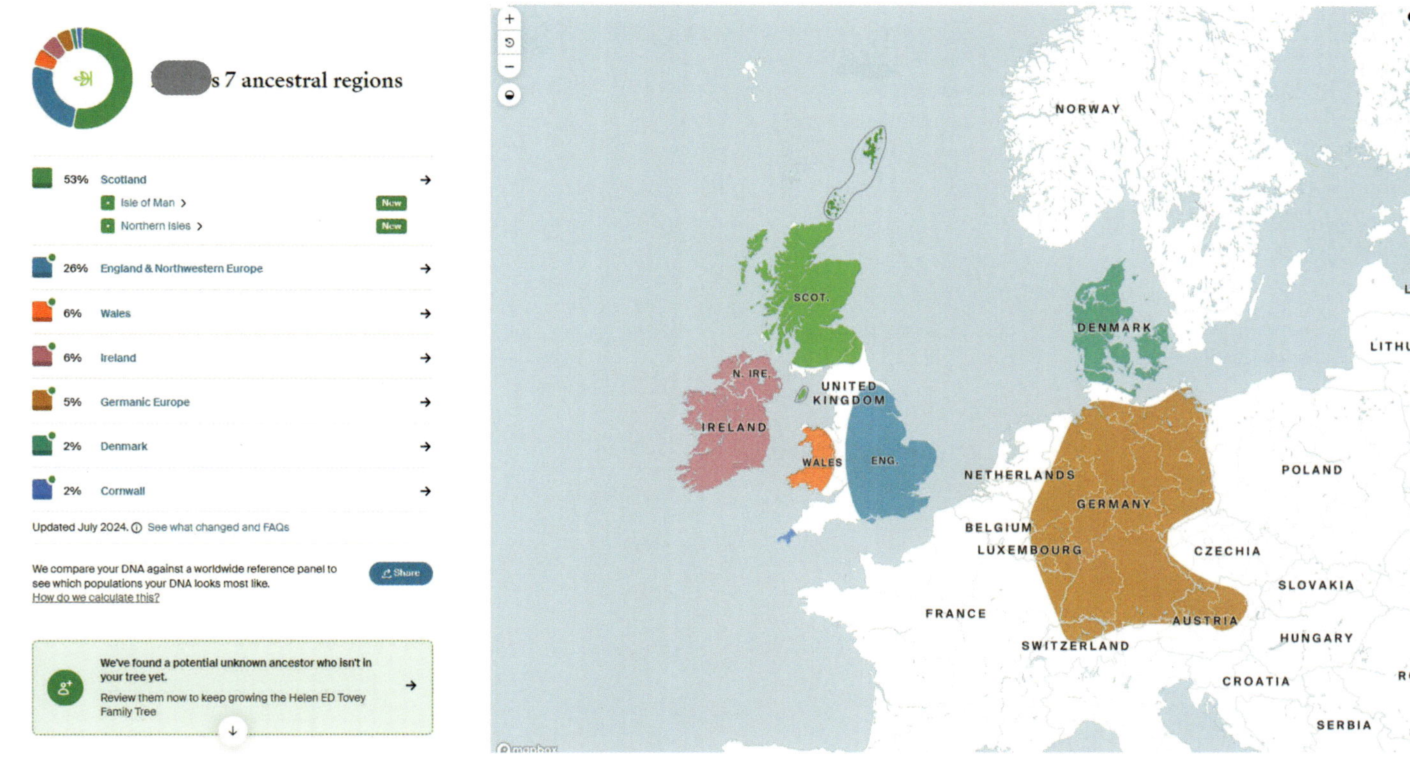

Figure 1: an example of the Origins reported for a person who has tested with AncestryDNA

'Origins'. Within it, you will find your Ancestral Regions, which provide a top-level picture, reporting percentages at a country level. For example, you may learn that your regions are reported as:

- 53% Scottish
- 26% England and North-Western Europe
- 6% Ireland
- 6% Wales

See Figure 1 for an example of the Origins reported for a person who has tested with AncestryDNA.

The percentages are arrived at by a process undertaken by Ancestry in which they look at 1,001 sections of your DNA and compare each of those sections with the DNA samples in the reference panel, assessing which ancestral regions your sections resemble.

Ancestry have divided the world into 107 overlapping regions and groups, and your DNA will be allocated to the most appropriate ones.

Ancestry advise that your genetic link to the regions 'can go back hundreds of years or even more'.

What is a 'reference panel'?

As the Ancestry website states, 'A reference panel is a set of people whose DNA is typical of DNA from a certain place or group'.

When you take a test your DNA is compared to the DNA in the reference panel. By way of example, let's look at Ancestry.

Currently the Ancestry reference panel used for defining ancestral regions has 116,830 DNA samples in it, to which your 1,001 sections of DNA are compared and then assigned a location-based designation.

This link (**https://support.ancestry.co.uk/s/article/AncestryDNA-Reference-Panel**) provides a useful breakdown of which countries the 116,830 DNA samples in the reference panel relate to. For instance there are just 24 samples for 'Indigenous Arctic' but 2,000 for Scotland, and 1,090 for Cornwall alone. Take a look and see how many samples are in the reference panel for the locations of interest to you (illustrated in Figure 2).

Why do my ethnicity estimates vary between the testing companies?

Your ethnicity estimates vary between the different companies because each has its own reference panels, methodology, and list of regions into which they have divided the geography of the world.

The approach of comparing a tester's DNA to a reference panel on MyHeritage is very similar to that on Ancestry, but MyHeritage's analysis is based on its own uniquely developed reference panel.

Most other DNA testing companies use academic reference population clusters in addition to their own company databases. For instance, FamilyTreeDNA, in addition to its own company (Gene by Gene) DNA testing database, used Stanford University's Human Genome Diversity Project's database, and other academic projects, to help to build their reference population).

Back to MyHeritage, a 'Founder Population Project' was established by MyHeritage; the reference panel was made up of 5,000 people each of whom had a family tree showing ancestors from the same region, or ethnicity, for at least six generations.

The MyHeritage reference panel now has 79 regions defined from around the world. Find out more at **www.myheritage.com/wiki/Reference_Populations**

FamilyTreeDNA, meanwhile, compares your DNA sample with 8,053 DNA samples categorised into 90 reference populations in the most recent iteration of its Origins (3.0) updated in 2020 (see page 16 of the white paper mentioned below).

As explained on the FamilyTreeDNA website (**https://blog.familytreedna.com/myorigins-3-is-here**), when the company first reported population percentages, back in 2014, there were just 18 population clusters and four blended clusters. So, as you can see the reference populations continue to be developed over time, thus accounting for the changes you will see in your ethnicity estimate percentages when the company you tested with provides an update to their reference populations.

In summary, the DNA testing companies each have a different tactic to arrive at a reference population, and they have divided the globe into a different number of regions (currently Ancestry 107, MyHeritage 79 and FamilyTreeDNA 90, for instance). So, for these reasons your ethnicity estimate percentages will vary from company to company.

Browse the list of Continent-level Populations, Super Populations and Population Clusters on the FamilyTreeDNA website: **https://bit.ly/ftdna-pop-clusters**

Figure 2: Ancestry provides a useful breakdown of which countries the 116,830 DNA samples in the Ancestry reference panel relate to. See: https://support.ancestry.co.uk/s/article/AncestryDNA-Reference-Panel

https://support.ancestry.co.uk/s/article/AncestryDNA-Reference-Panel

Here's the breakdown of how many people are in each of the 107 regions:

Region	# of samples
Aboriginal & Torres Strait Islander	54
Aegean Islands	1,305
Anatolia & the Caucasus	2,000
Arabian Peninsula	1,260
Ashkenazi Jews	2,000
The Balkans	2,000
Baltics	2,000
Basque	429
Bengal	1,146
Benin & Togo	1,138
Burusho	17
Cameroon	291
Central & Eastern China	359
Central & Eastern Europe	2,000
Central & Southern Philippines	2,000
Central Nigeria	700
Central West Africa	497

Read the (46-page!) white paper

Learn about Origins 3.0 and FamilyTreeDNA's ethnicity estimate methodology at: **https://bit.ly/ftdna-white-paper**

This white paper is a fascinating read explaining the science behind the FamilyTreeDNA ethnicity estimate update 3.0, but also providing extensive useful background reading for the keen DNA family historian. For instance, on page 11 we read the useful reminder: "Populations are groups of statistically similar DNA— they are not simple categories."

Why do they change?

DNA testing companies are continually looking to improve the accuracy of the ethnicity estimate percentages. To this end they periodically provide updates to the information they have previously provided. In February 2025, for instance, MyHeritage updated the number of regions from 42 to the 79 mentioned above. While it can be disconcerting to find that your ethnicity estimate has changed, hopefully it will gradually become refined, and more accurate, as time goes by.

Why are my geographic origins different from those of my siblings?

As you are probably aware, siblings only share in the region of 50% of their DNA with one another. This means that each of your siblings will have inherited some segments that you haven't. This will have an impact on the regional 'buckets' into which their DNA sections are put, and how many sections are put in each bucket. If you compare your DNA with that of a sibling, you may see that you have 53% Scottish, while they have 47% or 64% etc.

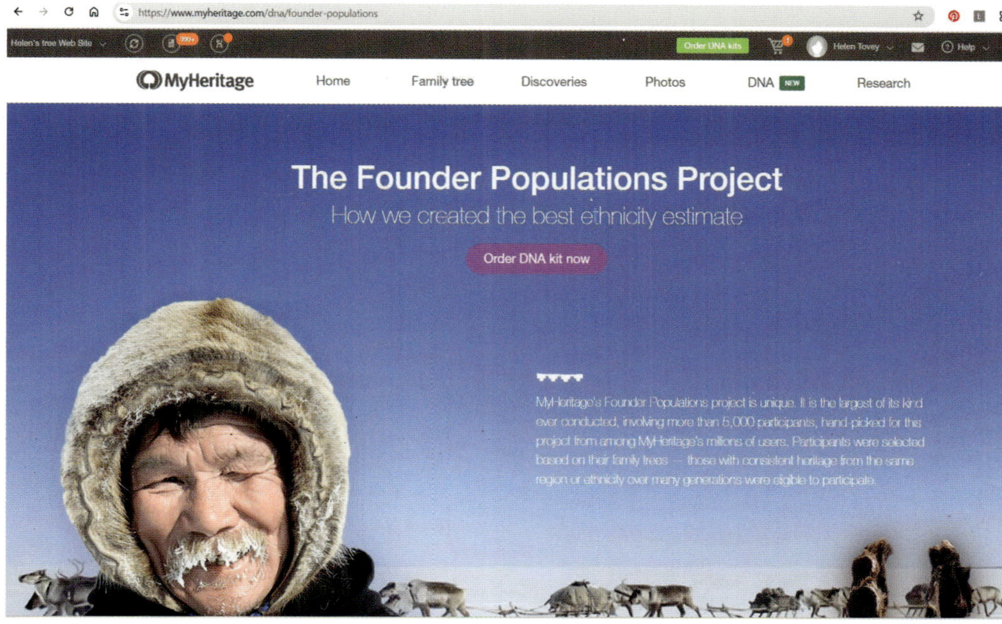

Figure 3: find out about the unique Founder Populations Project from MyHeritage at www.myheritage.com/wiki/Reference_Populations

How far can I rely on my ethnicity estimates?

These points can be helpful to remember.

1. Your ethnicity estimates will continue to evolve. They are just estimates.
2. As they become more precise you may feel that they have become more inaccurate. (For instance you may wholeheartedly agree that your ancestry is European, but when it's refined from 78% Scottish to 43% Scottish, you may not agree that your ancestry has become 'less Scottish' – particularly if you have many Scottish connections in your tree).
3. Any perceived inaccuracy will hopefully be resolved over time as reference populations and analysis continue to develop.
4. Don't set your heart on your ethnicity estimate percentages, and think long and hard before tattooing them on your body!

If they change will my match list change?

If your ethnicity estimates change, your DNA match list will not change. Your ethnicity estimate percentages and your list of DNA matches are calculated on a completely different basis to one another.

For your autosomal DNA match list, in the region of 700,000 of your markers (SNPs) are compared with 700,000 markers of other people in the DNA database of the testing company with which you've tested. Your match list is a list of the people with whom you match sections of DNA. As mentioned previously, for your ethnicity estimates sections of your DNA are compared with the reference panels.

> *DNA testing companies are continually looking to improve the accuracy of the ethnicity estimate percentages*

Hopefully this glimpse of the science and tactics that happen behind the scenes to arrive at your ethnicity estimates, will give you more clarity and confidence about what you are looking at.

A few words on Journeys, Genetic Groups & so forth

It was mentioned above, that as ethnicity estimates become refined over time you can sometimes feel as though they've become a little less accurate. Hopefully this is just a temporary situation to be resolved with a future company update.

There are aspects of ethnicity reporting from the DNA testing companies that are evermore precise and more accurate too. For example, consider Ancestry's Journeys and MyHeritage's Genetic Groups. Both of these tools are based on a comparison of your DNA and your family tree with that of the DNA and family trees of other testers in the respective company's databases of trees and DNA.

Ancestral Journeys are part of your ethnicity information from Ancestry that give you location-based clues about your ancestral inheritance over the past five to 20 generations. Typically the Journeys give insights over the past three centuries. They are not reported as percentages.

Combining analysis of the family trees of the 27 million DNA testers on Ancestry, and finding 'groups of interconnected DNA matches', the Ancestry Genetic Communities™ technology calculates locations that you are statistically very likely to find in your tree. For instance, you may learn not only that you are Scottish (as defined by the Ancestry Regions), but that, according to your Ancestry Journeys, have ties to the Northern Isles of Scotland. Much more precise information.

MyHeritage uses machine-learning algorithms to cluster DNA testers into groups of people who share segments of DNA, and analyses the trees of the DNA testers in its database, to calculate Genetic Groups. These reflect your ancestral inheritance over the past 400 years.

As the Ancestry Journeys and MyHeritage Genetic Groups reflect your ancestral inheritance within the past three or four centuries this is a suitable timeframe for which you may well have documentary evidence – and it's a great feeling when the DNA and the documents report the same thing!

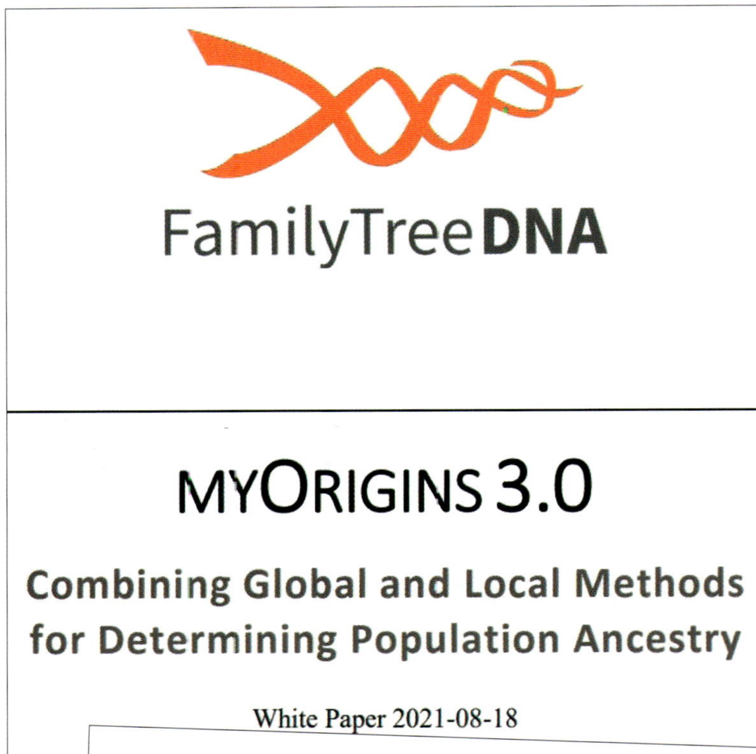

FamilyTreeDNA

MYORIGINS 3.0

Combining Global and Local Methods for Determining Population Ancestry

White Paper 2021-08-18

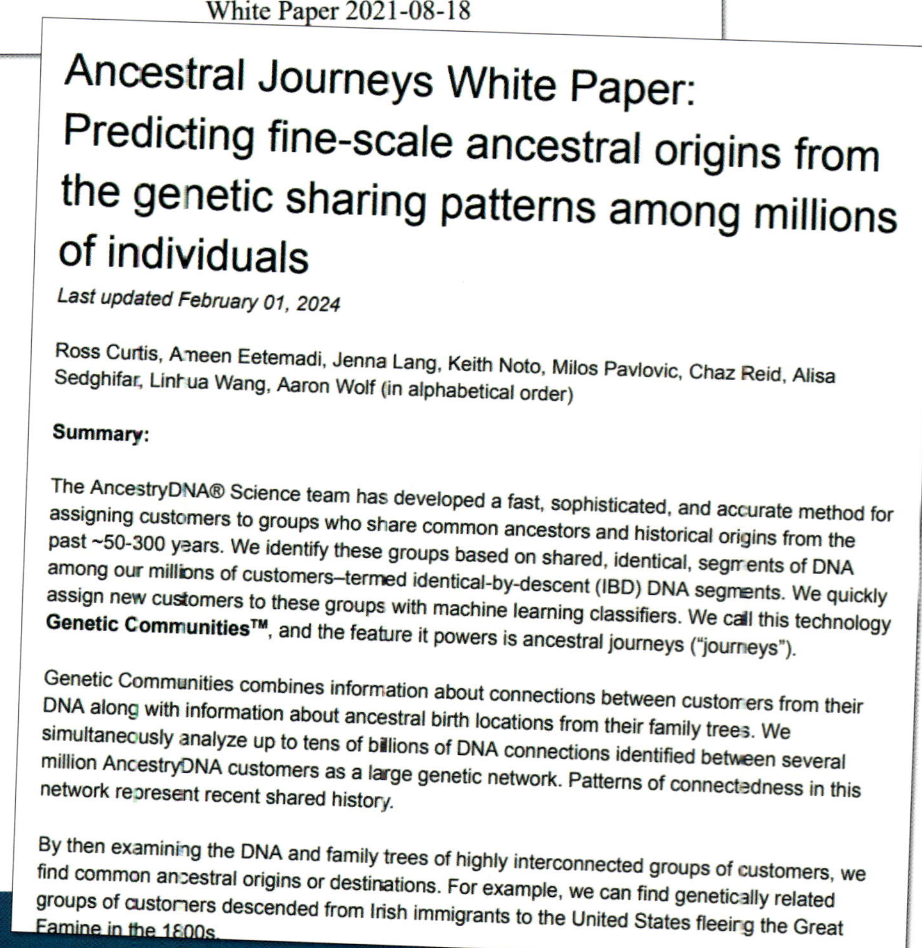

Ancestral Journeys White Paper: Predicting fine-scale ancestral origins from the genetic sharing patterns among millions of individuals

Last updated February 01, 2024

Ross Curtis, Ameen Eetemadi, Jenna Lang, Keith Noto, Milos Pavlovic, Chaz Reid, Alisa Sedghifar, Linhua Wang, Aaron Wolf (in alphabetical order)

Summary:

The AncestryDNA® Science team has developed a fast, sophisticated, and accurate method for assigning customers to groups who share common ancestors and historical origins from the past ~50-300 years. We identify these groups based on shared, identical, segments of DNA among our millions of customers–termed identical-by-descent (IBD) DNA segments. We quickly assign new customers to these groups with machine learning classifiers. We call this technology **Genetic Communities™**, and the feature it powers is ancestral journeys ("journeys").

Genetic Communities combines information about connections between customers from their DNA along with information about ancestral birth locations from their family trees. We simultaneously analyze up to tens of billions of DNA connections identified between several million AncestryDNA customers as a large genetic network. Patterns of connectedness in this network represent recent shared history.

By then examining the DNA and family trees of highly interconnected groups of customers, we find common ancestral origins or destinations. For example, we can find genetically related groups of customers descended from Irish immigrants to the United States fleeing the Great Famine in the 1800s.

Figures 4 and 5: read the white papers! For instance FamilyTreeDNA's coverage of MyOrigins 3.0 (**bit.ly/ftdna-white-paper**) and Ancestry's white paper on Journeys (**https://support.ancestry.co.uk/s/article/AncestryDNA-White-Papers**) both provide extensive detail of each companies science behind the scenes, and have many colourful and really explanatory diagrams, charts etc to illustrate key points clearly

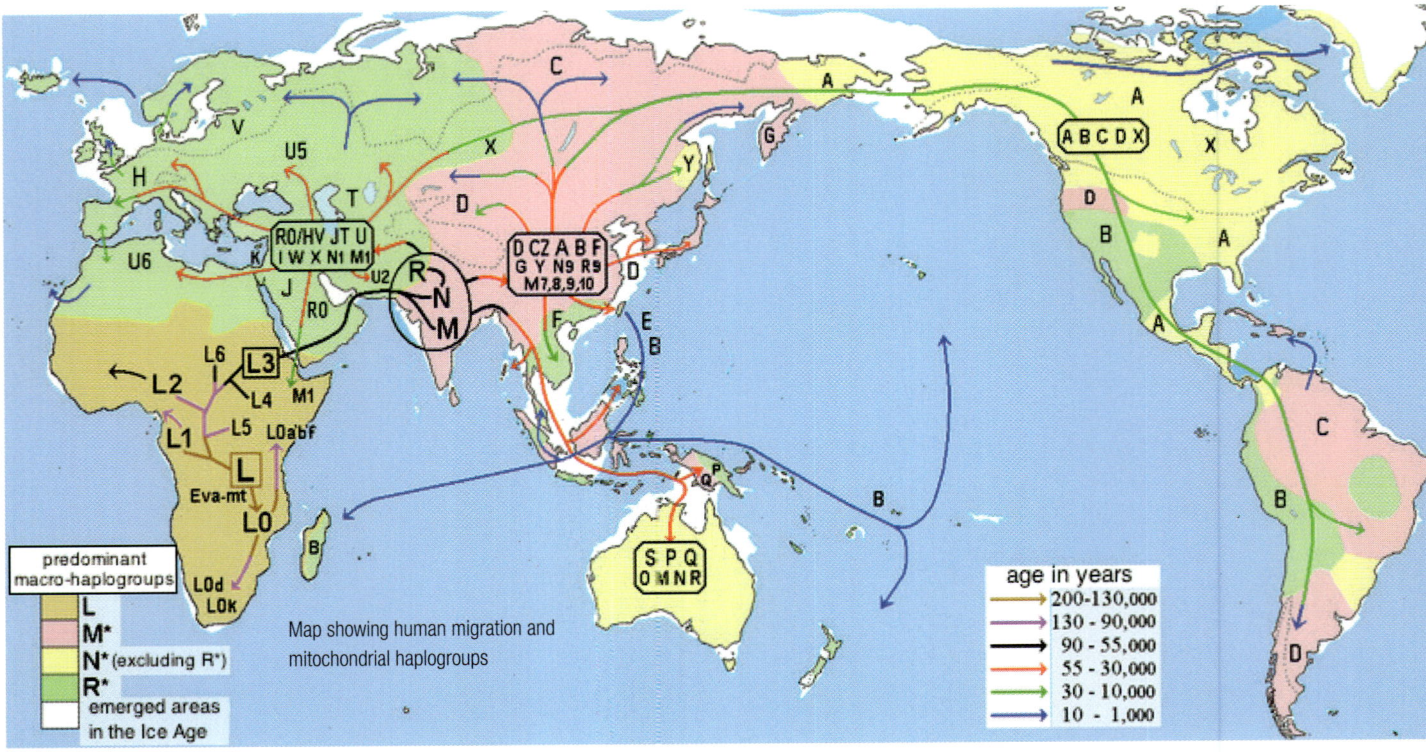

Map showing human migration and mitochondrial haplogroups

The tree of humanity

When thinking about and using DNA to trace family connections we are keenly aware of that sense of connection. For the past few decades the research community has been gathering DNA evidence, sorting it, and creating giant haplotrees. These reflect the genetic journey of humans through time, across specific lines of inheritance, as our guide explains

Why do the haplotrees only cover specific lines of inheritance?

Haplotrees, which are of interest to those studying DNA to learn more about their ancestors, cover specific lines of inheritance because they are based on the analysis of the Y-chromosome and mitochondrial DNA.

The Y-chromosome is studied to trace the direct paternal line; it is passed exclusively from father to son. Mitochondrial DNA (mtDNA) is studied to trace the direct mother line; while a mother passes mtDNA to both her sons and her daughters, only her daughters will pass it on to their children.

These two direct lines of inheritance are interesting to study as the Y-chromosome and mtDNA mutate very slowly. This allows lineages to be traced over vast tracts of time – tens of thousands of years.

When mutations occur, they can be mapped to create branches on haplotrees. This can provide fascinating broad-brush information about our ancestry, as explained on the 23andMe webpage (**https://customercare.23andme.com/hc/en-us/articles/235201447-Getting-Started-With-the-Haplogroup-Reports**): 'Before the age of European exploration – 500 years ago, people rarely moved between continents, so the report shows where people with a particular haplogroup lived for thousands of years.'

How far back do Y-DNA and mtDNA testing go?

'So far, all direct paternal (Y-DNA) lineages of humans alive today trace back to a common ancestor who lived in Africa 200,000 to 240,000 years ago,' states FamilyTreeDNA's FAQ guide (**https://help.familytreedna.com/hc/en-us/articles/360004593936-Y-DNA-Migration-Maps-Guide#do-all-direct-paternal-y-dna-lineages-trace-to-africa--0-5**). Meanwhile, the FamilyTreeDNA blog (**https://blog.familytreedna.com/mtdna/**) explains that: 'Mitochondrial DNA "Eve"… lived about 150,000 years ago and is the matrilineal ancestor of all humans.'

Where can I look at the Y and mtDNA haplotrees?

FamilyTreeDNA is the primary resource for exploring haplotrees. The company has the world's largest Y-DNA haplotree – with 90,000 branches and includes 674,000 SNP-tested users from the FamilyTreeDNA Y-DNA database. It also has the world's largest mtDNA haplotree – with 45,000 branches and 258,000 mt Full Sequences.

You can explore each of these public-view haplotrees freely online here:

- Y-DNA haplotree: **https://www.familytreedna.com/public/y-dna-haplotree**
- mtDNA haplotree: **https://www.familytreedna.com/public/mt-dna-haplotree**

To learn your place on the haplotree, you will need to

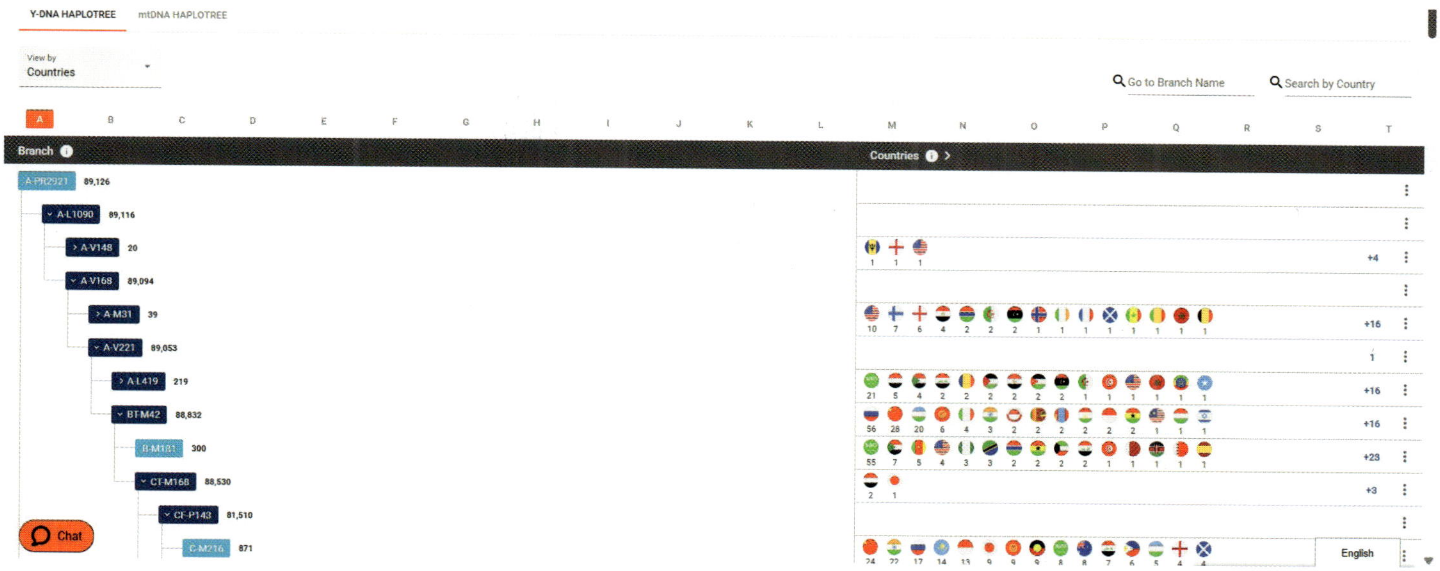

An excerpt from the public view Y-DNA haplotree on FamilyTreeDNA

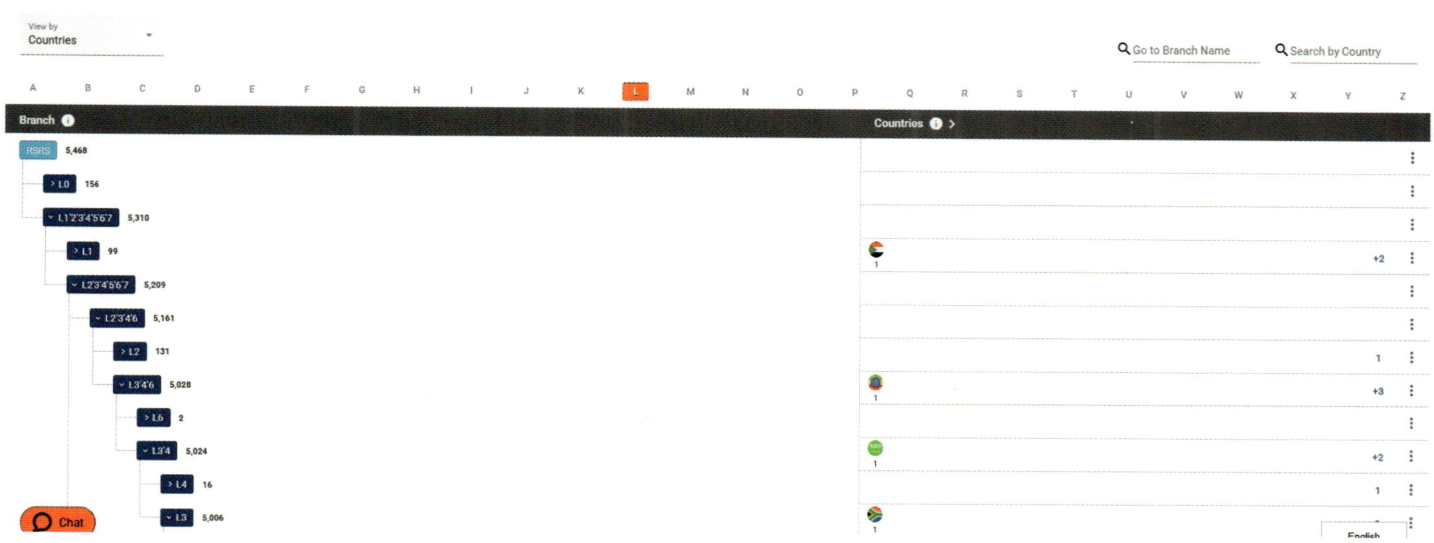

An excerpt from the public view mtDNA haplotree on FamilyTreeDNA

take the relevant DNA test. Males can be assigned to two haplogroups, one for their direct paternal line, one for their direct maternal one. Females can only be allocated to one haplogroup – that for their direct maternal line.

Some companies do report on haplogroup assignations when you do an autosomal DNA test (such as 23andMe and LivingDNA), but if you want to be able to find haplogroup matches – i.e. other people in your haplogroup – and be able to work with your DNA test results to that end you need to take a Y (males only) or mtDNA (males and females) test with FamilyTreeDNA, as they are the only company to provide databases of Y and mtDNA matches.

Haplotrees, haplogroups & haplotypes

Haplotypes can be grouped into haplogroups, and haplogroups are organised in a haplotree. The branch-and-tree analogy helps visualize how DNA samples are nested and organized in Y-DNA and mtDNA test results. When a mutation is identified within a haplogroup a subclade (i.e. a subgroup) is created.

As these databases develop over time – and further mutations are identified – the haplotrees, and haplogroups, will become increasingly detailed.

• For instance in 2021 the FamilyTreeDNA Y haplotree had 50,000 branches; now, in 2025, it has 90,000.

• In 2025, mitochondrial DNA studies saw a major development with the launch of Mitotree by FamilyTreeDNA. Mitotree includes 45,000 branches, and 258,000 mt Full Sequences. (Prior to Mitotree, FamilyTreeDNA used the academic mtDNA haplotree, Phylotree (**https://www.phylotree.org/**), which had just 5,400 branches and was based on 24,000 full and partial samples).

What is a haplotype?

The significance for people wishing to trace ancestry using DNA is that a haplotype is a genetic mutation (i.e. a letter change in your massive code of ACTG) that occurs somewhere on a single chromosome. Identifying such a genetic mutation in your DNA allows you to be placed in a haplogroup with others who share that haplotype (i.e. that letter sequence).

Read the full explanation here **https://www.genome.gov/genetics-glossary/haplotype**

How to create 'QUICK & DIRTY' TREES

Karen Evans gives us a guide to building 'quick and dirty' trees, and demonstrates how they can help to turbo-charge the results from our DNA matches

I have a confession and, even to me, it sounds odd. When I have a new DNA match, I actually don't mind if they have a small tree. Why? Because it gives me the chance to build 'quick and dirty' trees, and I adore building quick and dirty trees! I am not a masochist. I feel a thud of disappointment if a new match has no clues to get my teeth into, but a name and perhaps one parent on a tree and I can feel my heart beat a little faster with the thrill of the chase.

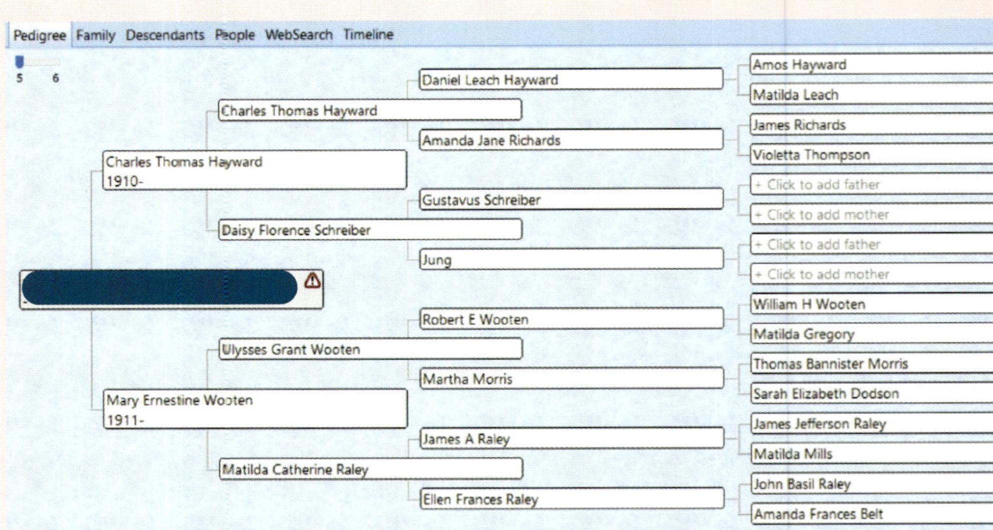

An example of a quick and dirty tree. You don't need to spend extra money on a tree like this and it can be assembled very rapidly. If you're lucky, it will suggest links to other trees you've created

What is a quick and dirty tree?

I define a 'quick and dirty' tree as one that is:

Quick: if I'm lucky, I want to get back to the match's 2 x great grandparents on all sides within a few hours. This isn't always possible!

Dirty: I'm using available online information to create a tree and not following the standards of proof I would with my own tree. I use hints on the sites and trees created by other users. Saying that, I do check that the hint is credible.

Ever growing: I have one database for all 'Q and D' trees. Each time I create a tree in this database I am looking for possible links to my known tree or other trees I've created which do not yet link to my known family.

Unsearchable for anyone else: There may be mistakes on this tree which I don't want anyone to inadvertently copy – so make sure you have set your tree, on Ancestry for instance, to 'private' and not able to be found in the Ancestry index.

Free: I don't spend money creating this tree but use the sites I have already have access to. I have a subscription for Ancestry and Findmypast so mine their resources, but I don't pay to access a site if only the search engine is free.

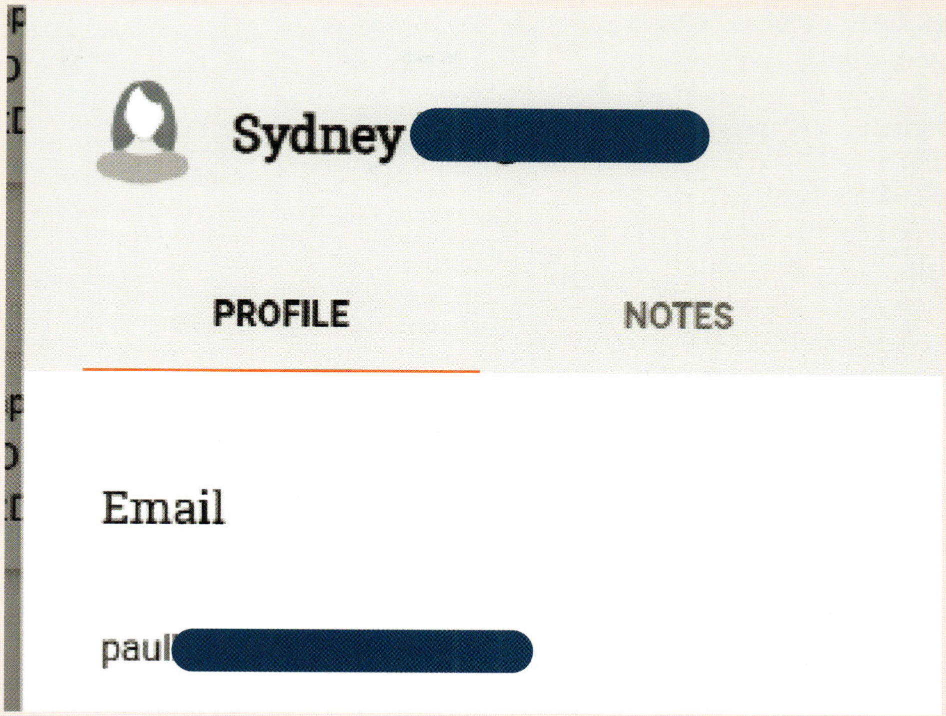

Sydney's profile on FTDNA, which indicated she was in the US, and also linked her to a man called Paul. These details provided clues that enabled Karen to conduct searches for further information

So, how do you go about Q&D tree-building?

You will have lots of matches with no trees. Firstly, check that there isn't a tree lurking in the background. If you tested with Ancestry it may be that a match hasn't linked their DNA test with their tree. You will see this marked as an 'unlinked tree' which may or may not be a tree that relates to the tester, for example your match may have taken a test but it is their partner managing it and the unlinked tree relates to their research. I have also found trees on sites such as FamilySearch and WikiTree or they have uploaded a GEDCOM to a site such as GEDmatch.

First steps to a Q&D tree

You may have checked and there is no tree. So which matches should you try to build quick and dirty trees for?

It's usually easier to find matches who share more DNA with you as the link to a family name or area could be more apparent. Look at your match's name. Look for high matches where the name is distinguishable. People often put their first name and surname together and add numbers which correspond to year of birth or age. Try to go for male matches, as women may be using their married name (though that's not always the end).

I remember the first quick and dirty tree I created which established the common ancestor between the match and my mother.

Here are some of the ways I use to build a tree with the limited information of only a name – Sydney Landerson.

Remember to use your testing site's tools. Check to see which side your match is from – if you have clustered your matches you may know which branch they belong to. Even if that cluster is unknown to you, there could be trees that give hints to a common surname or geographic area. If you are about to build a Q and D tree for a match who is in a cluster of matches where the Fletchers of Wolverhampton are popping up, it might be something to look out for. Sydney was in a group of matches that all pointed to my mother's paternal grandmother's line.

Internet searches

Google their name or username. Many people use the same username, regardless of site. Does their username pop up on any genealogical chat sites? I found a match who had asked a question about a family name on Rootschat, which gave me vital clues to surnames and places. On FamilyTreeDNA and Gedmatch the matches have an attached email address that you can also Google. At the very least the address could show the country where a match may be living. Sydney was on FamilyTreeDNA with a US email address which included the name of a possible son or husband, named Paul.

There are many websites dedicated to finding people, and their basic searches are free. If it's a US match there is even more information online which could include names, ages, possible family links and places of residence. Sites include:

- **www.fastbackgroundcheck.com/people**
- **mylife.com**
- **www.whitepages.com**

If it's a UK match, then you could use 192.com People Finder (**www.192.com/people**). A search for Sydney Landerson told me that she was born in 1937 and lived in Maryland; it also gave associated names, including Paul. Paul was shown as aged about 60, so more likely to be a son. Landerson was therefore probably Sydney's married name.

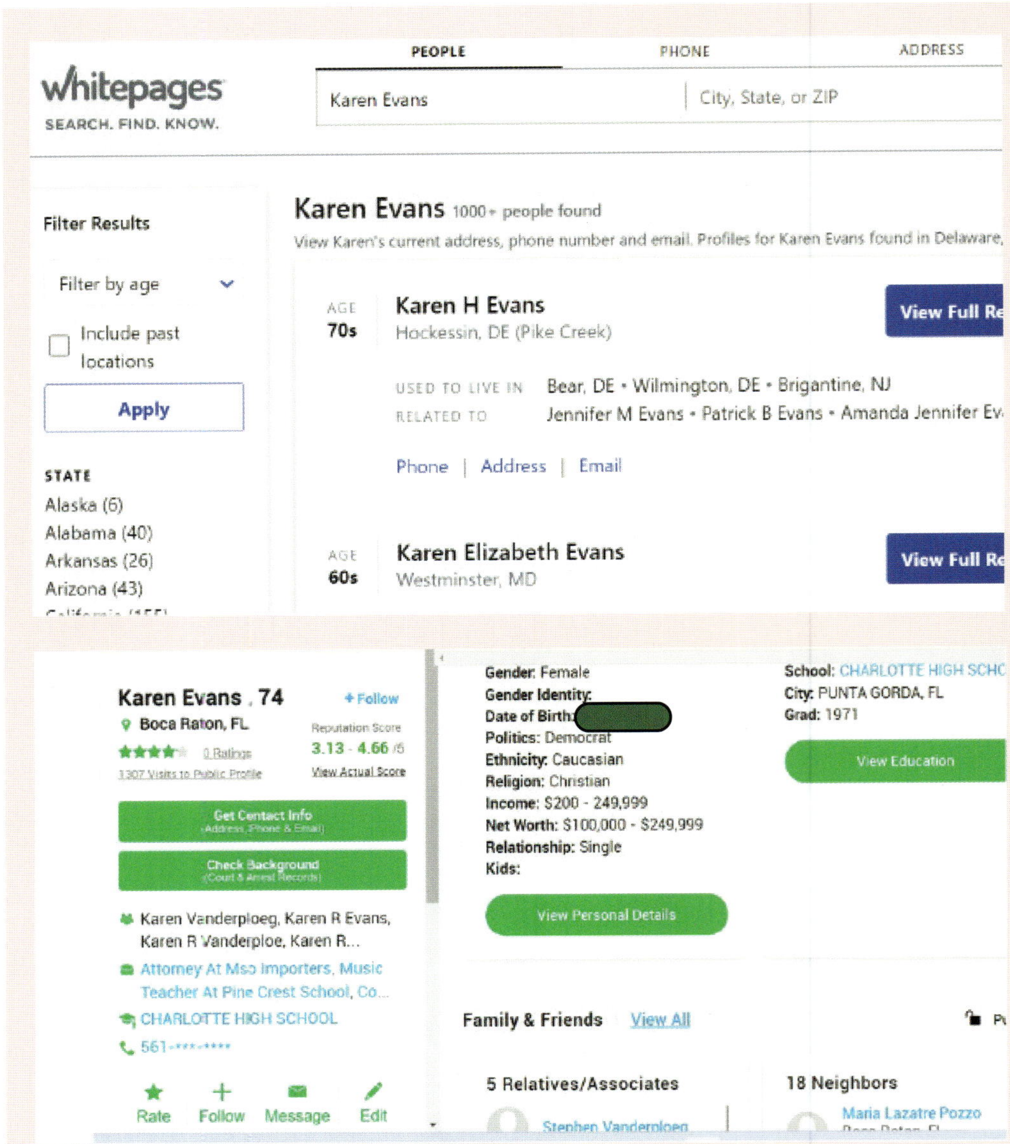

An example of a people-search website, which can yield valuable information on an individual's location, date of birth and family links. Many of these sites offer basic searches for free

Social media searches

I looked for them on social media. You can search for names in Facebook, Twitter, LinkedIn etc and see whether your match has a profile. This wouldn't work for John Smith, but I have found matches this way – one had even commented about her DNA results. Using their friends' list on Facebook you can sometimes build up a list of relatives' names, so you have living family groups. A bit like usernames, people sometimes use the same profile picture, so if a match has added a photo and you see the same one on Facebook you know you are on to a winner! Paul Landerson was on Facebook, which allowed me to work out family groups more clearly.

Weaving the clues

Using all my information I was able to find Sydney's marriage to a Kenneth Landerson on Ancestry and, with a maiden name of Hendry, I located her on the 1940 Census. Bingo! Sydney's mother was from England, and another marriage record established the family – Sydney was my 3rd cousin once removed. I emailed Paul armed with my information and I was soon swapping information and stories with him that brought long dead relations to life.

A simple 'Google'

Googling a match can also bring up marriage or death announcements, newspaper articles in which relatives have featured, places they may have worked – the list is virtually endless.

Find A Grave (**www.findagrave.com**) is particularly

useful, as family members have often added obituaries that can include generations of people related to the deceased.

Building a tree with the information

Often the hardest part to a quick and dirty tree is getting started. You need that first nugget of information that takes the match's name to their parents. Finding the age of your match is going to be important, since you need to get to records to build the tree. If I'm able to establish my match's birth on the civil registration birth index I will have a mother's maiden name and I can look for a marriage between the two names. Older matches will have parents included in the 1939 Register and I may find the mother with her maiden name and married name added. I do tend to look for first names that were more popular in the fifties and sixties, although I have been able to create trees for people who were born in this century!

Once I have been able to link my match to people in records I can then start building their tree in the same way I would build my own, looking at census, birth and marriage records, and any other documentation I can find online.

Searching Facebook and other social media sites may well lead you to one of your matches, and friend lists often contain the names of family members, giving you new leads. Look out for matching profile pictures – a sure sign that you have found the person you're looking for!

Quick and dirty trees – trouble-shooting

When you create quick and dirty trees, you are hoping to find a common ancestor to your own tree but this is not always the case. My paternal line is somewhat problematic. My paternal grandfather was illegitimate and so were my paternal grandmother's mother and grandmother! This meant that when I clustered my matches I had several groups who did not fit into my known tree. Fortunately, matches in my father's test identified grandad's father but the other lines were not so clear. The further you are genetically from an unknown ancestor the more difficult it is to find the DNA matches. This is because you are looking for any children they may have had who

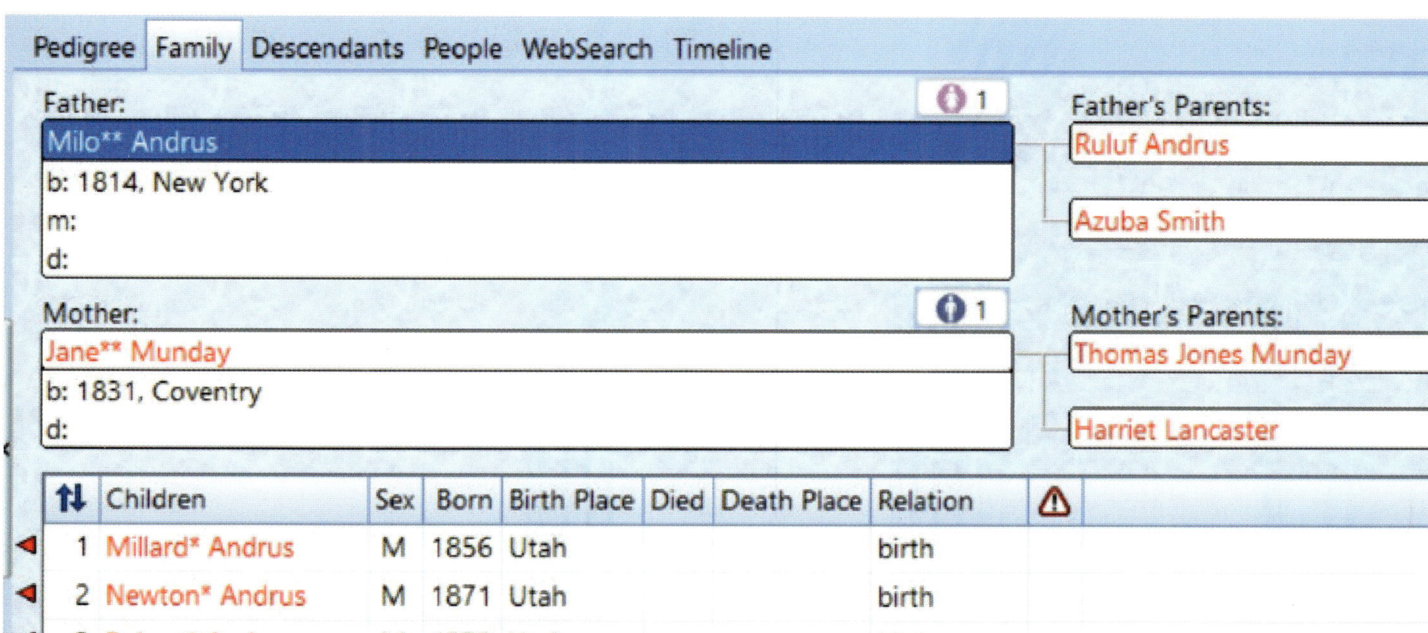

An unknown cluster of matches on my maternal line. Several Q and D trees have linked back to Milo Andrus and Jane Munday

Father:
William** Robinson
b: 1835, Chilson
m: 9 Mar 1857, Bilston
d:

Father's Parents:
Benjamin** Robinson
Sarah** Barnes

Mother:
Frances** Jones
b: 1839, Wrexham Wales
d: Jun 1913, Wolverhampton

Mother's Parents:
Robert** Jones
Mary**

	Children	Sex	Born	Birth Place	Died	Death Place	Relation	⚠
1	John Robinson	M	Mar 1859	Bilston			birth	
2	Mary Ann Robinson	F	22 Jun 1861	Bilston			birth	
3	Maria* Robinson	F	Jun 1863	Bilston	by 1911		birth	
4	Eliza* Robinson	F	Jun 1865	Bilston			birth	
5	Benjamin Robinson	M	Jun 1867	Bilston	by maybe 1871		birth	
6	George Thomas Robinson	M	Sep 1870	Bilston			birth	
7	William Robinson	M	Jun 1872	Bilston	by maybe 1874		birth	

Karen writes: 'I have DNA matches from both William and Frances' siblings and their parents' siblings'

are going to be half siblings to your known ancestor, or you are trying to identify the unknown ancestor's parents, who are even more distant. These matches will also share less DNA with you: the further you are from the common ancestor, the less DNA you will have in common.

One of my clusters had several matches, some of which shared over 50cMs with my father and my paternal aunts. When I looked at the trees available I noticed a link to Barrow-in-Furness. I began creating quick and dirty trees and saw the surname Jones in several of them, but as this is a common surname I couldn't be sure if this pointed to a possible line. However the Jones family in these trees was in Barrow and I therefore focused on it, looking for more clues. My hunch paid off – the family had moved to Bilston, which is where my paternal grandmother's line was from. I also saw that several quick and dirty trees were showing a link to a Robinson family from Chilson in Oxfordshire – it was a very happy day when I found a William Robinson from the Chilson line who married a Frances Jones from the Barrow line! I now know that, based on ages, my missing 2x great grandfather was one of their elder sons.

Some of my Quick and Dirty trees are little twigs with only a few names because I couldn't find any clues; others grew and flourished but show no sign of linking to my tree. The great thing about Q&D trees is they are an opportunity to find ancestors – even if they are not our own – and sometimes find the link that makes it all worthwhile. Why not have a go? You never know who you will find!

TOP TIPS & THOUGHTS ON Q&D TREES

Check for other trees

If your match has an unlinked tree, go and check their profile page. Sometimes they have more than one tree, and the information you need may be lurking on one of the others.

Build out your matches trees

Build out trees, looking for geographical places that are common to your own. My ancestry is very much around the areas of Staffordshire and Worcestershire; if a match's grandfather is born in Dudley and the other grandparents were born in Liverpool, I will concentrate on the Dudley grandfather's line first. This doesn't mean I'm guaranteed to find the common ancestor along this branch but it makes the most sense to follow this line.

Use your logic and concentrate on the most likely places

Similarly, if a quick and dirty tree's branches start showing links to European countries where I have no ancestry, I will build those out last.

Remember your matches may be descended from emigrant lines

Don't be put off if a match and their first few generations of ancestors are from America. I was surprised how many trees quickly led back to people who had emigrated, and this then gave me the most likely branch to pursue. Remember that the United States has released the 1950 census so your matches may be on it and there is a very good chance their parents are.

An alternative outlook with Living DNA

Living DNA offers a unique combination of approaches to genealogy, providing insights into your Neanderthal ancestors, wellbeing reports, a focus on British and African ancestry, and details as to how you fit on the haplotree. We spoke to Living DNA's Emma Smith to find out more

Whilst many of us will naturally opt for the larger genealogy organisations when choosing a DNA test, there are alternatives that can lead to new discoveries and a different assessment of your ancestry.

Living DNA's vision

Unlike many DNA testing companies that focus solely on ethnicity estimates and family matching, Living DNA was founded with a broader vision: to highlight human diversity while also emphasising our shared genetic connections. 'Living DNA was founded on the aspiration to combat racism,' Living DNA's Emma Smith tells us. 'We want to show as many people as possible how individual and diverse the human population is but also to demonstrate our similarities. To show that identity goes further than the colour of your skin or the location you grew up in.'

From the outset, Living DNA has been involved in projects such as 'Show Racism the Red Card' and 'One Family, One World', using genetic research to break down barriers between people and cultures. At a time when global divisions are growing, the company believes that DNA testing can help reconnect people with their roots and each other.

This world outlook also extends to the health data DNA tests can collect and share. 'Our health systems are nearing bankruptcy yet 80% of illness and disease is preventable and lifestyle-related,' says Emma. 'What if we could change that? What if through the power of DNA and the way it's delivered we are able to re-connect with ourselves and each other? What if as a result, we start to live a more enriched and healthy life? We see that as more than possible.'

The company's principles are clear, but how does Living DNA differ from other offerings and what can it provide to the family historian?

Discover your haplogroup

Both motherline and fatherline haplogroup and haplotype results are included in the Living DNA Full Ancestry testing costs, helping users determine where they fit on the haplotree.

The Migration Maps trace your mitochondrial DNA inheritance (received from your direct maternal line – i.e. your mother's mother's mother and so forth) and your Y-DNA inheritance (received from your direct paternal line, if you are a male). Your haplogroup and haplotype will help you gauge parts of your DNA inheritance over many thousands of years.

Note that a matching database is not provided, so you will not be able to see which other DNA testers on Living DNA share the same haplotypes as you. 'Living DNA currently does not offer MT and Y matching but we do offer space in the family matching section for users to add their Haplogroup for matches to view' Emma says. (FamilyTreeDNA is the only genetic genealogy company that offers a haplotype matching database for family historians).

KEEPING YOUR DATA SECURE

Living DNA offer a number of measures to ensure your DNA data is kept safe and secure, including:

- Strict GDPR data protection regulations
- Does not share or sell data
- Participation in research is entirely optional
- Aggregated data may be used to improve system quality, but personal information remains secure
- A two-step authentication (OTP) feature has been introduced, providing an additional layer of protection

Gain insights to your ancestral regions

The Living DNA test offers a focus on British and African ancestry and includes detailed reports, maternal and paternal haplogroups (usually female testers can only be assigned a maternal haplogroup), and can provide up to 150 regions across the globe, including sub-regional breakdown. Results can also be presented in a personalised book, intended as a keepsake or a gift for relatives.

Explore your archaic DNA inheritance

Going back much further in time, Living DNA also offer a 'Neanderthal' test, which shows you how your characteristics derive from Archaic Human DNA. 'Alongside all the benefits from Full Ancestry, we can provide you with Neanderthal & Denisovan scores. Your score represents the number of alleles (DNA letters) that you share with Neanderthals and Denisovans. Compare your level of Neanderthal DNA with the rest of our userbase, as a whole and by region,' explains Emma. The Neanderthal and Denisovan report is able to be purchased as an add-on to the Full Ancestry test, as are the Classical (Greek, Roman) and Viking reports.

Find & work with your DNA matches

Living DNA services include a Family Matching tool which helps users discover genetic relatives by comparing your autosomal DNA against potential matches, and a Chromosome Browser, available to users who opt for full autosomal analysis, which displays the genomic location of the DNA segments, as centiMorgans, that are shared between you and one of your matches.

Upload your DNA to Living DNA free!

Whilst you may have opted to test with a different testing company, your 'raw' DNA data isn't limited to that database, and can be uploaded to other websites, including Living DNA.

What advantages do you stand to gain by importing your DNA to Living DNA? 'Because each company uses unique methodologies and reference panels, results can vary,' a Living DNA spokesperson recently explained. 'A region that appears in one company's report may be entirely absent or look

Perfect for gifting, the personalised Ancestry book provides a keepsake experience. The book will provide you with your recent ancestry breakdown including both maternal and paternal (If you are genetically male) results

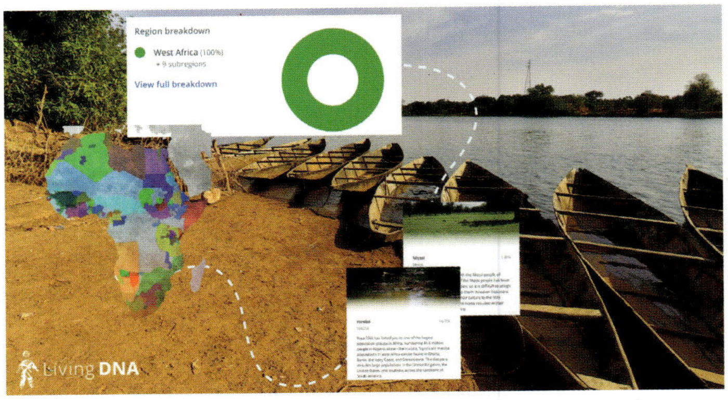

different in another. By uploading your DNA to other platforms, you can access unique analytical techniques, uncover hidden ancestral connections, or even refine your regional breakdown with greater accuracy.'

Living DNA accepts DNA test uploads from the following companies: AncestryDNA, 23AndMe, MyHeritage, FamilyTreeDNA (family finder), Gene by Gene, and Genographic (Geno 2.0). Unlock more of your DNA story by exploring the variety of updates available in the Living DNA store.

Upload your Living DNA data to Gedmatch

Living DNA data can also go the other way, and users can upload their results to the Gedmatch website (**www.gedmatch.com**), which allows you to analyse results and compare DNA shared with other users. (Note the law enforcement opt-out option if deciding to use Gedmatch, if you do not wish your DNA, once uploaded to Gedmatch, to be used to that end).

Your health

Living DNA's Wellbeing experience is available via an online portal, either as an upgrade or a standalone kit, and provides personalised insights into how genetics can influence various aspects of health and lifestyle. 'The focus on food intolerances, vitamin absorption, and muscle response seems especially practical for tailoring diet and exercise plans,' Emma says. As ever, such information should not replace professional medical advice, however.

Looking forward

'Living DNA has big plans for the next year or so,' Emma says. The next update promises to provide more detail to regions worldwide, specifically those with European and Asian ancestry. 'We are also continuing with building our panels and would love to improve other regions such as Ireland and France,' Emma adds. 'As part of building this, taking part in our research is vital. If anyone would like to get involved they can upload to us and opt into research.'

Future plans also include the ability to upload full NGS [Next-Generation Sequencing] data, more for family matching, and adding X chromosome reporting to the matching method. 'Furthermore we will be adding a clustering tool, and we will be making updates and improvements to our Viking product as well as releasing a new ancestry upgrade option.'

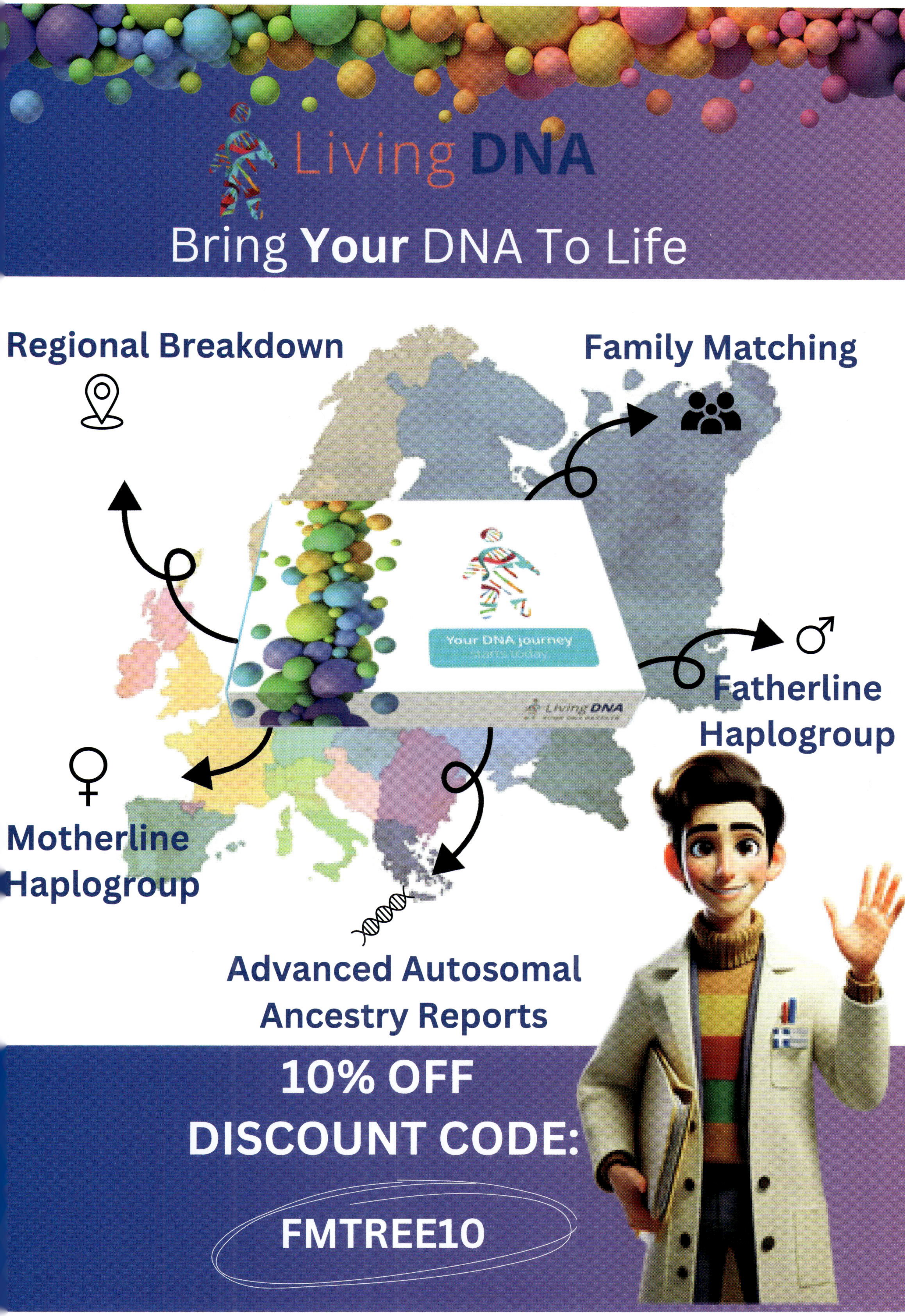
Living DNA
Bring Your DNA To Life
Regional Breakdown
Family Matching
Your DNA journey starts today.
Living DNA
Fatherline Haplogroup
Motherline Haplogroup
Advanced Autosomal Ancestry Reports
10% OFF
DISCOUNT CODE:
FMTREE10

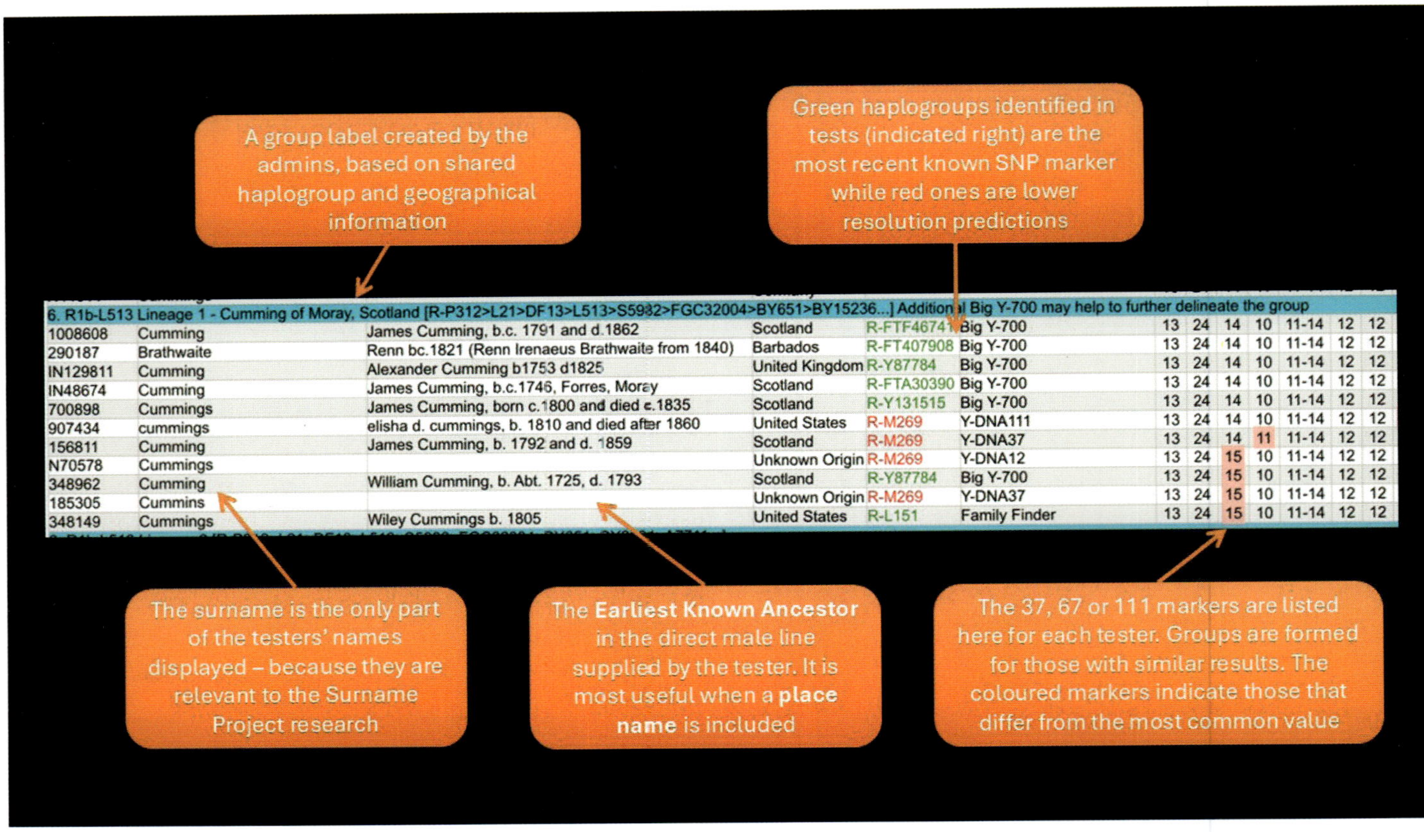

6. R1b-L513 Lineage 1 - Cumming of Moray, Scotland [R-P312>L21>DF13>L513>S5982>FGC32004>BY651>BY15236...] Additional Big Y-700 may help to further delineate the group												
1008608	Cumming	James Cumming, b.c. 1791 and d.1862	Scotland	R-FTF46741	Big Y-700	13	24	14	10	11-14	12	12
290187	Brathwaite	Renn bc.1821 (Renn Irenaeus Brathwaite from 1840)	Barbados	R-FT407908	Big Y-700	13	24	14	10	11-14	12	12
IN129811	Cumming	Alexander Cumming b1753 d1825	United Kingdom	R-Y87784	Big Y-700	13	24	14	10	11-14	12	12
IN48674	Cumming	James Cumming, b.c.1746, Forres, Moray	Scotland	R-FTA30390	Big Y-700	13	24	14	10	11-14	12	12
700898	Cummings	James Cumming, born c.1800 and died c.1835	Scotland	R-Y131515	Big Y-700	13	24	14	10	11-14	12	12
907434	cummings	elisha d. cummings, b. 1810 and died after 1860	United States	R-M269	Y-DNA111	13	24	14	10	11-14	12	12
156811	Cumming	James Cumming, b. 1792 and d. 1859	Scotland	R-M269	Y-DNA37	13	24	14	11	11-14	12	12
N70578	Cummings		Unknown Origin	R-M269	Y-DNA12	13	24	15	10	11-14	12	12
348962	Cumming	William Cumming, b. Abt. 1725, d. 1793	Scotland	R-Y87784	Big Y-700	13	24	15	10	11-14	12	12
185305	Cummins		Unknown Origin	R-M269	Y-DNA37	13	24	15	10	11-14	12	12
348149	Cummings	Wiley Cummings b. 1805	United States	R-L151	Family Finder	13	24	15	10	11-14	12	12

Figure 1: a lineage from the Cummings Surname Project showing the grouping of matching testers, most of whom share a surname and an ancestral origin in Northern Scotland. The image is from the public view, excluding members choosing to keep their results visible only within the Project

How might a DNA project help you?

DNA project manager, John Cleary, takes a look at DNA projects and answers useful questions, including what is a DNA project? Why are they useful? And how do you set one up? The focus of his attention will be on the projects run in association with FamilyTreeDNA

What are Projects?

Anyone researching their family history using DNA can develop a project bringing together different people's test results to answer a genealogical question. However, genetic genealogy Projects (with a capital P) are larger organised activities, often supported by the testing companies to help testers gain more value and information through sharing their results.

These are mostly associated with FamilyTreeDNA, which supports in excess of 10,000 of them on its Group Projects platform.

What information do the Projects study?

Among things commonly found in such Projects are:

- Sub-groups of testers with similar results, possibly indicating descent from a common ancestor (see Fig. 1)
- The typical or 'modal' marker values for each sub-group
- Information on surnames, possible ancestors' names, dates and places within each sub-group
- Background information, findings and news posted by the administrators
- An activity feed where members can post questions and information about their research, families and lineages of interest.

When are projects useful/less useful?

Projects are particularly useful for comparing Y and mtDNA results with individual marker values laid out in large results tables, where they can ►

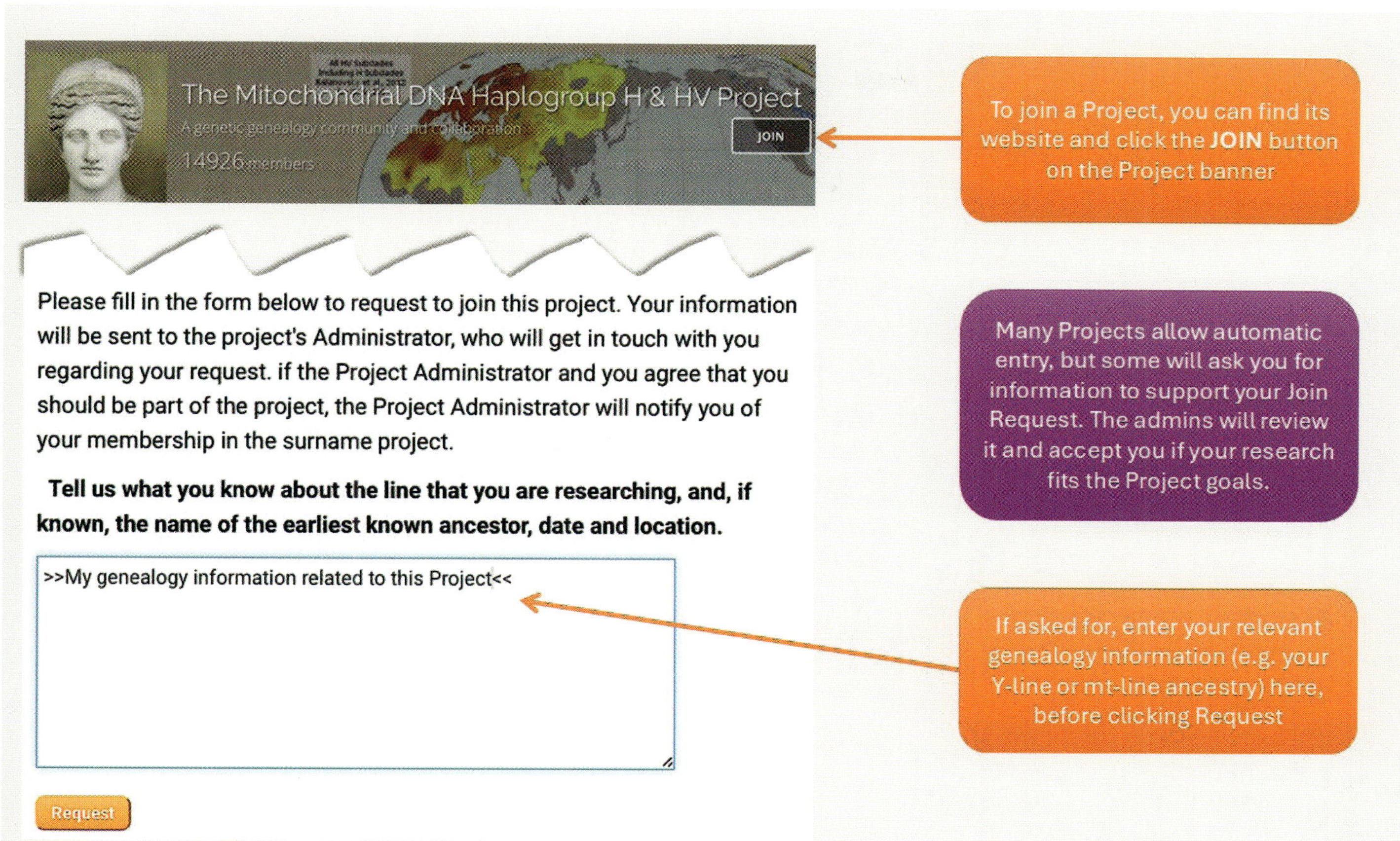

Fig. 2: join a Project by clicking its JOIN button. Some Projects may ask you for your related genealogical information in response before approving the request.

Types of Projects – and examples

To find the examples search online for the name of each Project + "DNA project"

Surname Projects (Y)

Dedicated to a shared surname or group of closely related surnames. Because most surnames have multiple origins, there may be several lineages in a Project that are not closely related within 'genealogical time'. Examples: Cummings, Gleason/Gleeson, Ó Cléirigh, Cruwys all arrange members into surname-lineage groupings.

Haplogroup Projects (Y/mt)

People who share a Y or mtDNA haplogroup marker. These can be huge projects recruiting carriers of ancient or prehistoric DNA markers. The R R1b ALL Subclades Master Project has over 33,000 members, the biggest single Project on FTDNA's platform. The mtDNA Haplogroup H & HV is the biggest mtDNA Project with almost 15,000 members.

At the other end of the scale, smaller haplogroups can be clusters of surnames with common ancestry just before surnames began to be adopted. The YP984-JACKS Project links approximately 5 surname lineages sharing a medieval pre-surname ancestry.

Lineage Projects (Y/mt/autosomal)

A focus on the descendants of a named historical person or ancestor. The Isaac Cummings Family Project (Y) welcomes the descendants of a man who emigrated from Essex to New England in 1635.

Geographical Projects (Y/mt/autosomal)

Testers with descent from a particular geographical location, or are themselves from the region. The aim is to build a collection of haplotypes or test results representing the region. While mostly for Y and mt, some administrators encourage autosomal testers to join if there is a geographical connection. The largest Geographical Project is Finland DNA (Suomi DNA), with 22,000 members. The Scottish, Ireland, Norway, Sweden, Polish and Germany Projects all have over 10,000 members.

Some like the Devon Project operate a requirement that members have a recent link to the region. The North of Ireland Project, run by local organisation NIFHS, strongly supports joiners who have taken autosomal DNA testing, or order it via the Project.

Heritage Projects (Y/mt/autosomal)

Related to a particular historical or cultural event and collecting multiple lineages descended from people linked to that event. The Scottish Prisoners Project researches descendants of prisoners taken by Oliver Cromwell's invasion of Scotland in 1650 and transported to New England. The African American Griot Legacy Project is open to testers who can identify ancestry from the Trans-Atlantic Slave Trade and African diaspora.

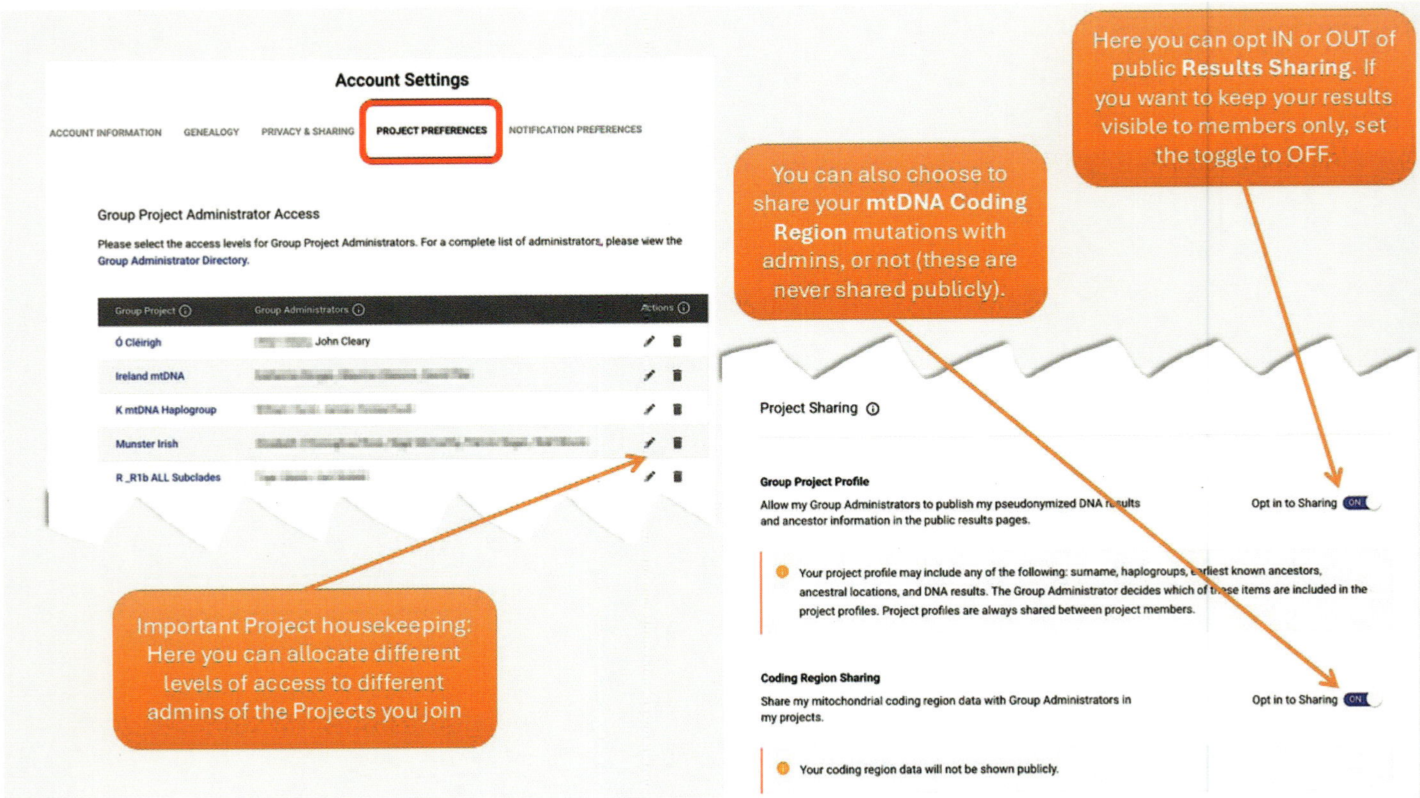

Fig. 3: Set your viewing and privacy setting for Projects in your FTDNA account.

► be compared for patterns of similarity, difference and marker inheritance.

Expanding your cluster of related DNA tests is a big benefit of joining a Project, along with gaining from the knowledge of the administrators, who will be experts on the surnames

Projects are less useful for autosomal DNA testers, as autosomal matching generally leads to research on branches of the tester's own tree. For this reason, specialist atDNA companies like AncestryDNA or 23andMe do not have similar Project platforms.

However, administrators of FTDNA's Y and mt Projects are usually happy to accept Family Finder testers to their Projects when there is a relevant connection, and some of them make active use of autosomal test information.

How to join a Project

You can join an FTDNA Group Project if you have taken an FTDNA test or want to buy one.

Projects can be found by searching on the WWW (see 'Types of project' panel, page 63) and a JOIN button is located on the front-page banner of each one (Fig. 2).

If you have not yet taken a test, you will be sent a message containing a link to buy a test, often with a small discount, and will automatically join when the test results are ready.

Having joined a Project, you can expect to see your name in a large table of results, usually broken up into sub-groupings (Fig. 1). The other members will be matches of yours, but, as administrators can see more distant matching than you can, some of them may be more distant than the usual 10/111, 7/67 or 4/37 genetic distances (for Y).

Expanding your cluster of related DNA tests is a big benefit of joining a Project, along with gaining from the knowledge of the administrators, who will be experts on the surnames, lineages, haplogroups or regions of interest.

Project housekeeping

Project privacy

It is important to note that most Projects are publicly viewable to some extent. Some are restricted to members only, but most admins give a degree of open visibility to maximise sharing

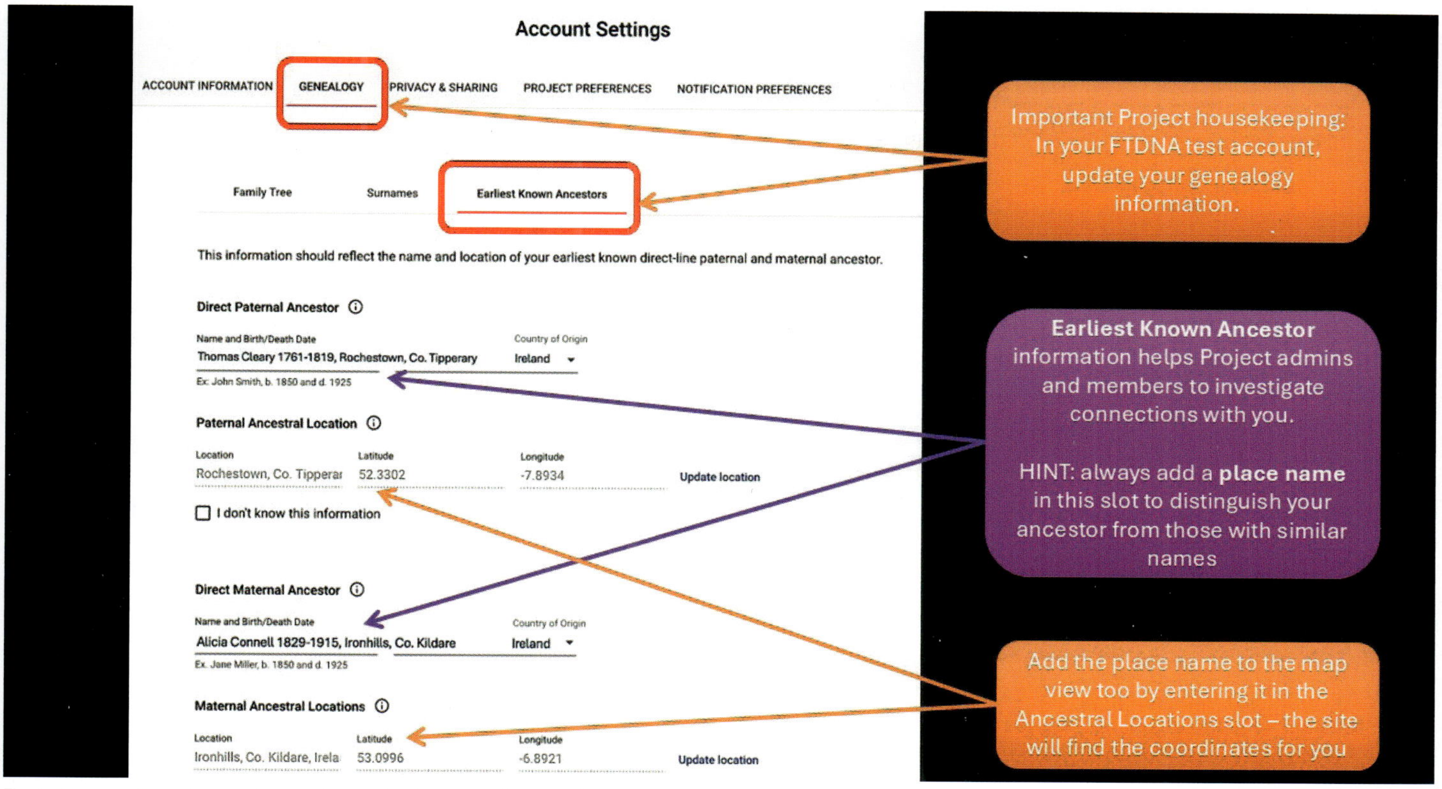

Fig. 4: Enter your Earliest Known Ancestor information for both the Y- and mtDNA lines

of information. Testers' full names are never shared in public, though their surnames may be in a Surname Project.

However, every tester may select the level of visibility they are comfortable with. You decide whether you want your test results visible to everyone or only to other Project members, by selecting the appropriate level of visibility in your project preferences (Fig. 3). Many testers are happy to share their results and genealogical information openly with other researchers.

Note though that mtDNA Coding Region results are never shared publicly as they are genetically sensitive, and you may decide whether or not to share yours with Project admins.

Project access rights

Members also decide whether to give their Project administrators Basic, Limited or Full access to their results (Fig. 3).

- Limited is recommended for most cases, as it allows administrators to review your test results and contact you with recommendations.
- Basic allows no access to your results, and administrators will probably ignore you if you choose this level.
- Full access is useful if you want an admin to handle your test for you, and usually occurs when you know an admin well and are willing to grant them your informed consent.

You decide whether you want your test results visible to everyone or only to other Project members

Earliest Known Ancestor information

Another important aspect of Project housekeeping is the Earliest Known Ancestor (EKA) information, which you enter into your Genealogy settings.

Our DNA test results leverage more profit when paired with genealogical information, so take a moment to enter your EKA for your direct paternal (father's father's father's) and direct maternal (mother's mother's mother's) lines (Fig. 4). You can also upload a family tree for autosomal DNA work – FTDNA now has a tie-in with MyHeritage to facilitate this.

Being an admin

The role of the admins

The administrators of the Projects – known as admins – are usually volunteers, testers who

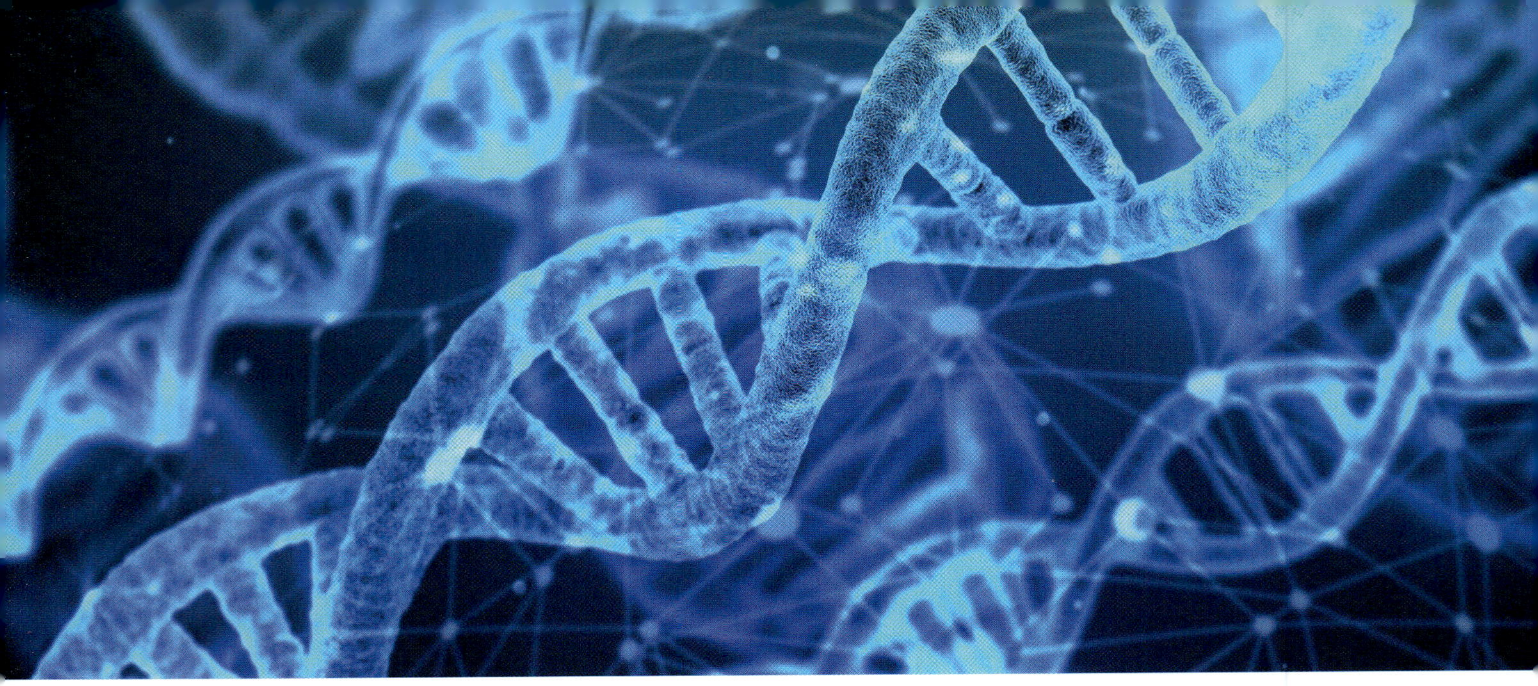

have cultivated an interest and offered their time to manage a Project or several. This means the Projects are dependent on the interest and commitment shown by their admins.

Sometimes Projects become orphaned – but you could consider stepping up and offering a little time if you find yourself in a Project without an active admin.

Admins are variously experts, advisers, coordinators, custodians, chairs of the welcome committee and diplomats. New members will value the guidance and advice on their results and what to do next. It is always worth checking with a friendly admin if you are considering further testing. If they have grouped you with other testers in the Project, ask them what their rationale is for doing it that way.

Ethical practice

Ethical practice is important: FTDNA created its GAP (Group Administrator Pages) Guidelines to guide admins on handling their members' data with due care and obtaining informed consent for any use they may want to make of it outside of the Project platform.

If you have a new idea – say, a surname without its own Project – contact FTDNA's GAP helpline, who will support you in setting up a new Project

Project funding

The Project platform also provides a General Fund facility which allows donations towards the costs of tests to be held by the Project. Active admins may use it to raise funds for a testing programme to advance the Project's goals.

Starting up your own DNA project

Learn the ropes

The best way to learn how to run a DNA Project is to volunteer as an admin, especially if you can collaborate alongside an experienced one. Start small, maybe as a co-admin on a surname project, and, if you enjoy the experience, consider offering more time to other Projects.

Avoid duplicating efforts

If you would like to set up your own Project, first check to see whether an existing Project already covers your topic, to avoid duplication (and ruffled feathers), and volunteer with it if one does.

Contact the admin helpline

If you have a new idea – say, a surname without its own Project – contact FTDNA's GAP helpline, who will support you in setting up a new Project.

Start recruiting members

You will need members! Be ready to recruit either existing testers, or new ones to test and join. This may involve researching the branches of the lineage and inviting key individuals from each branch to test.

Many Project admins work with family history societies and one-name studies to identify potential members with the enthusiasm to join a Project on their surname or lineage of interest. This can be a fascinating and exciting means of sharing research and collaborating on advancing new knowledge about families and lineages.

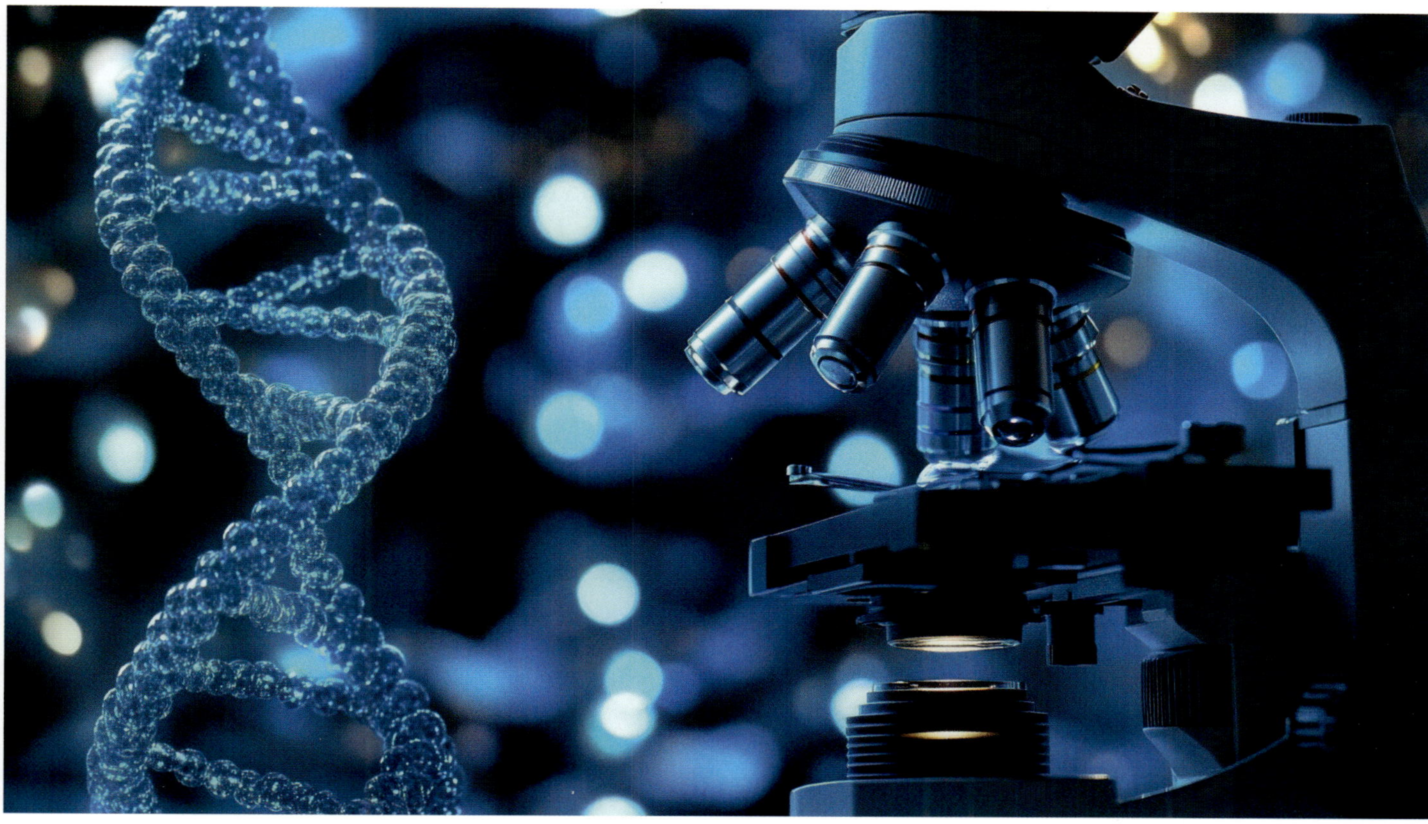

LEARN MORE ABOUT DNA

Books, bloggers, courses, groups, talks, events & useful websites

Whatever stage you are at on the genetic genealogy journey, there are always new DNA things to learn. To follow are ideas of ways in which you can keep discovering more about the subject – from books to courses, bloggers to talks, and – of course – useful websites for DNA family history research.

We would recommend that you employ a range of tactics to help you learn about DNA for family history.

Reading about DNA – whether online or in useful publications such as this one – watching presentations and taking courses are all very helpful ways to help you learn more about DNA and how to better understand your DNA test results.

Read on to learn how to get expert DNA help and advice, and ways to grow your DNA know-how, online.

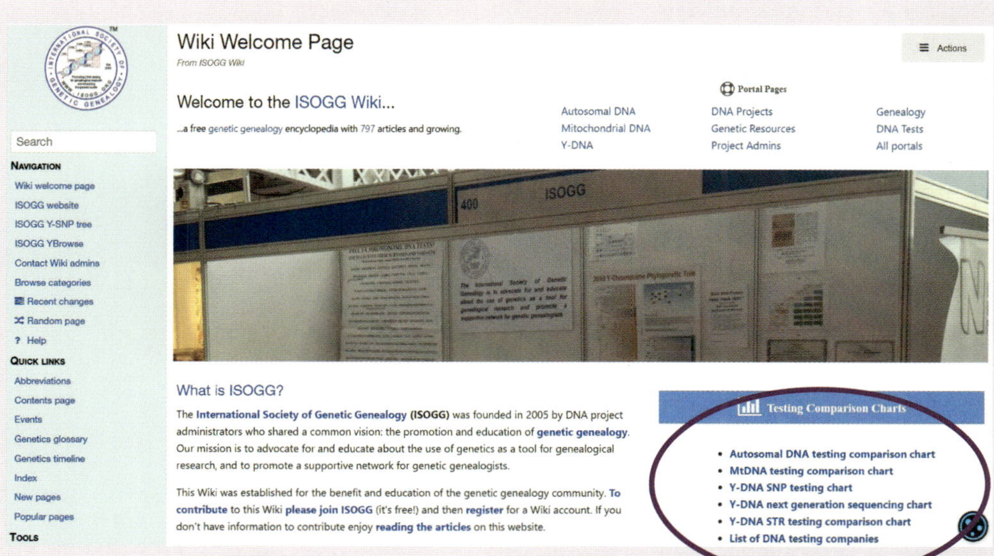

When you visit the International Society of Genetic Genealogy's Wiki, don't miss the extremely useful testing comparison charts (found on the right-hand side of the window)

Join the DNA Club

Join Family Tree Plus, the online membership from Family Tree, and you can access the monthly DNA Club webinars. Each session includes the latest DNA news, an expert presentation, and the chance to ask questions. Find out more at: **www.family-tree.co.uk/membership**

Join the DNA society – ISOGG

The International Society of Genetic Genealogy (**https://isogg.org**) Internationally respected, the society is a reliable source of information about using DNA for family history, to suit researchers of all levels of knowledge, and it's free to join.

Browse the DNA Wiki

https://isogg.org/wiki/Wiki_Welcome_Page

With approximately 800 DNA topics covered, the ISOGG Wiki is an invaluable source of DNA knowledge for numerous aspects of genetic genealogy.

Explore DNA experts' websites

There is a growing body of experts who write about DNA and share news of their discoveries online.

We all have different learning styles, and each of the experts have their own particular angles of research interest too, so we would recommend periodically browsing them all, to make sure you're not missing out on useful and fascinating DNA material to read.

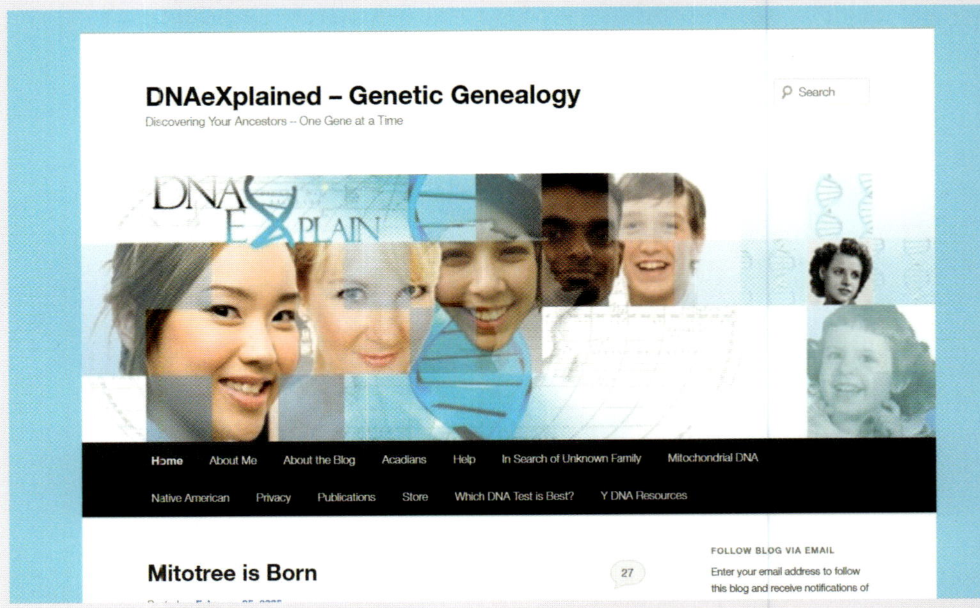

In addition to providing very careful, detailed instruction, the website of Roberta Estes is valuable for up to the minute DNA news-related announcements. Explore her website: **https://dna-explained.com**

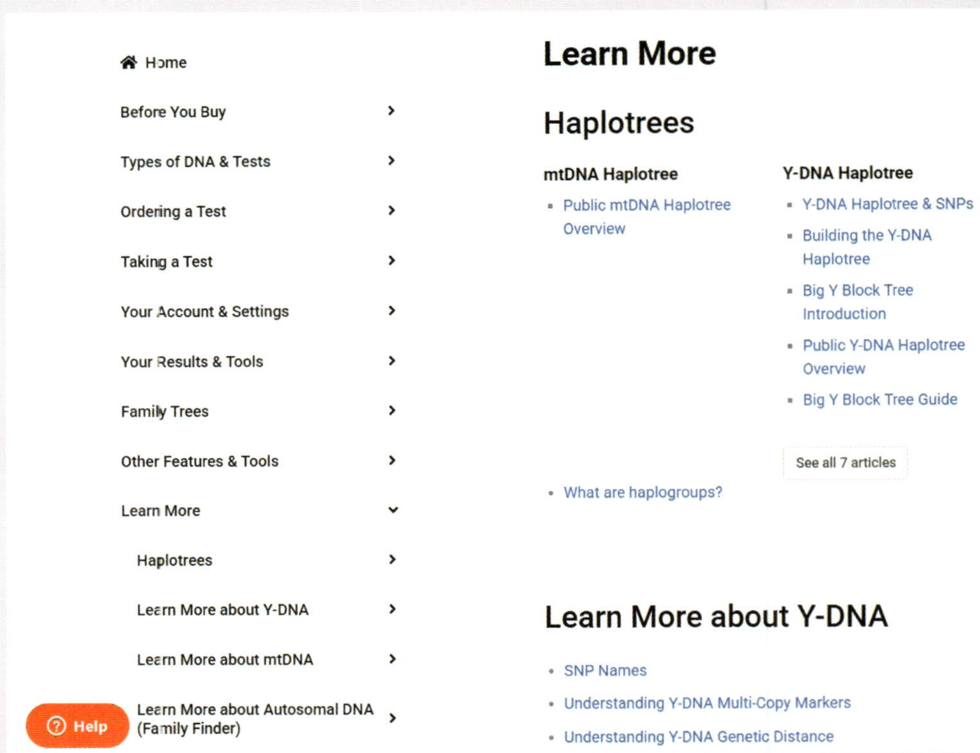

Learn about mtDNA, Y-DNA and autosomal testing, SNPs, STRs, haplogroups, Investigative Genetic Genealogy and more at the FamilyTreeDNA 'Learn More' web pages: **https://help.familytreedna.com/hc/en-us**

Interesting expert websites include:

- Blaine Bettinger **thegeneticgenealogist.com**
- Kitty Cooper **kittycooper.com**
- Roberta Estes **dna-explained.com**
- Janna Helshtein **dnaateyelevel.com**
- Maurice Gleeson **dnaandfamilytreeresearch.blogspot.com**
- Leah Larkin **thednageek.com**
- Dana Leeds **www.danaleeds.com**
- Michelle Leonard **www.facebook.com/genesandgenealogy**
- Donna Rutherford **donnarutherford.com**
- Diahan Southard **www.yourdnaguide.com**

See pages 91-96 of this guide

to learn more about our expert contributors too.

Study the DNA testing company websites

You will have heard of the main DNA testing company names, as used in the world of family history, but be sure not to miss the free online learning resources that some of them provide.

Many of the DNA test companies provide extremely helpful posts to explain how their DNA tests work; how to interpret the results; news of updates and developments and more.

Explore the learning pages

Be sure to take time to investigate this helpful material. Useful web pages are, for instance, in particular:

- Ancestry DNA Learning Hub **www.ancestry.co.uk/c/dna-learning-hub**
- FamilyTreeDNA Learn More **https://help.familytreedna.com/hc/en-us**
- MyHeritage Knowledge Base **https://education.myheritage.com/learn/dna**

Take the tool tutorials

In addition to the DNA testing companies, there are other DNA companies that provide online tools to help you work in a more organised or advanced way with your DNA results and matches.

Below are examples of some of these companies. As with the DNA testing companies, many of these provide detailed, helpful guides and reading material to help you understand their tools and resources.

Useful tool manuals

See, specifically:

- BanyanDNA **www.banyandna.com/docs/quickstart-guide**
- DNA Painter **https://dnapainter.com/tools**
- GEDMatch **www.gedmatch.com/how-it-works/**
- Genetic Affairs **www.geneticaffairs.com/faqs.html** and **www.geneticaffairs.com/images/Manual_Genetic_Affairs.pdf**

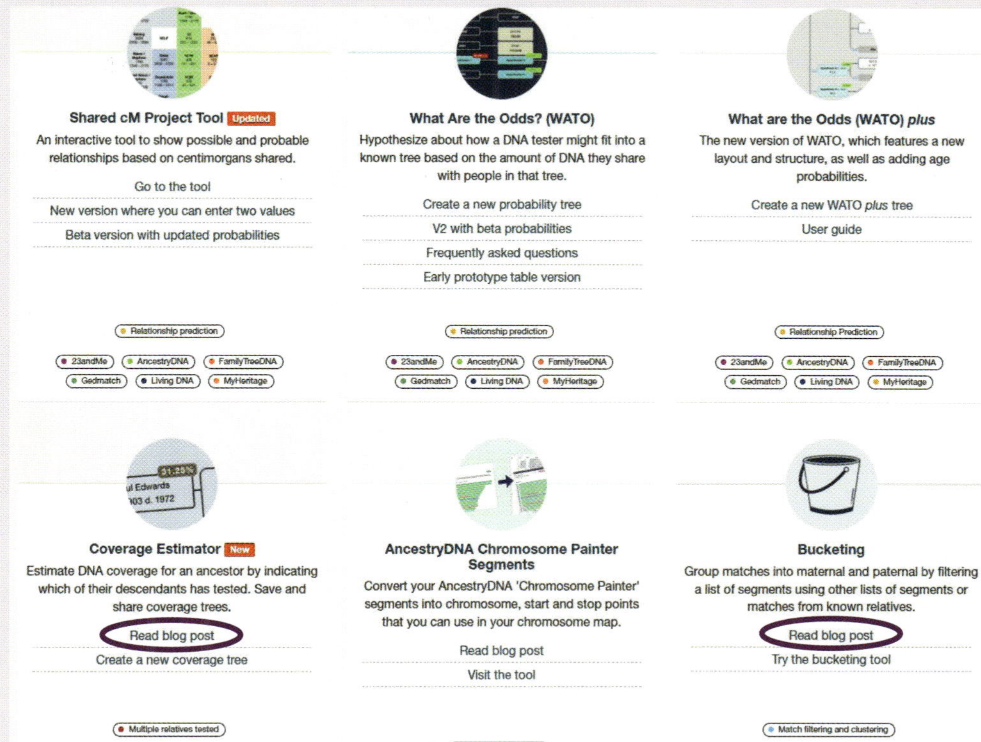

Numerous DNA tools are available on the DNA Painter website. To see the full range of tools go to https://dnapainter.com/tools. For each tool further guidance is given, to help you understand how to use the tool, what to expect from it, and the way in which it can enhance your DNA research. See for instance the links to the relevant blog posts for the 'Coverage Estimator' and 'Bucketing' to highlight just two such guides.

Read about the golden rules of genetic genealogy

A decade ago the Genetic Genealogy Standards were drawn up to help guide those involved in using DNA for family history, to help us all work in the most ethical way. Find out more about the standards at **www.geneticgenealogystandards.com**. Click 'document' on the home page of the website to download the three-page standards document.

In addition to the testing companies, there are other companies that provide online tools to help you work in a more organised or advanced way

Join a social group

Social media platforms can have extremely useful groups, allowing you to ask questions

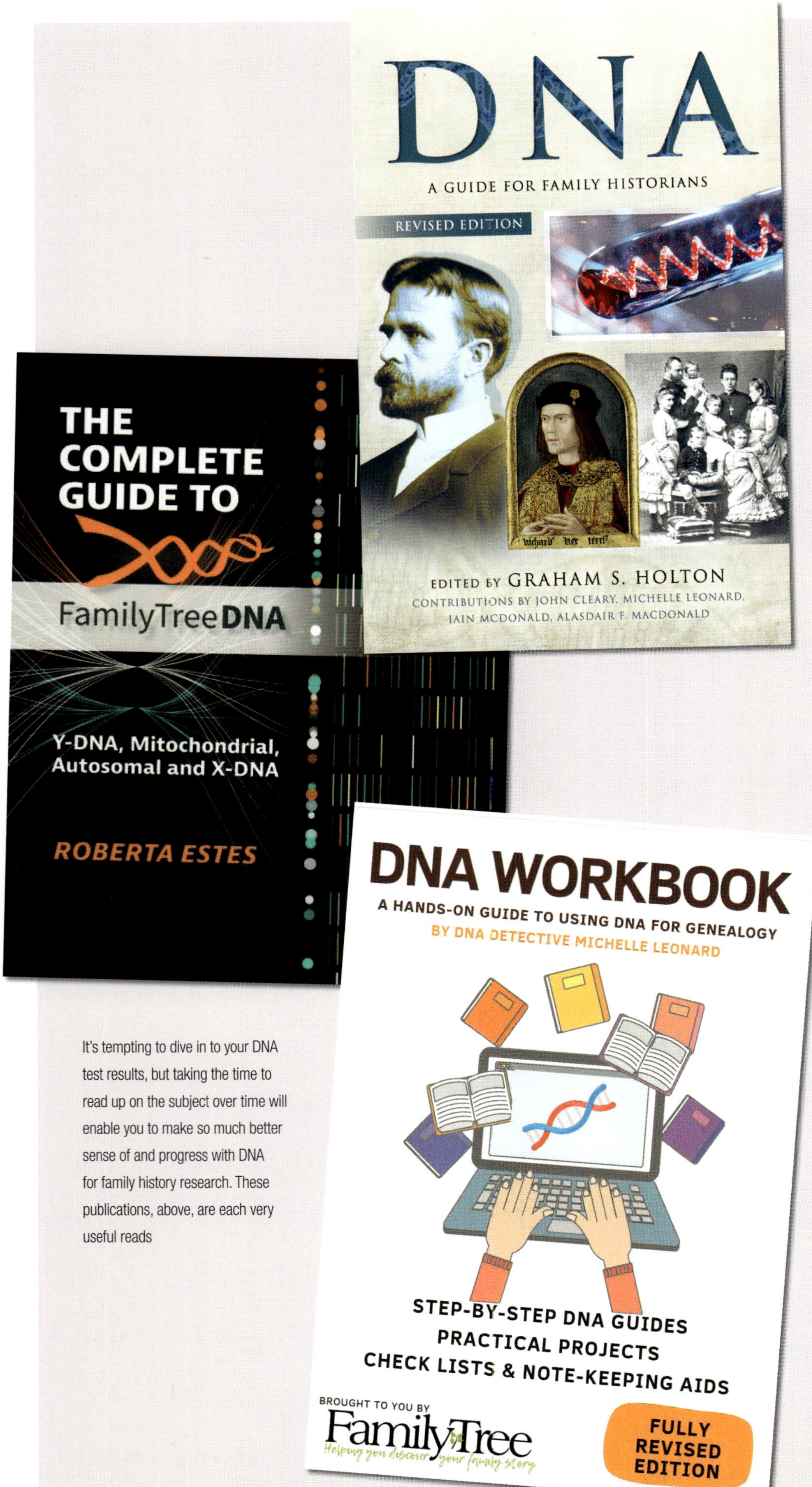

It's tempting to dive in to your DNA test results, but taking the time to read up on the subject over time will enable you to make so much better sense of and progress with DNA for family history research. These publications, above, are each very useful reads

and learn from the answers provided to fellow group members too. Look out for general-interest family history DNA groups, such as:

DNA Help for Genealogy (UK) **www.facebook.com/groups/AncestryUKDNA** (admins: Donna Rutherford & Seth Rogoff-Johnson)

Invest in your knowledge

Where to study DNA online? Look out for online talks, events & courses.

- Don't miss the five-week bitesize course on DNA, free to readers of this guide. Turn to page 34 for more details, or simply sign up online at: **bit.ly/free-dna-course**
- As mentioned, Family Tree Plus includes membership to the DNA Club. This meets monthly, for a one-hour presentation, DNA news and question time: **www.family-tree.co.uk/membership**
- Family Tree also runs DNA masterclasses, and courses, such as the online DNA Bootcamp course: **www.family-tree.co.uk/how-to-guides/webinars**
- Legacy Family Tree Webinars provides numerous presentations on DNA (some are available free; a subscription is available for greater access): **familytreewebinars.com/webinar-library**
- The Northern Ireland Family History Society runs a DNA summer school week each year: **www.nifhs.org/courses**
- The Society of Genealogists' runs DNA presentations. See their calendar: **https://members.sog.org.uk**

DNA Club online learning sessions are open to all members of Family Tree Plus. You may also buy a one-off ticket if there's a talk that particularly interests you, but you don't yet wish to join the club. Many of the authors of this guide are global experts on their DNA fields and have provided excellent presentations at the club sessions. Illustrated here are just some examples of talks that club members have enjoyed in the past. To find out about forthcoming talks at DNA Club, see https://www.family-tree.co.uk/how-to-guides

- Pharos Tutors offers two online courses in DNA: 'Demystifying DNA for family historians' and 'Advanced DNA strategies with autosomal DNA'. Visit **www.pharostutors.com/courses** and filter on 'DNA'.

- The FutureLearn course 'Genetic Genealogy: Researching your family tree using DNA' is a six-week free (on a limited time basis) online course from the University of Strathclyde: **bit.ly/strathclyde-dna**

- The IHGS is launching a new DNA assessed qualification – **bit.ly/ihgs-dna-course**. Tutored by Dr Sophie Kay this six-week online course 'is designed to help you acquire new skills and techniques in genetic genealogy, and put them into practice'. It's aimed and amateurs and professional family historians.

Recommended reads – DNA books

DNA: A Guide for Family Historians edited by Graham S. Holton and co-authored by John Cleary, Michelle Leonard, Iain McDonald, and Alasdair F. MacDonald. This extremely popular publication from Pen & Sword is now in its 2nd edition, fully revised and updated, published in March 2025. (Pen and Sword, 2025, 280 pages) **www.pen-and-sword.co.uk** Be sure to check out the special offer on page 33, giving you an exclusive 35% discount on this revised edition.

The Complete Guide to FamilyTreeDNA (Y-DNA, Mitochondrial, Autosomal and X-DNA) by Roberta Estes. This is a detailed, practical publication covering the full range of DNA tests and

> *'Genetic Genealogy: Researching your family tree using DNA' is a six-week free online course from the University of Strathclyde*

resources from DNA testing company FamilyTreeDNA. This is the only company to provide DNA match databases for the full range of DNA tests. (Genealogical Publishing Company 2024, 247 pages). **www.amazon.co.uk**

The DNA Bootcamp Workbook – by Michelle Leonard. Published by Family Tree this popular guide is updated regularly. Packed with practical step-by-step instructions and tips to help you work with your DNA test results this workbook is aimed at people new to DNA testing, or those who would welcome a hand working with their DNA match lists. (Family Tree 2024, 52 pages) **https://bit.ly/dna-wkbook**

Ancestry white papers

Ancestry publishes detailed, formal reports for some of the DNA-related developments that it undertakes. White papers are available for Ancestry's DNA traits, DNA regions, DNA journeys and DNA matches. **bit.ly/ancestrydna-whitepapers**

Family Tree magazine

Founded in 1984, *Family Tree* is your monthly genealogy guide and each issue features the popular DNA Workshop with expert Karen Evans. Join Family Tree Plus and you can read the latest issue and search through an archive of back issues. **www.family-tree.co.uk**

Create a word list

As you read and learn about genetic genealogy you are likely to come across many words that are unfamiliar to you. Why not create your own DNA word list, rather as you might do if learning a foreign language? By writing down the words that are new to you, and including a definition, you will help to fix the new knowledge in your memory. See the glossary at the end of this guide (page 97) for ideas of the sorts of words you may like to include, and add further words to your own DNA word list.

Why not create your own DNA word list, rather as you might do if learning a foreign language?

THE EVER-ADVANCING WORLD OF Y & MTDNA
& how it can help you

"As well as vastly expanding databases, the tests themselves have evolved to become more genealogically useful than before," explains **Martin McDowell**, Education Officer at the North of Ireland Family History Society, adding: "If you were thinking that things have changed in the world of Y and MT-DNA in the last decade you'd be right." So what are these changes, and in what ways can they help with family history research? Martin shows how.

In this article I'll be demystifying and explaining how these FamilyTreeDNA Y and MT tests can help you. FamilyTreeDNA is the only company with a large matching database of Y and MT test results and therefore there isn't the same concept of uploading your DNA to other databases – they have a worldwide database and the vast majority of results are already there.

Y and MT tests provide unique access to information about your ancestors that you don't get from companies such as Ancestry or MyHeritage which solely provide autosomal DNA tests.

People have a number of different questions that they may want to answer with a DNA test. One person could be an adoptee trying to find their birth family, another may be trying to discover the unknown father of an illegitimate ancestor, whereas somebody else might be trying to push back a brick wall on a specific line of their family. All of these questions may be solved through a Family Finder (FamilyTreeDNA's autosomal test), Y or MT test. It's a case of knowing which test is most suitable for the research requirements.

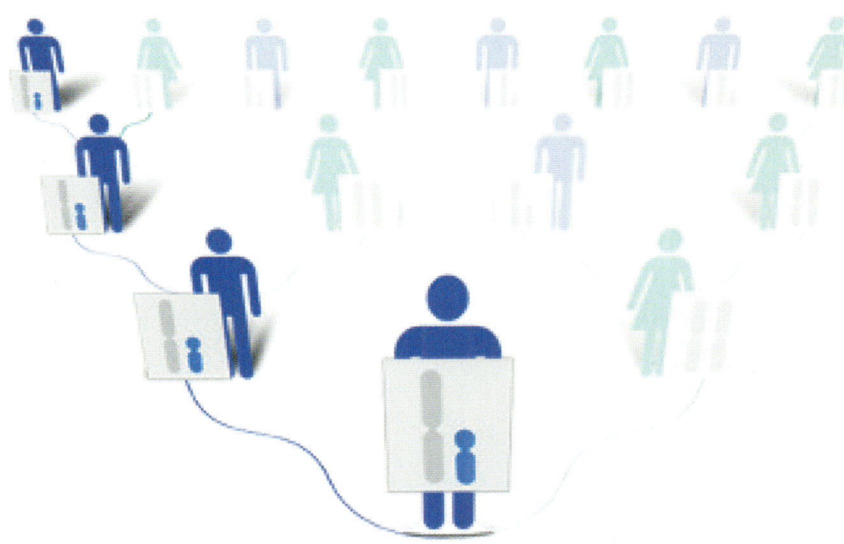

Figure 1: Y-DNA is passed down from father to son to grandson just like a surname is, so only males can do this test

The massive genealogical research potential of Y-DNA

Let's look at Y-DNA for a moment. Y-DNA is passed down from father to son to grandson just like a surname is, so only males can do this test.

A Y-DNA test is effectively tracing the surname line and takes you much further back than an autosomal DNA test can. This has massive potential for genealogical research as it can help you uncover both the recent – and distant – past of your family line.

You will find matches back at least 24 generations and there is no end to the discoveries you can make when you go even further back. You may find out a surname has changed somewhere back in your direct line and you may be able to link this to a specific time period.

The advantage of Y-DNA is it is a deep dive into a specific line in your family tree. To find out about another line in your family (that isn't your surname line) you have to source the right person to take a test for you – someone who is a direct male descendant of the line you are looking to find out about.

How can Y-DNA be used for genealogy research?

Y-DNA uses the mutations – or changes – in your DNA to estimate how closely you are related to each of your matches. There are three different levels of test you can do:

- Y-37
- Y-111
- Big Y-700

Each one is testing a different amount of your Y-DNA and it is always better to compare as much Y-DNA as you can as this increases the accuracy of the results.

Budget is obviously a factor, however for best results I would advise you to test to the highest level that you can afford.

Figure 2: with your Y-111 test result you receive a table which shows a number of options of how far back your common ancestor is with each match. The one appropriate to the connection between you and your match is highlighted

When you test at Y-111 level, for example, you can compare with people who have tested to Y-111 and people who have tested to a lower level (such as Y-37).

Bear in mind that it is also possible that you could have no surname matches at a lower level of testing but get them at a higher level so comparing as much DNA as possible is definitely recommended.

Genetic Distance	Y-111 TMRCA
0	1850 CE (1750 - 1950 CE)
1	1850 CE (1700 - 1900 CE)
2	1800 CE (1650 - 1900 CE)
3	1750 CE (1600 - 1900 CE)
4	1700 CE (1500 - 1850 CE)
5	1650 CE (1450 - 1800 CE)
6	1600 CE (1350 - 1800 CE)
7	1500 CE (1200 - 1750 CE)
8	1450 CE (1100 - 1700 CE)
9	1350 CE (950 - 1650 CE)
10	1250 CE (800 - 1600 CE)

Figure 3 (below):

1. Timescales are often available for the most recent generations but in the example below we are looking at a mutation that occurred around 300AD.
2. What this is telling you is that 2,271 people have this mutation and are direct descendants of the person in which this mutation occurred.
3. It also allows you to see the countries where proven descendants – testers – are found. This example indicates an origin in the British Isles – Ireland – which might have been previously unknown.

All of this is updated weekly as more people's results are added to the database.

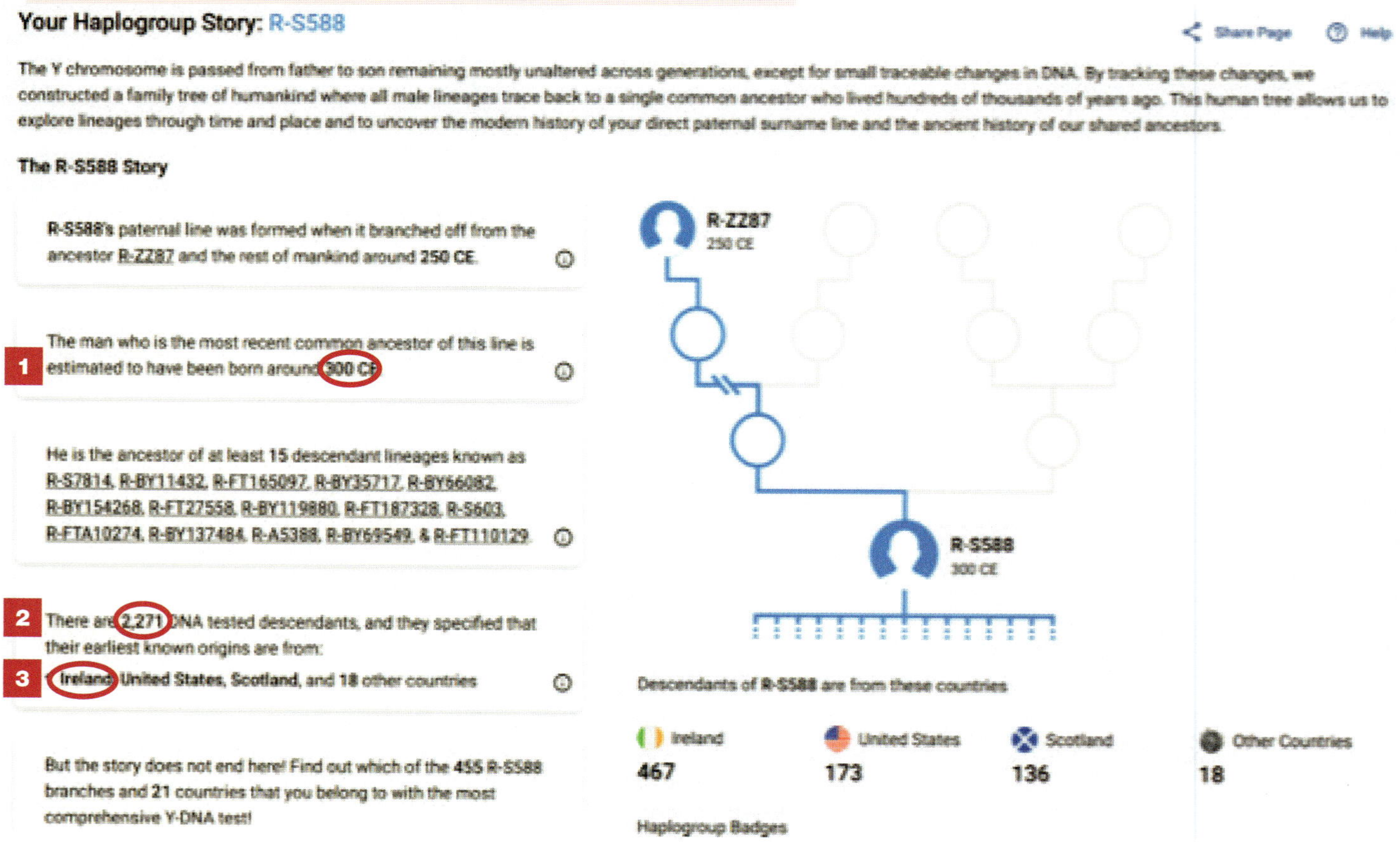

What do your Y-DNA results look like?

Firstly, you get the all-important match list. This gives you the names and contact details of people related to you on the Y line and you can see their family tree, if they have shared one.

You also get a timescale prediction for each match indicating the date at which your common ancestor may have lived. The timescale predictions for Big Y-700 are much more refined than those for the lower levels of testing as they are based on specific mutations inherited from your ancestors.

For example with Y-111 you get a table (Figure 2) showing a number of options of how far back your common ancestor is with each match. The one appropriate to the connection between you and your match is highlighted.

However, at Big-Y level this information is much more refined. Big Y-700 identifies all the specific mutations – or haplogroups – which occurred in your ancestors and then shows you matches descended from these lines. It can also differentiate between your matches, telling you who is closer to you than others.

> **What is a haplogroup?**
> A haplogroup is a genetic group of people who all descend from one individual on either the patrilineal (Y) or matrilineal (MT) line.

As part of your Y-DNA results you will also gain access to 'FTDNA Discover'.

FTDNA Discover is a publicly accessible database which can be used to explore your DNA. As well as the haplogroup story shown (Figure 3) it also provides lots more interpretation of your Y-DNA story.

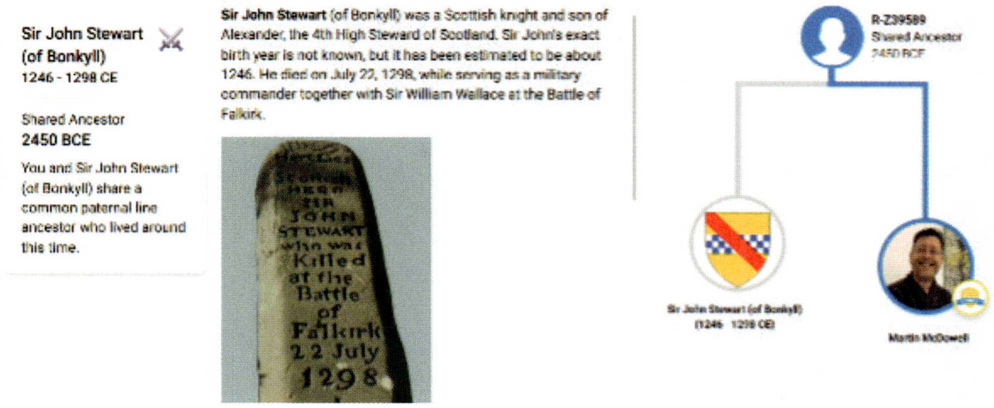

Figure 4: notable connections are both fun and fascinating, showing you shared Y-DNA connections between figures from distant history and historic figures in recent times. Martin has a DNA connection to a 13th century knight, Sir John Stewart of Bonkyll, via a shared connection about 4,500 years ago!

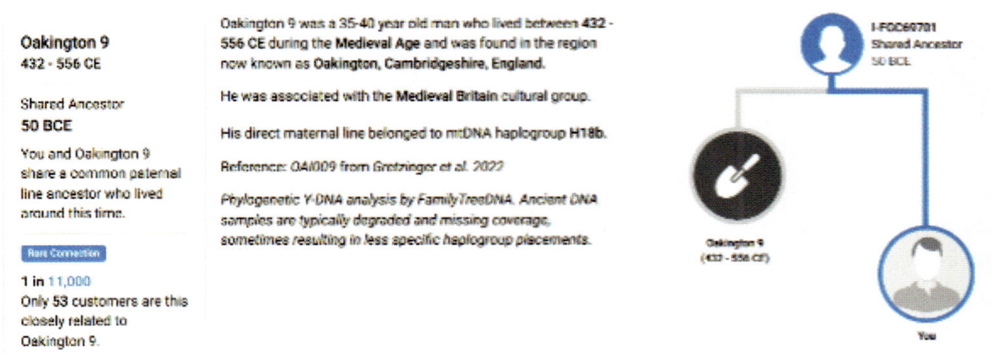

Figure 5: ancient connections show your connection to archaeological remains and again give you a predicted time for when your common ancestor lived, and may indicate which countries your ancestors lived in, in centuries past

Figure 6: see a customised video showing the migration and retreat, in the face of an Ice Age for instance, of your Y-DNA ancestors over tens of millennia, using FamilyTreeDNA's Globetrekker

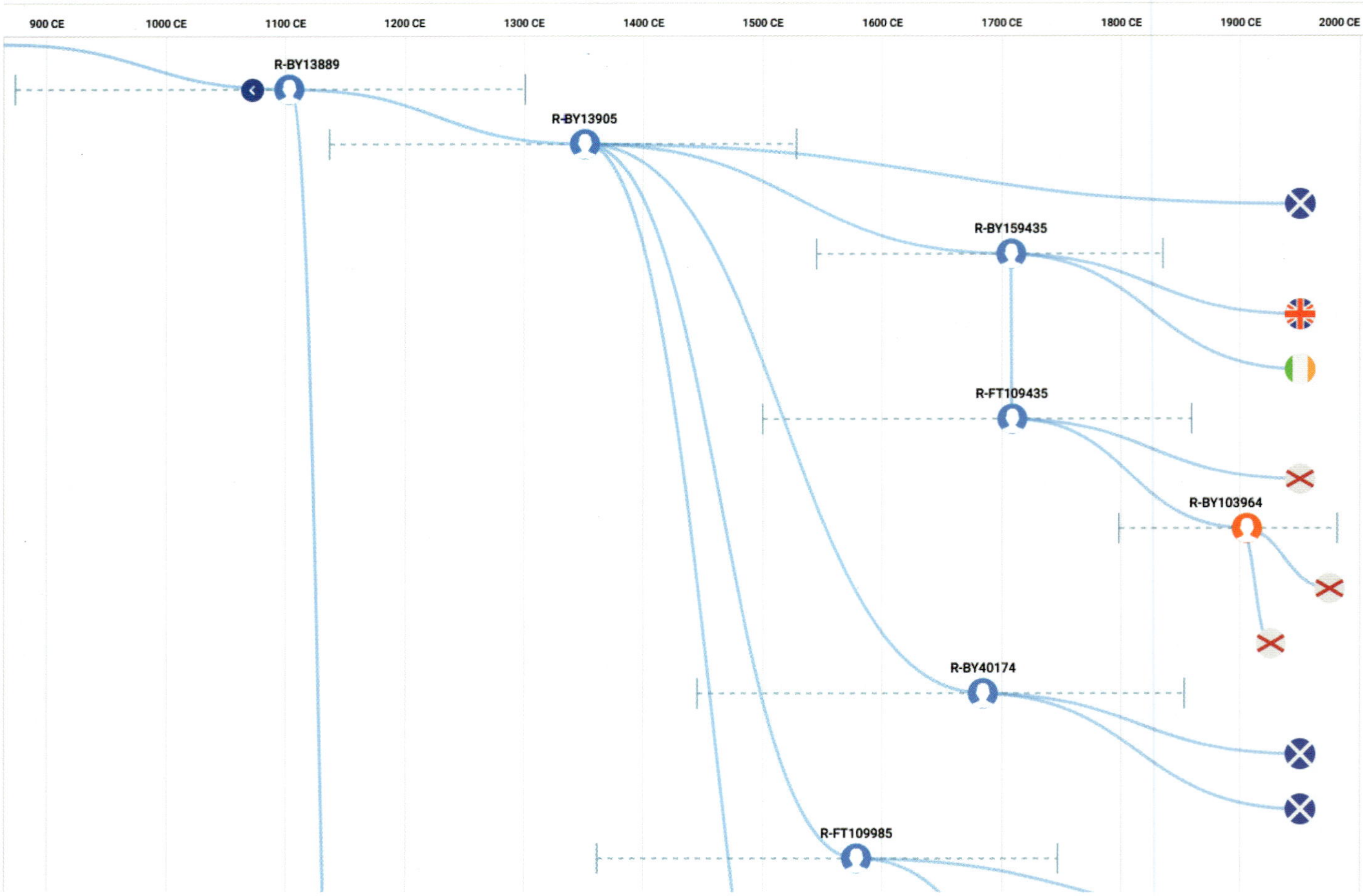

These include **notable connections**, **ancient connections**, **Globetrekker** and a **time tree**. Big Y testers will find a world of new information open up before their eyes.

Who says Y-DNA can't be fun? **Notable connections** show you connections to people whose Y-DNA lines are known – people as varied as Gregory Peck, Tutankhamun, Neil Armstrong, Beethoven and Matthew Perry! Figure 4 shows one of mine.

Ancient connections show your connection to archaeological remains and again give you a predicted time for when your common ancestor lived. Examination of these may indicate which countries your ancestors lived in, in centuries past (Figure 5).

Globetrekker allows you to trace the migration paths of your ancestral line based on the mutations found in your DNA. Globetrekker provides a personal video (Figure 6), which shows the passage of time including the advancement, and retreat, of the polar ice caps.

Figure 7 (above): time tree shows you the country of origin of your matches and shows how they all interconnect to you and each other.

A diagram such as this helps you visualise the connections across the centuries

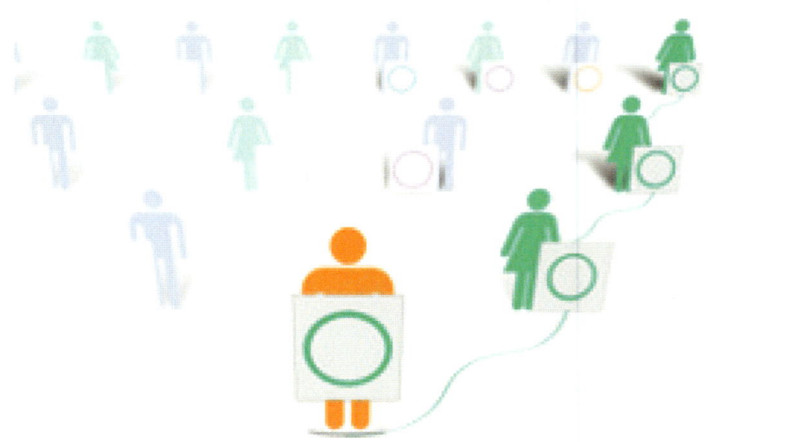

Figure 8 (right): everyone inherits MT-DNA but it is only passed on by mothers to her children. This means anyone can test their mitochondrial DNA, male or female, to trace their direct maternal line

This fascinating feature can be amended to show ancient connections, can be played at various speeds and has a zoom feature for more detail.

The **time tree** provides another way to explore your Y-DNA matches. Figure 7 shows you the country of origin of your matches and how they all interconnect to you and each other. A diagram such as this helps you visualise the connections across the centuries.

MT-DNA – 'more useful than ever'

And now let's move on to MT-DNA. Everyone inherits it but it is only passed on by a mother to her children. This means anyone can test their mitochondrial DNA, male or female. It traces the matrilineal line back many generations (Figure 8).

In the past MT-DNA has not been considered as genealogically relevant as other types of DNA, however recent advancements are starting to make it more useful than ever before.

It can be used to find out whether two lines are connected or just to explore where you came from.

How the Million Mito Project is helping MT-DNA researchers

MT-DNA is more stable than Y-DNA and therefore mutations do not happen as regularly. Up until now this has meant that matches can be related to you many generations back, however the Million Mito Project is changing all that: the tree of womankind has been redrawn with many more haplogroups added. In fact there are now more than 40,000 haplogroups, thus providing more definition and more genealogically relevant matches.

New: mt-DNA Discover

A version of FTDNA Discover has been built for MT-DNA and launched in February 2025. Anyone who tests now will have full access to mtDNA Discover.

mt-DNA Discover includes the following features: Haplogroup Story, Country Frequency, Ancient Connections, Notable Connections, Migration Map, Time Tree, Ancestral Path, Classic Tree, Suggested Projects, Scientific Details, Compare Haplogroups. The Match Time Tree is also available as a mtFull Exclusive tool, and Globetrekker and Group Time Tree will be similarly mtFull Exclusives. Learn more about the range of mt-DNA Discover tools at: **bit.ly/mt-DNA-Discover**

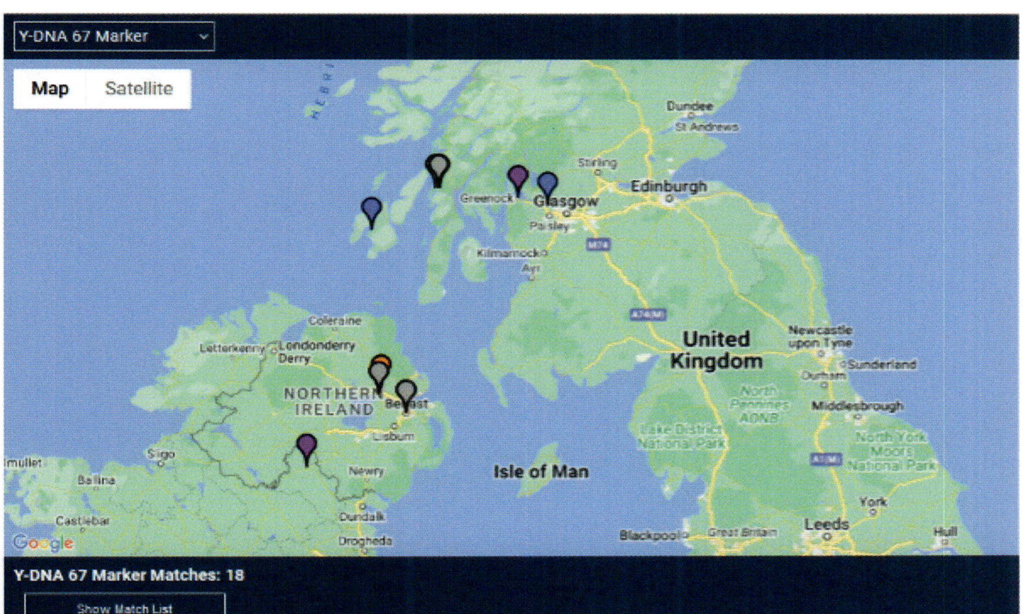

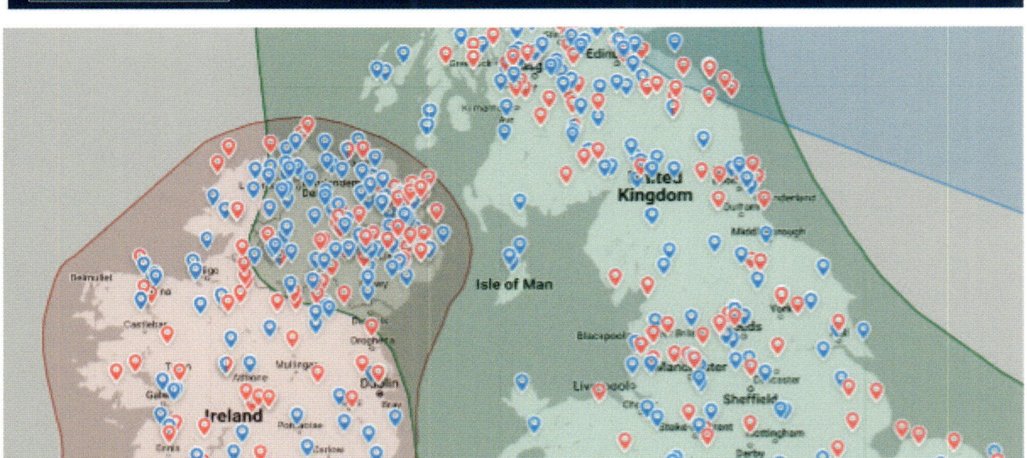

Figure 9 (top): see your Y DNA matches on a map. Figure 10 (above): use the 'compare origins' feature to see the Y and MT ancestors of your autosomal matches plotted on a map

What do your MT-DNA results look like?

MT tests have got lots to offer, in addition to the list of matches.

Currently Y and M- DNA testers each have the option to add the location of their earliest known ancestors to a map. This allows you to examine your matches geographically. The colours of the pins on the map indicate the genetic distance between matches and when you click on a pin it tells you the name of the match to which it refers. Matches' maps can help you identify an area that a specific family line came from and as you zoom in closer you may find multiple pins appearing from behind others (Figure 9).

Integrating Y, MT and autosomal DNA

Let's end our exploration of what is available with an exciting integration of Y and MT-DNA with autosomal DNA. The 'compare origins' feature allows you to see the Y and MT ancestors of your autosomal matches plotted on a map (Figure 10).

You can zoom in and out and each pin is clickable, revealing the name of your autosomal match, their predicted relationship to you and the name of their earliest known ancestor.

I hope you can appreciate how much potential there is in doing a Y or MT test. What could you discover?

All tests mentioned above can be purchased directly from FamilyTreeDNA. Alternatively Y-37 and MT tests can be obtained from **www.familyhistorybooksonline.com**

All images courtesy of FamilyTreeDNA.

ANCIENT DNA FOR GENEALOGY

Pushing back the boundaries of pre-history, Diane Brook takes the long view, combining her interests in archaeology and genealogy to piece together an account of our shared human past as revealed by artefacts, remains and DNA

In the family history world, DNA has become a major part of tracing ancestors and linking living relatives. I well remember an early conference on the subject, organised by the Guild of One Name Studies held in Oxford, about 2005. One very elderly gentleman (I am elderly now but he seemed very old to me then) raised his hand. In horrified tones, he asked, 'You are not digging people up, are you?'. We laughed and assured him that, no, we were just comparing the DNA of the living to find the links to our deceased ancestors.

On the other hand, archaeologists dig up the remains of people all the time and have done for centuries. In general, no one could say much about them except what the shapes and damage to bones could say. Now, we have ancient DNA as well but when did this become available?

In 1991, genetic tests were done on the possible remains of the Romanovs, last Tsar of Russia, and family. Comparisons with living royals including Prince Philip showed these were indeed their bones. Work on early man, Cheddar Man and Neanderthal remains followed in 1997.

Extreme care is needed to avoid contamination with modern human DNA which was a problem with the first attempts to get DNA from an Egyptian mummy. Special techniques are used to identify sections of DNA and then group them correctly.

Since the late 1990s ancient DNA techniques have evolved and improved, costs have dropped and many museum specimens as well as new finds have been tested.

Understanding historical & archaeological timeframes

I studied archaeology to further degree level so am very used to thinking in terms of the various periods of history and prehistory but readers may not be so familiar. Here are three timelines to show the periods and lengths of time involved against which to set the ancient DNA findings.

First there are the British historical periods, the last 2,000 years back to the Romans which covers almost all the time when we have anything written about

British individuals, barring a few Celtic coins and some mentions by Julius Caesar in his account of two abortive attempts to conquer Britain in 55 and 54 BC. Most of our genealogical knowledge is confined to the Modern Period with a little in the Later and Early Middle Ages.

Archaeology and ancient DNA can take us much further back. British archaeological periods go back continuously to the end of the last Ice Age. The Neolithic is the 'New Stone Age' when farming came to Britain, the Mesolithic the 'Middle Stone Age', after the Ice Age but before farming, and the Palaeolithic the 'Old Stone Age', the Ice Age and before, of mammoths, woolly rhinoceros and cave paintings.

Before this, humans and their earlier ancestors came and went from the British Isles in the warm periods between earlier Ice Ages so that we must look to Europe and the wider world for our deepest ancestry.

All over corded beaker. Ancient DNA studies are shedding light on the nature of the migration of Beaker people in the Early Bronze Age

Genetic terminology decoded

- Genes are the set of DNA letters ACGT in a specific sequence.
- Where a set of genes is typically inherited together in a population group they form a haplotype.
- The population of matching haplotype individuals form a haplogroup.
- Relating the different haplogroups to each other across place and time is assembled into a haplotree.
- Most work has been done on male-line haplogroups (tracing Y-chromosome inheritance) as these are almost completely unmixed with other parts of the genome, and mutations over time can be used to create a family tree. The male haplotree links all male lines back to 'Y-DNA Adam.' An excellent tool showing this is the SNP Tracker website (http://scaledinnovation.com/gg/snpTracker.html). *See also page 60 for coverage of the mtDNA Discover Mitotree.*
- SNP (pronounced 'snip' – Single Nucleotide Polymorphism) is a way to map haplotype changes; it occurs when a mutation, in the form of a change of a letter in the code, occurs.
- The female haplotree for mitochondrial DNA (mtDNA) has also been developed and work linking it to ancient DNA is continuing.

Seeking answers 1,000-plus years ago

Let us proceed now in correct genealogical fashion, from the present backwards, and, archaeologically, from the top of the soil, layer by layer, down into the past. Later medieval people can have their DNA sequenced but we tend to know a good deal about the history of these relatively recent populations. Once in the early medieval period, about 410 to 1066 CE, there are large questions to answer about British populations.

Vikings (793 CE – 1066 CE)

The first question is 'how much ancestry did the Vikings contribute to British and Irish populations?'.

A study of ancient DNA showed that there was considerable input, and, various areas of Scandinavia contributed to different regions of the British Isles with more Danish in England and Norwegian in Ireland and parts of Scotland. A difficulty is that the Anglo-Saxons were originally Danish as well so there is overlap in DNA types.

English and Welsh (c.410 CE – 1066 CE)

Another migration question is 'How big was the Anglo-Saxon migration into Britian?' and therefore, was there much survival of the native British population in areas that became England and southern Scotland.

A study published in 2022 examining 278 aDNA samples from England, the rest of Britain and Ireland, and the continent, from 200 to 1300 CE, showed that the English population suddenly showed a great deal of continental DNA from the beginning of the early Middle Ages while Wales did not. There was mixture and survival, though as studies of some Anglo-Saxon early graves showed that some

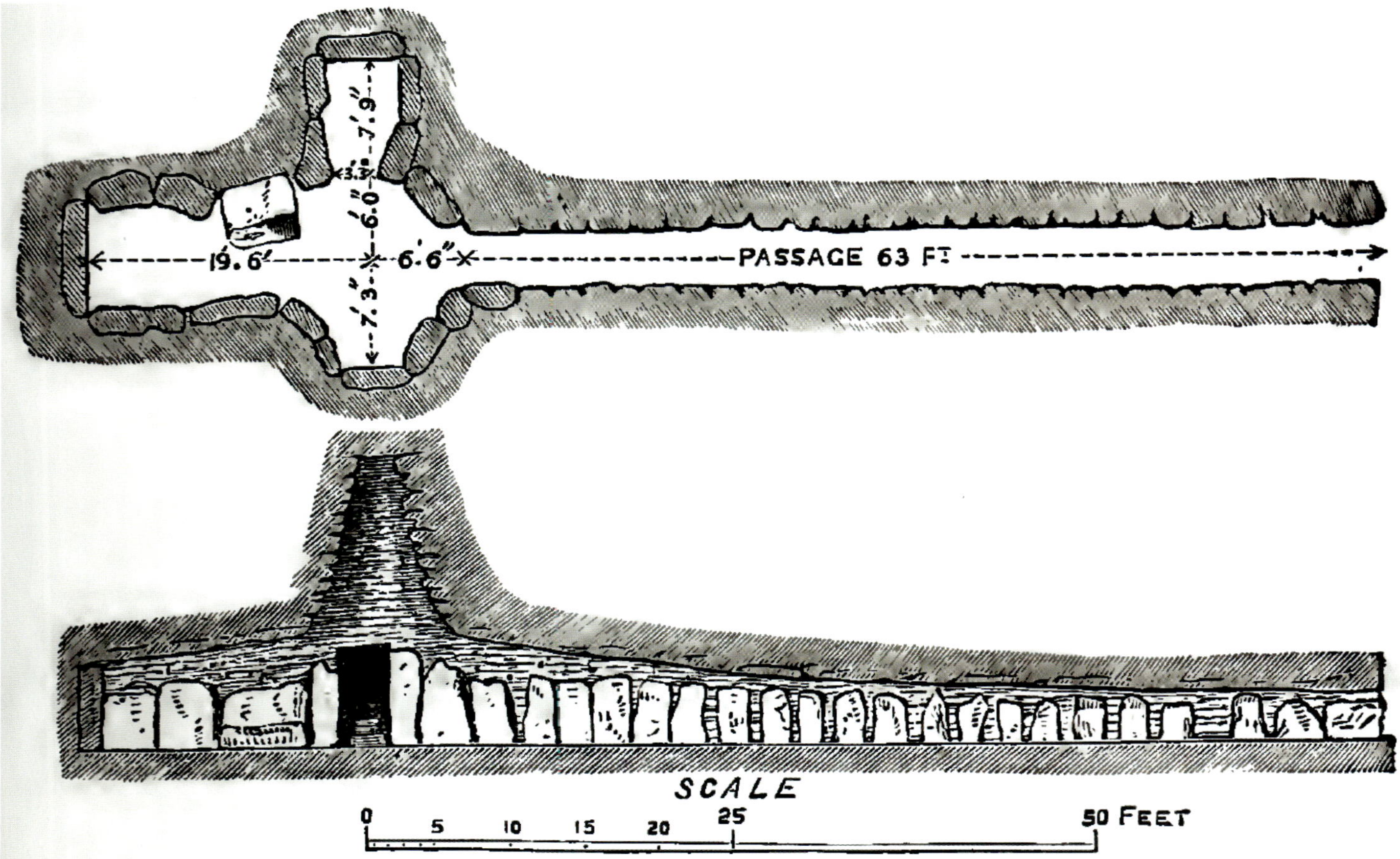

Plan and Section of Chamber in Newgrange Tumulus.

had recent continental ancestry while others were native British.

Romans (43 CE – c.410 CE)
There are some DNA studies of burials from the Roman period in Britain, proving that the Roman Empire was very diverse, bringing people from one end of the Empire to the other.

One study showed a man, possibly a gladiator, came from eastern Europe or the Middle East, and a woman had north African links. To date, there does not seem to be much input in modern British populations but studies continue.

Iron Age and Bronze Age (2500 BCE – 43 CE)
British people spoke a Celtic language when Julius Caesar first recorded details in 55 and 54 BC. It had an Iron Age culture, iron coming into use in Britain about 700 BCE.

Ancient DNA now points to a large-scale migration into England and Wales during the period c.1000-875 BC (the very end of the Bronze Age). The study in 2021 suggested this brought DNA from what is now France and may have brought Celtic language, light skin and more lactase persistence (ability to digest milk as an adult).

Beaker People & the Early Bronze Age (c.2500 BCE)
When I first studied archaeology in the 1970s, invasions in prehistory were out of fashion, the emphasis being on continuity with culture change happening naturally over time. This was a reaction to the terrible misuse of archaeology by the Nazis including their views on invasions. 'Pots are not people' became the mantra.

British antiquaries of the 19th century often suggested early invasions (not being averse in the British Empire to a bit of invading themselves!), especially of the first metal users in Britain, the so-called Beaker People, from the distinctive pots in their burials. The antiquaries noted not only the change in pottery from the previous Neolithic period, but changes in burial rite from cremation cemeteries to individual barrow burials, and, a change in skull shape. Even this latter was explained away by the continuity fashion, as a change in infant head shape management.

A cross-section of Newgrange tumulus chamber, from *Wakemans Book of Irish Antiquities*, 1903. Three ancient Irish stories refer to incest in royal families and events involving Newgrange. DNA now seems to be bearing this out

A change in Early Bronze Age perspective: evidence of invasion & culture change

Then came the Amesbury Archer burial. This elaborate Beaker burial had five beakers, not just the usual one, as well as metal work and other items. When his teeth were analysed with isotope studies, it showed the man had not been born in Britain but probably somewhere around Switzerland. Ancient DNA studies of Beaker burials followed, and invasion could no longer be ruled out. In fact, most male lines in the British population were replaced by the new people over the following 400 years.

The new people were linked to migrations over a few hundred years from what is now eastern Ukraine, from a group named the Yamnaya, bringing metal use, chariots and horse riding from the steppes into northern Europe. The cultures developed over time and spread across northern Europe with cultures in the Iberian Peninsula adopting Beaker pottery and culture and mixing into the northern groups. Thus, both invasion and culture change are true.

The male line signature type, R1b, once thought to be original to the first farmers in Europe, and so common in the west geneticists named it the 'Atlantic Model Haplotype', proved not to be. Ancient DNA shows that R1b did not occur in Europe before the Yamnaya cultural change. The Yamnaya may have brought the Indo-European languages but this is still under discussion.

Another surprise was the apparent crash in the existing population in Britain before the Beaker people arrived. A new analysis of some late Neolithic tooth plaque showed *Yersinia pestis*, the Black Death, so an epidemic may have swept away much of the existing population. The Yamnaya may have been more resistant or even brought the disease with them, much like European colonists bringing new diseases to the native Americans with devastating results.

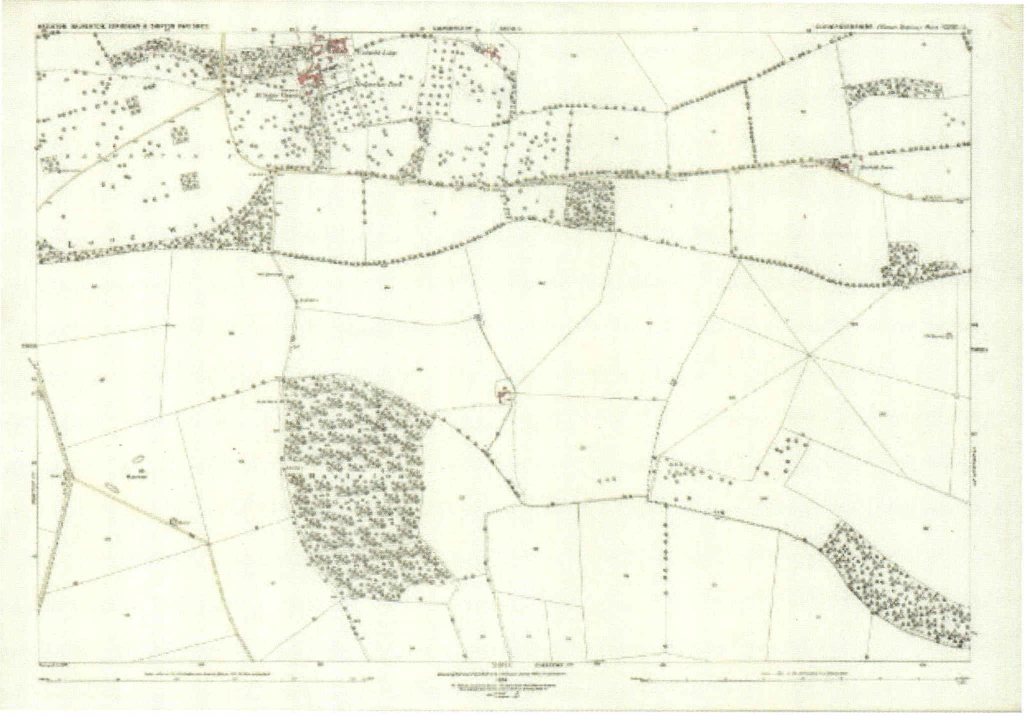

A map of Gloucestershire from the late 1800s showing the location of the Hazleton Long Barrow. DNA now reveals that this is the burial site of one man, his four wives and their children, children's partners and grandchildren. Explore a Zoomable version of the map at https://maps.nls.uk/view/109725091

The Neolithic, the New Stone Age, the First Farmers (4000 BCE – 2500 BCE)

The first people to bring farming to Britain and Ireland arrived about 4000 BCE, 6,000 years ago. Farming had been invented in a number of places around the world but ours came from the Middle East where it began at least 10,000 years ago, spreading across Europe over the millennia. Again, the ancient DNA shows that there was invasion with almost no descents from the earlier hunter-gatherer Mesolithic people.

These new people were the first to leave existing monuments in our landscape, Stonehenge and other henges, stone rows and the huge burial monuments, long barrows and chamber tombs.

Neolithic family burial insights

Archaeologists have long wondered if the tombs which held many burials (where still untouched until modern times) were tombs of the whole community, an elite, or one kindred. Ancient DNA is starting to answer these questions, showing why keeping materials in museums is an excellent idea. The Hazleton long barrow in Gloucestershire, excavated in 1979-82, held 35 burials. The DNA now shows that there was a one man with four wives and their children and grandchildren with others the partners of the children. Each wife and her descendants were in a separate area of the tomb. In this case, an elite single family were provided with this huge monument, in use for only about a hundred years from 3700 to 3600 BCE.

Evidence of incest

Another study, of chamber tombs in Ireland, from 3900 to 2500 BCE, showed smaller, simpler tombs did not contain related people between different sites. The major tombs, far apart, did have related male burials, two in Sligo, and one each in Meath and Down, strongly suggesting a powerful elite. Most interesting is the New Grange burial, about 3200 BCE of the man in the most special position just to the side of the passage end, by the carved stones where the mid-winter sun hits.

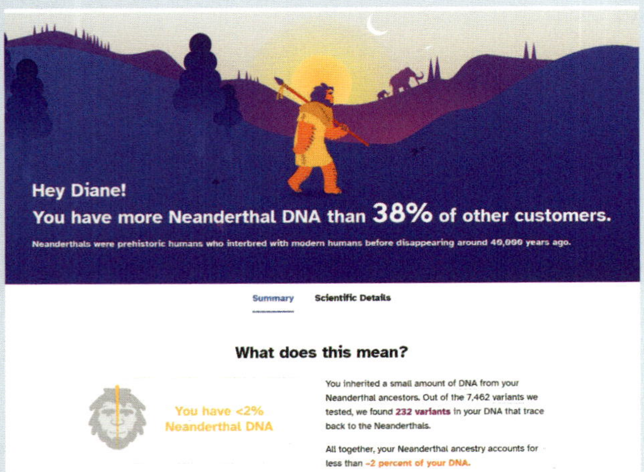

23andMe give customers insights to their Neanderthal DNA

LivingDNA share information about early populations, such as 'Viking' results...

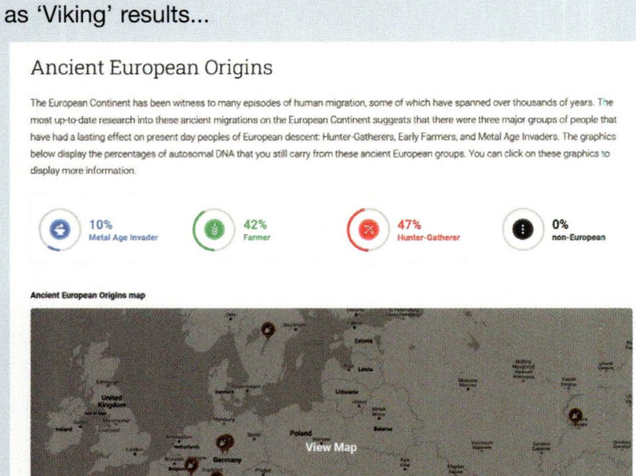

FamilyTreeDNA provide clues about ancient origins, and information about paternal line and maternal line haplogroup information

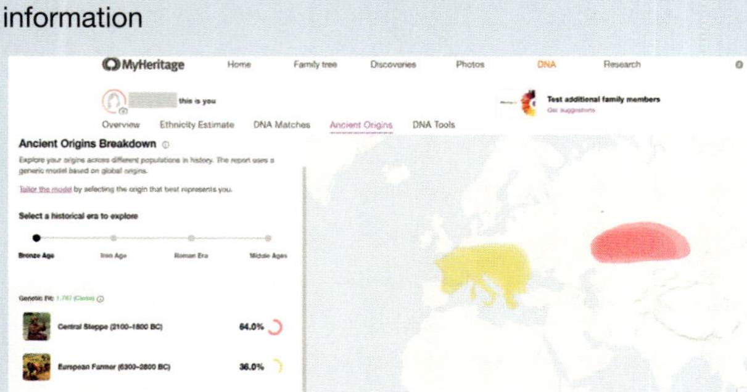

MyHeritage also provide Ancient Origins insights too

His DNA showed he was the product of incest; parent-child or brother-sister. This is usual only in royal elites such as the Pharaohs and Hawaiian royalty. Three ancient Irish stories refer to incest in royal families and events involving Newgrange. It is hard to believe this is continuous tradition but I would love to think Irish ancient 'history', treated as mythology, has some basis in fact.

Mesolithic, the Middle Stone Age (9700 BCE – 4000 BCE)

Cheddar Man, dated to the Mesolithic, about 8000 BCE, was the first and much publicised ancient DNA study in Britain in 1997.

New research shows he was not in a group providing much current British ancestry. Early studies used only mitochondrial DNA (MtDNA), the easiest to get good samples from. Now improved techniques mean ancient samples can include autosomal analyses as well. Cheddar Man had light eyes and dark skin, and was lactose intolerant, a pattern being found in other Mesolithic Europeans of the same period.

Palaeolithic, the Old Stone Age (before 9700 BCE)

Britain was uninhabited during several of the coldest phases of the last Ice Ages with occasional visitors in warmer times, hence we only have continuous occupation from about 9000 BCE. Before that we must look to Europe for our ancestors. A study of ancient DNA from 35,000 to 5,000 years ago, from many different groups, showed change over time in groups and migrations. These are the cave painters, reindeer and woolly mammoth hunters – now knowable as our ancestors.

Neanderthals

We are now in the realm of 'a really long time ago'. Modern humans arrived in Europe about 45,000 years ago.

At this time, the Neanderthal people were still living in Europe where they had been established for about 400,000 years. The Neanderthals were not stupid or stooped. They probably spoke but whether it was fully conceptual language we do not know. They had culture, tools, and some basic art.

Archaeologists again wanted to know how closely related they were to us, and if we mixed with them at any point. Svante Pääbo and his team answered these questions by developing techniques to study very ancient DNA. He was the first to work out Neanderthal DNA in 1997 and received a Nobel Prize. In 2010, he and his team identified the Denisovans as a separate early hominin group.

The Neanderthal answer turned out to be that Neanderthal genes do survive in us; there was mixing. It is thought about 20% of the Neanderthal genome survives in modern humans while any one individual has from 1 to 4% Neanderthal genes. Some Africans have some, many have none. If you have Neanderthal genes, you really are a European.

Denisovans

Denisovans are another ancient human type, only recognised from ancient DNA recently, from 2010. They have an eastern distribution, and overlapped with both Neanderthals and modern humans, all of whom mixed.

Finding your own ancient DNA matches

We can now find our ancestral links to these ancient people and migrations.

The male and female DNA

origin maps had already been established by studying modern DNA patterns but the location and dating of groups, as discussed above, has been revolutionised by ancient DNA studies. The good news is that some of the online genealogy services also offer ancient DNA comparisons. This is a fast-developing field and no doubt more options will be provided in future.

At present, 23&Me, LivingDNA, FamilyTreeDNA, and MyHeritage offer ancient DNA comparisons with your own DNA. Gedmatch also has Archaic DNA matching but takes uploads from other testing sites only. AncestryDNA and uploads to Geneanet DNA do not currently offer ancient DNA matching.

The presentation of results differs on each site.

23&Me

23&Me information is under the 'All Ancestry reports' menu option. It offers Neanderthal DNA comparison from autosomal DNA. Neanderthal genetics are shown as a percentage compared with other 23&Me customers and, a set of Neanderthal-linked traits with a chromosome map are included under 'Scientific Details'.

LivingDNA

LivingDNA offers several comparisons with your autosomal DNA results: Viking, Neanderthal, and now 'Classical' – ancient Roman, Greek and Egyptian results. The Viking result has an overview, results and map. The results are given as a percentage or scored circle chart and a map showing best match area or closest match ancient find as well as each section having historical background and scientific explanations.

Viking results are based on 446 ancient examples from across the Viking world including Britain and Ireland but also Scandinavia and eastern Europe.

The Classical results are also from a wide variety of samples for the ancient Roman and Greek worlds with scored results and showing your nearest match on a map; my Roman was buried in Yorkshire so may well have been a British person in the Roman period. My Greek was from Spain on the Mediterranean coast near the French border, so probably a Greek descendant or local person of the period. Egyptian results are only for the last 700 years BCE, not the ancient pyramid builders, and are not yet localised within the Nile valley as more samples are needed.

LivingDNA shows your Neanderthal descent as a circle chart, a percentage of your autosomal DNA and the nearest match amongst ancient burials, now with some traits and references as well. I am 1.8% Neanderthal, apparently.

Living DNA also offers Denisovan DNA comparison, under the Neanderthal menu heading. The results are, a bit confusingly, with percentiles compared with other groups around the world, by continent. My score is 0.23% Denisovan.

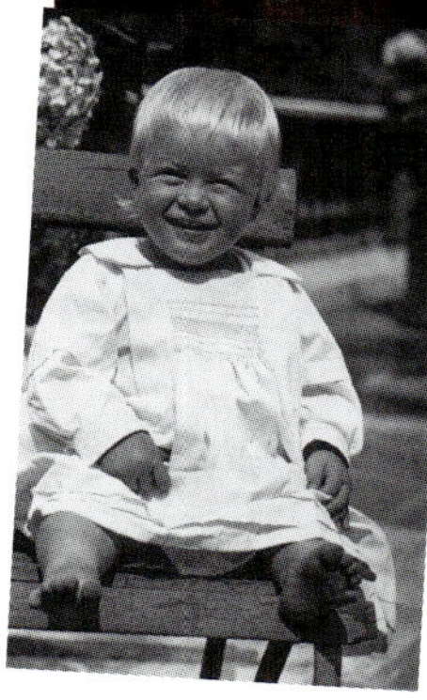

Nicholas II and children (with Cossacks of the Guard). Inset: Prince Philip in 1922. In 1991 genetic tests on the remains of what were thought to be the Romanov family were proved to be so by comparison with members of the living royal family, including Prince Philip

FamilyTreeDNA

FamilyTreeDNA, the most long-established genetic genealogy service, now offers the most complete matching with ancient European groups; Western Hunter Gatherers (WHG), Early European Farmers, (EEF), Metal Age Invaders (the Yamnaya), and Non-Europeans. The results are in the form of percentage circle charts and maps with linked migration routes and archaeological sites with explanatory text. These are shown under Ancient Origins on the Autosomal DNA results menu.

FamilyTreeDNA Y-DNA results provide more directly genealogical information.

Both Y-DNA and mtDNA results have migration maps for all migrations and any chosen haplogroup. Both also have a link to Public Haplotrees, linked from the Home Page. The mtDNA tools allow search by country of origin but not, of course, by surname.

The FamilyTreeDNA Y-DNA haplotree states 'Discover the countries of origin and surnames for each branch of the world's largest Y-DNA Haplotree. Currently, the tree includes

79,000 branches, 701,000 variants, and 303,000 SNP-tested users from our Y-DNA database.' Options include single surname search, which shows which haplotrees have the surname, so far amongst those tested. The surname report for each haplogroup lists all tested surnames associated with the group with the proviso that there must be at least two instances of the same spelling, not something we normally pay much attention to. Clearly this is a powerful link between the Y-DNA story back through time and present-day surnames. The FTDNA haplogroup information being made available to Family Finder testers will make for fascinating new discoveries for many.

[Turn to page 46 to learn more about haplotrees.]

MyHeritage

MyHeritage now provides information on Ancient Origins: 'View a percentage breakdown of your origins from ancient populations across different historical eras, from the Bronze Age to the Middle Ages.'

Gedmatch

Gedmatch is an upload site for detailed chromosome comparisons with other users and includes many tools. One of the free options is Archaic DNA Matches where single instances of ancient DNA have genetic maps compared with your own autosomal DNA. Many samples of different dates and places all the way back to Neanderthals and many ages in between are included and sometimes updated. I have scattered matches from Neolithic finds, the first farmers, but much more from Bronze Age Ireland, for example, which makes sense as I have much recent Irish ancestry.

All the humans

We are all part of this ancient story. Modern humans are now known to go back at least 300,000 years, the earliest fossil found to date, in Morocco. Neanderthals developed in Europe from earlier forms, about 400,000 years ago. The Denisovans, discovered in 2010, are another ancient group, living from about 500,000 to 50,000 years ago. We are all mixtures.

The Flores 'hobbits', discovered in 2003 are still mysterious as DNA does not preserve well in the tropics so their place on the human tree is still speculation. They survived until about 54,000 years ago but don't seem to have mixed with other humans.

And our friends, ancient DNA of animals & plants

Ancient DNA studies of animals and plants are well underway. An early dog from about 2500 BCE from an Orkney tomb was tested as well as an Irish Neolithic dog; both had very similar genetics to modern dogs. A quick internet search shows ancient DNA is being studied in cats, cows, horses, sheep, maize, wheat, barley, and no doubt others. These studies will illuminate further our history and migrations as well as theirs. And, within recent years, it is now possible to get an Ancestry DNA test for your dog!

The Future

New discoveries and studies are appearing regularly; keep Googling 'ancient DNA human'.

The prestige science journal, *Nature*, regularly features new studies where the abstracts are freely available online. Check also the ISOGG website and Facebook pages where these studies are noted and discussed. By the time this article is published no doubt there will be more new and exciting discoveries. Our ancient family tree is getting ever more detailed.

Genealogical Traits

I was amused to note one of my Neanderthal Traits on 23&Me – 'You have one variant associated with having difficulty discarding rarely-used possessions.' I wasn't surprised – is this a trait shared by all genealogists!?

Find Out More

Books:

- *Who We Are and How We Got Here*, David Reich, Oxford University Press, 2018.
- *My European Family, the First 54,000 Years*, Karin Bojs, Bloomsbury Sigma, 2017.

Websites:

- Timeline of Prehistory - https://en.wikipedia.org/wiki/Timeline_of_prehistory
- Human DNA - https://en.wikipedia.org/wiki/Human_genetic_variation
- International Society of Genetic Genealogy - https://isogg.org/tree/

Tasting your DNA

West Midlands stand-up comedian Darren Harriott and *MasterChef* finalist Hasan Semay recently embarked on a unique DNA journey with the results being brought to life in an unusual way: through food.

Think of the your favourite meals and you're likely to pick an array of delicacies from around the world, ingredients that you first tasted whilst on holiday, on a business trip, perhaps, as well as those familiar comfort foods that are closer to home. This exciting melting pot of flavours neatly reflects the marvellous mishmash of heritage and culture that we explore via family history, and particularly with DNA. It's this celebration of diversity and connection that inspired 'DNA Kitchen'.

The pilot episode of the show, produced by Ancestry and available to view on YouTube, stars Darren Harriott, a regular on the British comedy circuit and TV shows like *Live at the Apollo,* as he discovers the results of his DNA test. But rather than simply log in to the website to see the results, Darren is treated to a culinary masterpiece from chef Hasan Semay (also known as 'Big Has'), who uses ingredients inspired by Darren's 'Ancestral Regions' results. He doesn't simply take a test, he tastes it. Then it's onto the London streets to see if the general public can identify the ingredients… and Darren's heritage.

Given just four days to come up with a menu based on the results, Has had no idea who he was catering for, but he rolled up his sleeves, put on his chef hat and started creating. 'I quite like the fact that we were given the chance to look at the DNA results, and then I got to do research and dive in and be like, "Oh, what can we mishmash, and where can we pull inspirations from?"' Hasan says.

The results gave the cook a mix of African ingredients (including Nigeria (48%), Mali (3%), and Ghana(13%)) alongside a subtle taste of England (3%), Scotland (1%) and Ireland (3%), and Has chose to base his recipe on jollof rice, a West African staple, adding in smoked haddock to create a delicious African-Scottish kedgeree. Who knew DNA results could taste so good?

The results of the test were not a huge surprise for Darren, but gave him a welcome sense of belonging. Growing up in the UK with Jamaican roots, he often faced questions about his background. 'They would always ask, "What's your African name?"' Darren explains with his trademark smile, 'and I'd respond, "It's Darren!"'

'I'd always known there was a possibility my Caribbean heritage could have links to other parts of the world, but to finally have a clear snapshot of where, has given me a true understanding of who I am.'

When Darren tasted the meal, he was struck by how accurately it represented his heritage, even if his culinary preferences often lean toward Jamaican. 'I was hoping for something strongly Jamaican,' he admits, 'but the

African influences made perfect sense. I loved the inclusion of rice – it's my favourite food in the world! It felt very much like me. My DNA was on that plate.'

One of the highlights of the episode is the public's reaction to the meals, as strangers recognise flavours and ingredients from their own cultural backgrounds. 'To see people enjoy it made all the effort worthwhile,' says Hasan. 'It was almost like they were eating a part of me!' Darren laughs.

Hasan was rightfully pleased with the creation. 'To cook jollof for the first time and get it right, I was quite proud of myself,' he says. 'Food is something that we hold so closely, with dear love, and I didn't want anyone to be like, "Oh, why have you made this?" Or "Why have you done that?" What I wanted to do was celebrate the differences, celebrate migration, and celebrate people being able to live and stay wherever they wanted.'

But the experience also gave Hasan the chance to discover his roots. Born to a Turkish Cypriot father and a white British mother, Hasan grew up immersed in multicultural influences. 'I wanted to know if we stemmed from Greek or Turkish descent, given Cyprus's divided history,' he explains.

But Hasan's DNA results were much more diverse, spanning regions from the Balkans to Turkey, Greece, and even parts of Africa. These findings connected Hasan's culinary instincts to his ancestry. 'My love for tomatoes, olive oil, and onions... it all makes sense now,' he says. 'I wouldn't say finding my results makes me look at the world any differently, but it is something I feel like I'd bring up over a couple of pints every now and again, like at a dinner party, I'd be like, "Oh, by the way, I'm 2% African. Therefore, I can cook jollof properly."'

For Darren the project highlighted the obvious intrigue and rewards of exploring your DNA. 'To see where my dad's family came from and how strong those genes are with me, it made me feel emotional,' Darren says. 'My family are strong Jamaicans, but they were really impressed. My auntie did her DNA test, and it came back nearly the same as mine, heavy Nigerian. It's nice to know where my dad's family comes from and how strong those genes are.'

The experience reinforced the idea that food is more than sustenance; it's part of our history and identity, a medium for storytelling and connection. 'There's always something about food that's a talking point,' Hasan says. 'Whether it's an argument among uncles or a celebration among aunties, food brings people together in a way nothing else can.'

The pilot episode has proved popular online and with the obvious connections between DNA results and the world's food, it has every chance of coming back to our screens. 'I'd love to do this again,' Has says. 'There's this whole topic of food that's not spoken about, and it's about migration, it's about celebration, it's about identity – all those little things that make breaking bread with people that much more enjoyable.'

Interview: Karen Evans
Additional words: Matt Hill

More about DNA Kitchen

The pilot features Young MasterChef Judge and Chef, Hasan Semay and British stand-up comedian, Darren Harriott. Having grown up only knowing of his Caribbean heritage, Hasan sets Darren the challenge of sourcing ingredients in London's Tooting Market to unveil his culinary heritage and the true intricacies of his DNA. Looking for clues and making guesses along the way, Darren's DNA results offer interesting discoveries and open his taste buds to fresh flavours and dishes, through the creativity of Hasan's imaginative cooking skills.

Watch Karen's full interview with Darren and Hasan at: www.youtube.com/@familytreeplus

Family Tree

Helping you discover your family story

JOIN TODAY!

DNA Discoveries is brought to you by the team behind Family Tree; our mission is simple, we want to help you discover your family story.

No doubt you agree, family history plays such an important part in our lives, and we want to give you all the information and inspiration you need to continually improve your research. And we want it to be fun too!

These simple goals inform everything we do, from our magazine to the masterclasses, courses, workbooks, podcast, webinars, and our online membership Family Tree Plus.

As reading habits and technology continue to evolve, we've introduced new ways to help you on your family history adventure, as detailed here. So whether you prefer paper or digital, or like both, there's a membership option to suit you.

Continue learning, get support and advice from experts and fellow researchers, and find more of those family stories. We can't wait to help you!

OPTION ONE

Online membership and magazine archive

Family Tree Plus

Join Family Tree Plus, read the magazine digitally and also enjoy monthly webinars, on-demand videos, and more…

- ✓ **Live monthly webinars (worth £40/month)**
- ✓ **Over 100 hours of on-demand video**
- ✓ **Searchable archive of *Family Tree* magazine**
- ✓ **Every new issue added to the digital library**
- ✓ **Exclusive discounts on masterclasses, workbooks & more**
- ✓ **Your members-only newsletter, filled with expert tips**

SPECIAL OFFER!

WORLDWIDE
JUST £5 FOR YOUR FIRST TWO MONTHS

THEN £9.99/month

DNA and DIPLOMACY

Professional genetic genealogist, **Laura House**, explains how to communicate effectively with DNA matches and prospective test-takers

One of the biggest differences between traditional and genetic genealogy is the extent to which genetic genealogists negotiate relationships between living people. Some of those relationships are extraordinarily distant; Y-DNA studies span centuries, connecting tenth, twentieth, thirtieth cousins, and beyond. Sometimes, however, we navigate relationships as close as parent and child.

Whether you are a professional researcher or using DNA to enhance your own family tree, you will face sensitive conversations requiring your best diplomatic and communication skills. These include contacting DNA matches for information about their family or reaching out to potential relatives for the purposes of targeted DNA testing.

AncestryDNA is mentioned a couple of times in this article, but many of these strategies are applicable to any testing company.

When to contact a DNA match

Direct-to-consumer DNA tests provide you with a list of every person in the database with whom you share a meaningful amount of DNA. These are your 'DNA matches,' and we use matches to: support documentary research; extend our genetic family tree; and identify misattributed parentage.

However, this is only possible if we know our relationship to the match.

You can determine your relationship to a DNA match by examining your shared matches and their family trees.

On the other hand, if your matches have private, limited, or no online trees, you might need to ask them for more information.

Before you contact a match, you should research their ancestors yourself, as this may be quicker and easier than waiting for them to respond to your message. Even if your match has no tree, there are steps you can take to figure out who they are.

1. Check their profile for identifying information

Almost all the DNA testing companies have user profiles. AncestryDNA's user profiles can include the test-taker's name, their age, where they live, their research interests, and the names of their online trees. You might find that this is enough for you to identify them and begin researching their pedigree.

2. Enter their name or username into a search engine

You might find your match's name or username is associated with multiple online platforms. Use closed quotes to ensure you only get results for that exact username (for example, "Funnigenie04" or "Jane Smith" rather than Funnigenie04 or Jane Smith). Sometimes the username forms part of their email address (for example, 'funnigenie04@email.com').

3. Find them in civil records indexes

Search for your match in the births and deaths indexes for their country. Indexes for the UK and Ireland are available across Ancestry, ScotlandsPeople and Irishgenealogy.ie, among many other useful websites. Search the marriage index for a person with the match's forename marrying someone with the match's surname to discover whether they might be going by their married name.

4. Take screenshots!

People can be fickle and unpredictable, and they might block you after you contact them, even if they have no apparent reason to do so. They can also delete their DNA data and profile information from the database, so before you contact a match be sure to preserve anything that could be useful for your future family history research.

Before you contact a match, you should research their ancestors yourself, as this may be quicker and easier than waiting for them to respond to your message

After these steps...

If you complete these steps and still need more information about your DNA match, it's time to make contact.

How to contact a DNA match

Be friendly & respectful

Keep your tone friendly, light-hearted, and respectful. Address your match by their name or username and make your message personal so they don't think you're sending 'copy-and-paste' communications to everyone on your list.

If you want your match to go to the effort of answering your questions, you will also need to invest time and energy into the conversation.

Be patient

Many DNA test-takers wait months or even years to reply to a message, but if you send frequent follow-up messages and demands for information, the recipient could feel hassled, which might make them less likely to reply. Wait as long as you can before sending a follow-up message.

Ask broad, open questions

One common error is asking matches closed questions, like: "Do you have ancestors with the surname Jones?" There are two problems with this approach. Firstly, the match can just reply, "No," and then you've learned nothing useful about them or their family. Secondly, even if they tell you about their Jones ancestors, this only gives you information about one branch of their family. You might actually be related to the match via different (or multiple) ancestral lines, and you have no way of knowing without more information.

Consider asking open questions, like, "Can you share any information with me about your parents or grandparents so I can figure out how we might be related?". The response to this question will give you the

information you need to build their complete tree, allowing you to:

- identify the match
- reduce the risk of confirmation bias
- and increase your chances of discovering all your recent common ancestors.

Asking someone to take a DNA test

Advanced genetic genealogy projects often require multiple sets of DNA results to support the research and conclusions. Much of the guidance outlined above applies here, but there are additional factors to consider when you ask someone to test for your genetic genealogy project.

Ensure the tester is making an informed decision

First and foremost, you must ensure the potential test-taker can make an informed decision to participate. When you contact them, outline your project and how their DNA results will help you achieve your goal, so they fully understand the importance of their contribution. If they feel important and well-informed, they will be more motivated to help.

Reassure the tester about privacy concerns

People are often anxious about privacy, so reassure them that they will have full access to and control over their results. They can anonymise, privatise, or delete their DNA data. Explain how the results could benefit them, especially if they are interested in family history. This could revolutionise their research!

If you can, offer to pay for the test

You might feel reluctant to pay for the test, but if you offer to do so from the outset, your potential test-taker will be far more likely to participate. People love a freebie! Don't sabotage your chances of getting that crucial data by putting the potential test-taker under financial pressure.

Plan for unexpected discoveries

Finally, explain that the test could reveal unknown genetic relatives, and that when you review the results, you might find that they are unrelated to their documented family. Ask them how they feel about this, and if they want you to tell them about any such findings. This ensures that you are both prepared for any outcome, and you can enjoy making exciting discoveries with confidence.

Making connections with a DNA match can be rewarding, but you should always approach with caution; their enthusiasm and curiosity might not match yours

Not every communication will be a success – be kind to yourself

These are complex conversations, and you are often dealing with complete strangers, which makes the communication unpredictable. If you follow this advice, your messages, emails, and letters will be polite, open, and ethical, but that does not guarantee success. Many of your requests will go unread, unanswered, or unfulfilled, and this lack of response can be frustrating, and at times, devastating. I hope that this guidance will help you to avoid some of the most common pitfalls, giving your genetic genealogy projects the best chance of success, and allowing your newly discovered family relationships to flourish.

YOUR DNA GOAL & who to test

The two topics of deciding on 'your DNA goal' and deciding 'who to test' are very closely intertwined, so let's look at them together to help you make the most of your DNA testing experience…

What is your DNA goal?

DNA testing is more popular than ever, but what you get out of it can vary greatly from person to person. Like any family history research, you'll benefit most if you start with a clear goal in mind. Taking a moment to define what you're hoping to discover will keep your efforts focused – and help you make real progress. So why do you want to take a DNA test?

We look at 'why take a test' on pages 6 and 7 of this guide. Yet it's a useful question to ask yourself when it comes to setting your DNA goal.

So, why do you want to take a DNA test?

- Have you been doing family history research for years, and you're feeling that you're missing out?
- Perhaps you'd like to take a DNA test to see what insights it can add to your family history research?
- Maybe you'd like DNA to verify your document-based findings?
- It could be that you've been gifted a DNA test, and are now wondering how to proceed.
- Perhaps you have a family mystery you'd like to resolve?
- Maybe you're seeking a close relative (a parent, grandparent, sibling, half-sibling, for instance) and feel that DNA can help you find them?
- Possibly you would just like to give yourself the challenge of learning about DNA for family history as you think it will be interesting.

Like any family history research, you'll benefit most if you start with a clear goal in mind. Take a moment to define what you're hoping to discover

Whatever your reason, each is a valid motivation for considering a DNA test.

Maybe you have a very specific goal in mind – such as seeking a close relative (as mentioned above), or perhaps you have a brickwall relating to a particular ancestor or branch of your tree, and you're wondering whether DNA may be able to provide new clues.

Whatever your reason for taking a test, it will help to focus your DNA goal. This will mean that when you are working on your DNA test results, rather than feeling a little overwhelmed and wondering where to begin, you will have your goal at the forefront of your mind, and so will be able to use your research time more effectively.

Who's best to test?

Leading on from setting your goal is the question of who's best to test. Testing yourself is clearly an idea that appeals to many of us. But, depending on the nature of the research question you wish to answer (your goal), it may be that a person other than yourself makes the best test candidate.

Since only males inherit the Y-chromosome from their fathers, Y-DNA testing can only be done by men. If you are not a direct male descendant of the paternal line you're researching, you'll need to identify a male relative from that line and ask them to take the test on your behalf.

Similarly with mtDNA testing, if you are curious about the genetic inheritance on a direct maternal line, then you will need to choose a relevant person. As both males and females inherit mitochondrial DNA from their mothers, you may be the eligible person to take the test.

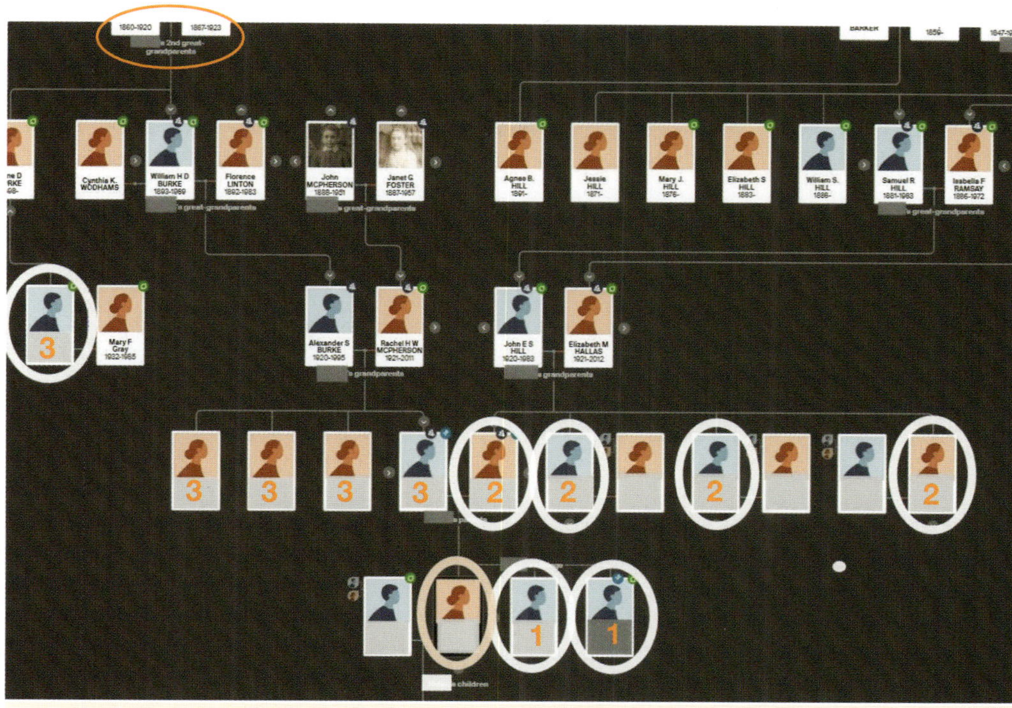

CASE STUDY

Let's think about who's best to test. In this instance, imagine that you are the person circled in pink and are female.

1 If you wished to learn about your direct paternal line, and presuming that your father had passed away, then, in this instance, your two brothers would be the best people to take a Y-DNA test for you. (In this instance, your father had only sisters – so you don't have a paternal uncle, who is that one generation closer to the ancestors, to ask to test).

2 If you wished to learn about your direct maternal line, here you could ask your mother or your maternal aunt to test, and, as males inherit mtDNA too, you could ask either of your maternal uncles to test.

3 Imagine you are interested in researching your paternal grandfather's paternal branch (ie the couple you can just see in the top left-hand section of this family tree, circled in orange), then there are a few people who could help you.

Your father (if not deceased) and your three paternal aunts would all be useful candidates to test, taking an autosomal DNA test – in addition, so would your first cousin twice removed.

That 'twice removed' is crucial here as he is two generations older than you, and one generation older than your father and aunts. While you will only share in the region of 221 centiMorgans with your first cousin twice removed (see **https://dnapainter.com/tools/sharedcmv4**), your first cousin twice removed will have a significant proportion of your paternal line 2x great-grandparents' DNA. For instance, you will only have inherited roughly 6.25% of each of your 2x great-grandparent's DNA. However, that couple (your 2x great-grandparents) are your first cousin twice removed's grandparents – so that person will have inherited roughly 25% of each of their grandparent's DNA.

Use the Shared centiMorgan Project tool, in the url above, to explore how much DNA you are likely to share with your relatives.

When it comes to autosomal testing (ie the mainstream DNA tests from Ancestry, MyHeritage, 23andMe, LivingDNA and the Family Finder test from FamilyTreeDNA) then it can be very helpful to test the older members of the family. This is particularly the case if these older relatives are on a branch of your family tree that you are especially keen to gain DNA clues about. Clearly, that older family member will only be shedding light on part of your tree (eg if they are on your paternal side, they will provide no DNA clues about your mother's side), but they will have inherited segments of your paternal (in this instance) ancestors' DNA that have not been passed down to you.

Is it the X-chromosome you're after? The X-chromosome has a unique inheritance pattern meaning that it can be extremely helpful in specific situations. Think back: males have an X and a Y chromosome, the Y inherited from their father and the X from their mother. When they pass on an X to their daughter it is unchanged from the X that they have inherited from their mother. (When a mother passes on an X to her daughter, that X is a mixture of the X she inherited from her father and the X she inherited from her mother).

Create your own X chart

Download a copy of genetic genealogist Blaine Bettinger's template X charts. Fill in the details with your ancestors' names, and see which lines are of most relevance.
https://bit.ly/dna-x-charts

To find X matches upload your DNA to FamilyTreeDNA or take a test directly with FamilyTreeDNA: www.familytreedna.com

Don't forget your siblings! While your siblings are in the same generation as you they can still provide additional clues to the ancestors' DNA as they will have inherited segments of DNA that you haven't, and vice versa.

Your DNA goal will help you decide who's best to test, so it's important to have a plan.

Where possible, test as many family members as you can, keeping an eye out for DNA test offers to make this more affordable. When inviting relatives to test, be sure to avoid any pressure and ensure they understand the potential outcomes, including the possibility of unexpected discoveries, such as previously unknown relationships.

Get more DNA advice with our free bitesize course. Sign up at: bit.ly/free-dna-course and we'll send you a series of emails to help you continue your learning

Top tips from the DNA DISCOVERIES EXPERTS

The DNA experts we are proud to feature in *DNA Discoveries* are authors, speakers, researchers and professional genealogists. Find out more about how they got into DNA and why they are so passionate about DNA research for family history with our mini interviews

Dr Sophie Kay

How did you first get in to DNA?

I remember being fascinated by the idea of DNA from the age of about six – but my first professional steps towards working with DNA happened when I was 22, when I got to extract and sequence my own DNA in a lab as part of my training as a research scientist (yes, we're talking white coats and lab specs – the lot!). Once you've done this first-hand, you're into a world of endless wonder.

What do you really enjoy about DNA?

DNA is gloriously versatile, but for me the human element is the most important. Genetic genealogy gives us a means of seeing how we're connected to one another, of finding lost relatives and birth families, and understanding how we each fit into the vast sweep of human history.

Can you recall a lightbulb moment, when using DNA?

So many – usually from working on unknown ancestor mysteries for private clients! The moment when you see how the puzzle pieces fit together and can identify the person you're looking for brings a feeling I'll never tire of.

What's your top tip you'd like to share, for people using DNA for family history?

We call it genetic genealogy for a reason – so the genetic evidence of how much DNA you share with your matches, who matches with whom and on which DNA segments, should always sit at the heart of your arguments for identifying an unknown ancestor. Tree-building for your matches is a vital skill, but don't let the distraction of names and places override what the DNA is telling you!

Tell us about the DNA education activities you're involved in

DNA teaching is fun for the discussion it prompts! Right now I'm busy writing two brand-new distance-learning qualifications in genetic genealogy for the Institute of Heraldic and Genealogical Studies (IHGS, **www.ihgs.ac.uk**), where I'm the specialist tutor in DNA. They're called the Intermediate and Advanced Certificates in DNA and Genetic Genealogy and will open to students later in 2025. I also have a blog, The Parchment Rustler (**www.parchmentrustler.com**) where I write about family history research and how we can do it well – good research shouldn't ever be dull!

Tell us about any DNA projects or organisations that you're involved with

It's a delight to be the new Scientist in Residence for The Mixed Museum (**mixedmuseum.org.uk**), a digital space which curates and shares the histories of mixed-heritage people in Britain through the ages. I'm developing a range of genetic genealogy resources for them, to help people navigate DNA testing in search of recent unknown ancestors.

I'm also the 'Ancestry & Genealogy Expert' for popular archaeology show, *Time Team*, which lets me combine the joys of genetic analysis with traditional archival work in pursuit of the past.

Find out more about Sophie's research services at www.khronicle.co.uk

Diane Brook

How did you first get in to DNA?

I was fascinated by my ancestry from at least 11 years old and by archaeology, geology and palaeontology from about the same time. I was also a 'horsey' teenager and someone bought me a book on the evolution of the horse. One of the chapters featured the basics of Mendelian genetics illustrated by horse colour genetics. I was hooked. Then Dr Brian Sykes wrote his books and started Oxford Ancestors [now no longer trading] so I tested then and have carried on ever since.

What do you really enjoy about DNA?

Finding and linking new distant cousins and sorting our possible ancestors, and, the constant flow of new testers on the various testing platforms. I subscribe to most of them.

Can you recall a lightbulb moment, when using DNA?

When I realised there was a match on a brick wall line I had been working on for 40 years which broke through and gave me a whole new ancestry in a new county.

What's your top tip you'd like to share, for people using DNA for family history?

Don't forget, the person you need may test tomorrow – keep checking. And, the person who doesn't answer your message may just not be that interested, or ill, or worse. Be patient, and try another relative.

Tell us about the DNA education activities you're involved in

I have spoken about DNA off and on for decades. Before the modern tests, I did a talk called 'Does it run in the family?' on inherited traits. More recently I have given talks to Glamorgan Family History Society and the Guild of One Name Studies.

Tell us about any DNA projects or organisations that you're involved in

I have joined some FamilyTreeDNA projects. One is trying to find the British ancestor of Miles Morgan of early New England. I am descended from Miles, not on a male line, but am very interested in any results. Another is a much more recent brickwall of mine. I got my recently contacted third cousin, a male line descendant, found through DNA, to test and join the surname project. Result? He doesn't yet match anyone else! More patience required. I also belong to some genetic genealogy private Facebook groups which sometimes suggest matches and keep me up to date on developments.

Donna Rutherford

How did you first get into DNA?

I did my first DNA test in 2015 as I was really curious about this new 'technology' and started to teach myself about all things DNA.

What do you really enjoy about DNA?

It brings a new dimension to genealogy, a new source of evidence that is completely different to anything else we've had.

Can you recall a lightbulb moment?

Not really, it was quite a lot of learning to start with but I made a big notebook and kept adding questions I wanted to find answers to. Slowly I realised I was answering the questions not writing them anymore.

What's your top tip you'd like to share, for people using DNA for family history?

Spend your time on higher matches, even though we have less of them they are closer relatives and solving those matches will give high confidence evidence for your known tree. If you don't know your tree, for example if you have unknown parentage such as adoption, foundling, NPE, or surprise results, then the high confidence matches are going to help you solve your case.

Tell us about the DNA education activities you're involved in

I speak at a lot of events which I love, especially the in-person events. As well as that I'm working towards freeing up some time to create more YouTube content. I'm very interested in streaming which would allow people to join me live and ask questions in the chat. Watch this space! Making DNA complex topics easy to understand is something I'm very passionate about.

Tell us about any DNA projects or organisations that you're involved with

I belong to Society of Genealogists organisations both in the UK and New Zealand. As well as that I like to work closely with chosen genetic genealogists to share ideas, discuss preferred methodologies and generally stay abreast of any new tools and features that get rolled out.

In addition, I'm very involved in using AI (Artificial Intelligence) for genealogy (including presenting on this topic). I'm currently working on using AI for DNA research – looking at how this evolving technology can help us work smarter and faster with our genealogical and DNA research. Exciting times!

Find out more about Donna's family history and specialisms at www.donnarutherford.com

Karen Evans

How did you first get in to DNA?

My paternal grandfather was illegitimate and I really wanted to identify his father. I'd been dithering about buying a test and when I saw a special offer for a FamilyTreeDNA test at a genealogical show I decided to take the leap.

What do you really enjoy about DNA?

There are so many things! I love the excitement of new matches or when a DNA tool is released – I couldn't sleep the day Ancestry Pro Tools landed! It's amazing when I work out how a match fits into my tree (especially when the answer isn't obvious) or when I 'solve' a puzzle for someone. Meeting new cousins and sharing stories and ephemera is lovely. There is a real sense of satisfaction to know that every match I find validates the tree I've spent decades on.

Can you recall a lightbulb moment, when using DNA?

I can! I'd been staring at my results for a month or so and really scratching my head. One evening I chose a match with a fairly unusual name and started creating a tree for her (I didn't know that was called a 'quick and dirty' tree then) After about an hour, I spotted a link to my family, I couldn't believe it!

What's your top tip you'd like to share, for people using DNA for family history?

Take time to understand what your match list means and be prepared to do a lot of genealogy in the shape of quick and dirty trees.

Tell us about the DNA education activities you're involved in

I have several talks which I present to groups and societies. These can be beginners' talks or delving into a specific area of DNA. I also love my involvement with DNA club [**www.family-tree.co.uk/membership**], there is always something new.

Find out more about Karen's interests & talks: www.publicspeakerscorner.co.uk/karen-evans

Michelle Leonard

How did you first get in to DNA?

I first got into DNA back in 2009 through my work on the ground-breaking Fromelles Genealogy Project. I spent several years tracking down appropriate DNA donors to help identify WWI soldiers buried in a mass grave in Northern France. I had never really thought of myself as a 'science' person, but I threw myself into learning how the different types of DNA worked and became completely fascinated. That foundation gave me a huge head start when DNA testing took off in the genealogy world – I was excited by the possibilities and ready to dive in thanks to Fromelles!

What do you really enjoy about DNA?

I enjoy the mystery-solving aspect the most! I think that's why I like the term 'DNA detective' as it perfectly describes what I do. I love nothing better than working on a fresh set of DNA results, immersing myself in an unknown ancestor mystery and being able to piece together the genetic jigsaw puzzle. Every case is different, and the thrill of discovery never gets old!

Can you recall a lightbulb moment, when using DNA?

There have been so many that it's hard to pick just one! A major moment came early on after I received my first autosomal DNA results when I proactively built out the tree of a DNA match, identified our connection, and it dawned on me that I could try to do this over and over again with so many other matches! That was the moment it truly clicked that DNA could be the key to breaking through my own brick walls. That first success set me on the path to making DNA a core part of my genealogy work.

What's your top tip you'd like to share, for people using DNA for family history?

Test your older generation relatives whenever you can! They carry more of your ancestors' DNA than you do, so their results are incredibly valuable for identifying connections and unlocking family mysteries. Once their DNA is gone, so is that opportunity – so don't wait!

Tell us about the DNA education activities you're involved in

I create and teach a range of DNA courses and webinars throughout the year for family history organisations worldwide, including Family Tree Plus (DNA Club), Family Tree, Family History Academy, Legacy Family Tree Webinars, and more.

Tell us about any DNA projects or organisations that you're involved with (either as a member or admin)

I'm an FTDNA project admin, though in more of a backseat role at the moment due to other commitments. I'd love to dedicate more time to it in the future, as these projects can be incredibly valuable for genetic genealogy research.

Find out more about Michelle's forthcoming talks at www.facebook.com/genesandgenealogy

Laura House

How did you first get into DNA?

I started researching my own family history in 2011, while I was doing my bachelor's degree. DNA testing was fairly new in the UK at that time, and I tested my relatives as soon as I realised it was becoming a useful resource for people with British and European heritage. I first tested my two surviving grandparents and my parents, and then my extended family. Four years later, I began my postgrad in genealogical studies, and then I specialised in genetic genealogy.

What do you really enjoy about DNA?

I've worked on hundreds of unknown parentage cases, and every one is different. Each case is as fascinating as the last, and there is no such thing as a boring set of DNA results. On top of this is the knowledge that the answer to the client's question is somewhere in those results, if I just put the pieces together in the right way. There is nothing more exciting than that.

Can you recall a lightbulb moment, when using DNA?

Hundreds! But the biggest moment was when I compared the DNA of my great-aunt to the DNA of my mother and her siblings and realised they had a half-relationship. That's when I discovered my grandmother was conceived outside her parents' marriage.

What's your top tip you'd like to share, for people using DNA for family history?

Education is so important. Everyone makes mistakes when they start researching their family, but the stakes are much higher with DNA. Take courses and workshops, read books, articles, and blogs, and apply everything you learn to your research.

Tell us about the DNA education activities you're involved in

I've written many articles, and I always have a presentation, workshop, or public speaking gig on the go somewhere, many of which are recorded and can be found online. I've also just started a TikTok series on Ancestry's channel called Epic Genetics with Laura. Check it out!

Tell us about any DNA projects or organisations that you're involved with (either as a member or admin)

I run the Weddige Y-DNA project at FamilyTreeDNA. 'Weddige' is my patrilineal surname, and it's an unusual one, so if you know any Weddiges then I'd be grateful if you could send them my way.

Find out more about Laura's specialisms at www.qualifiedgenealogists.org/profiles/house

John Cleary

How did you first get in to DNA?

Someone suggested I take a Y-67 test many years ago as I was interested in surname history. I was sceptical then, but the results were fascinating, and since then I have done all the tests.

What do you really enjoy about DNA?

Solving mysteries and puzzles over how people are related.

Can you recall a lightbulb moment, when using DNA?

The release of the original WATO calculator back around 2017, showing how we could crack mysteries by crunching results from multiple DNA tests together.

What's your top tip you'd like to share, for people using DNA for family history?

Always have a particular family mystery you want to solve, and use all the evidence you can, like documentary research and family knowledge, alongside the DNA tests you do.

Tell us about the DNA education activities you're involved in

I have just been working with the other authors on the new edition of *DNA – A Guide for Family Historians*, published by Pen & Sword.

Tell us about any DNA projects or organisations that you're involved with

I am involved in surname projects for my own surname (in its Irish form) Ó Cléirigh, Kemp (my mother's surname), and Cummings – partly because I have been researching the history of the Scottish Comyn and Cumming families. I also assist with the big geographical Scottish DNA Project, and I advise a US-based lineage society for the descendants of an English Puritan-era settler, Isaac Cummings, on their DNA research.

Find out more about John Cleary's specialisms at www.qualifiedgenealogists.org/profiles/cleary and at https://researchportal.hw.ac.uk/en/persons/john-cleary

Martin McDowell

How did you first get in to DNA?

I did my own test in 2012 in an effort to get back beyond the 1800 brickwall that lots of us have in Ireland. I couldn't believe how helpful this proved to be!

What do you really enjoy about DNA?

It gives you the evidence that you haven't been spending hours tracing the wrong people. The ultimate satisfaction is in proving your tree is correct when it coincides with your genealogical research. For me its both about getting that level of proof and pushing the boundaries of known lines as far as I can.

Can you recall a lightbulb moment, when using DNA?

Lots of them! One in particular stands out; I found a book on Family Search that was written about 100 years ago and gave some information on a Taggart family located in Donegore in County Antrim. This gave information back into the 1500s which is very unusual for a farming family in Ireland. Whilst at first sceptical about its content, I investigated further and started to extend the branches of the tree in the book down towards the present day. I then found it led into different surnames and that many of my DNA matches were descended from these lines showing this was indeed the Taggart family I also descend from. It has helped me prove a new source which has extended my line dramatically and given me information I couldn't have got any other way.

What's your top tip you'd like to share, for people using DNA for family history?

My top tip is to use all types of DNA. It isn't enough to just use autosomal DNA as other types of DNA (Y, MT and X) can prove evidence from a different perspective that can either prove your theory or totally refute it. If you don't do these tests you'll never know what you may have missed!

Tell us about the DNA education activities you're involved in...

I am chairperson of the North of Ireland Family History Society and we run courses on DNA throughout the year. Our most popular event is our annual DNA Summer School in late August each year via zoom. This is suitable for people of all skill levels, all talks are recorded and we cover all types of DNA. We also have a YouTube channel here: **www.youtube.com/@dnaatnifhs/videos**

Tell us about any DNA projects or organisations that you're involved in...

I am DNA officer for the Federation of Family History Societies and am very keen to help people use DNA properly. As well as doing more testing we need to ensure that people have the ability to interpret their results correctly and make the right conclusions. As part of this I want to see people test more widely in their own communities and approach DNA testing geographically. By testing more people in an area where people have lived for generations you can find connections no-one knew about and uncover lost family links.

Find out more about Martin's role as DNA Officer at the Federation: www.familyhistoryfederation.com/whos-who

ABOUT THE AUTHORS

Dr Diane Brook grew up fascinated by her grandfather's family history of her Smith family and started seriously researching her own, her husband's (and almost anybody else's) family tree more than 40 years ago. She is a founder member of what is now the Glamorgan Family History Society and has written, taught and spoken on the subject for decades. On the academic side, she has a PhD in early medieval archaeology.

Associate professor **John Cleary** is speaker and writer on using DNA in ancestral research based in Scotland, and is a contributing author to the very popular book published by Pen & Sword *Tracing Your Ancestors Using DNA: A Guide For Family Historians*. He has presented on genetic genealogy at events in the UK, Ireland and the USA including Genetic Genealogy Ireland, Family Tree Live and seminars for the Guild of One Name Studies. He is involved with a number of Y DNA surname projects including the names Cummings, Kemp and Ó Cléirigh.

Karen Evans is a long-time family historian and in recent years she has enlisted DNA to help her work on, and solve, some of her family mysteries. Karen Evans is DNA advisor to *Family Tree* magazine, in which she writes a monthly DNA advice column featuring step-by-step advice and reader case studies. Karen is also the DNA Club news anchor and host at the monthly DNA Club meetings provided to members of Family Tree Plus.

Laura House has an MSc. degree in Genealogical, Palaeographic and Heraldic Studies from the University of Strathclyde. Her specialisms are genetic genealogy and unknown parentage, and she writes articles and delivers talks on the subject of DNA testing for genealogy. She appears on BBC Three's 'Stranger in My Family' (2023), SBS's 'Every Family Has a Secret,' and ITV's 'The Queen and Her Cousins with Alexander Armstrong' (2021). Her research is showcased on many TV shows, including 'Who Do You Think You Are?', 'DNA Journey', and 'Coronation Street's DNA Secrets,' and she has been interviewed about her work on television and radio. Laura is a spokesperson for Ancestry and is the primary genetic genealogist on AncestryProGenealogists's International team.

From DNA to historical maps, from research methods to historical occupations, **Dr. Sophie Kay** is a professional genealogist and geneticist at Khronicle who loves all manner of family history research challenges. She's the Ancestry and Genealogy Expert for popular archaeology show, 'Time Team', and the specialist DNA Tutor for the Institute of Heraldic and Genealogical Studies, where she leads their Certificate qualifications in genetic genealogy. She's a Member of AGRA, a UK organisation of professional genealogists, and also specialises in research methodology and historical maps. Sophie's family history blog can be found at The Parchment Rustler, where she shares tips, tricks and strategies for making the most of your ancestral research journey.

Michelle Leonard of Genes & Genealogy is a Scottish professional genealogist and DNA detective. She specialises in solving adoption and all manner of unknown ancestor mysteries using DNA but also undertakes traditional genealogical research, living-relative tracing, historical and television research, tutoring, webinars and speaking engagements. She is also known for her work identifying WWI soldiers especially with The Fromelles Genealogy Project. She is a regular speaker at major international genealogy events and is also one of the co-authors of *Tracing Your Ancestors Using DNA: A Guide For Family Historians*, and author of *The DNA Bootcamp Workbook*, which accompanies Michelle's 8-week online DNA Bootcamp course.

Martin McDowell is the Education Officer of the North of Ireland Family History Society and DNA Officer on the Executive Committee of the Family History Federation. He started family history at primary school and has found DNA an essential tool in proving the connections within his family tree.

Donna Rutherford is a New Zealander with English, Scottish and Irish ancestry. Many of her family were New Zealand pioneers. Donna is co-owner and admin of a DNA facebook group where they help people with questions about their own results. She is also co-admin in a Y DNA project (the Rutherford project). She specialises in trying to make the complex side of DNA testing easy to understand for people who are new to genetic genealogy.

DNA Discoveries image credits: P4-5 Person in academic clothing © thenort/AdobeStock; P6-7 DNA helix tree © alex/AdobeStock; P8-9 Images credited on the page; P10-19 Testing companies attributed on the page; P21-27 graphics created by Dr Sophie Kay; P28-32 Testing companies attributed on the page; P34-35 Person in academic clothing © thenort/AdobeStock; P36-38 Testing companies attributed on the page; P40-44 Main image ©max_776/AdobeStock; Testing companies attributed on the page; P46-47 Main image published under the Creative Commons licence 3.0; Testing companies attributed on the page; P48-52 Main image © JR-50/AdobeStock; P56-60 graphics created by John Cleary; P61-66 Main image © Botahry Dex/AdobeStock, closing image © peshkova/AdobeStock; P67-71 Images referred to in the copy; P72-78 All over corded beaker CC BY-SA 4.0 National Museum Scotland, Newgrange tumulus chamber, cross-section, Wakemans Book of Irish Antiquities 1903 public domain, map of Gloucestershire SSVIII 13 Surveyed 1883 published 1884 Hazleton Long Barrows CC BY reproduced with permission of the National Library of Scotland, Nicholas II and children with Cossacks of the Guard, cropped Romanov Collection, General Collection, Beinecke Rare Book and Manuscript Library, Yale University; P84-86 Main image © New Africa/AdobeStock; closing image © Rido/AdobeStock; P88-90 Main image © Valentyna/AdobeStock.

DNA DISCOVERIES GLOSSARY

As you'll have seen throughout this guide, when it comes to using DNA for family history, you're likely to come across many new ideas and terms. Master the jargon and get quick facts with our helpful glossary

2 PER CENT Our 20,000-25,000 genes represent only 2% of our DNA; the other 98% of our DNA is non-coding.

22 This is the number of autosomes we have (chromosomes 1 to 22). We each also typically have a pair of sex chromosomes (XY for men; XX for females). Kinefelter's is an example of an intersex syndrome in which the person has 3 sex chromosomes (rather than a pair) – ie XXY – and usually has the male phenotype.

37 the number of individual genes contained within mtDNA.

46 The number of chromosomes humans typically have per cell, in 23 pairs. Genetic variations include, for instance, people with Down's Syndrome who have 47 chromosomes per cell – as they have an additional copy of chromosome 21 (ie they have not just a pair of chromosome 21s, but 3 copies of chromosome 21).

16,568 The number of base pairs in mtDNA.

25,000 The number of genes a human has. Our genes code instructions for our body.

46.7 MILLION The number of base pairs that chromosome 21 consists of. Chromosomes vary in size, varying in the number of base pairs and number of genes they each contain. Chromosome 21 is the smallest (smaller than chromosome 22).

600,00-700,000 The number of DNA markers that are tested when you take an autosomal DNA test. Each marker is the location of an SNP (pronounced 'snip', this stands for Single Nucleotide Polymorphism). Each marker is the location of a single letter difference (see more on the letters, ATGC, under 'Base pairs' below).

AUTOSOMAL SHARING STATISTICS You will 100% match your second cousins. There is a 90% chance that you will match your third cousins (with whom you share 2 x great-grandparents). There is a roughly 50% chance that you will match with fourth cousins (with whom you share 3rd great-grandparents). There is a tiny chance you will match 6th cousins. Thus from a family history DNA perspective it is well worth researching as many of your 3 x great-grandparents and their descendants as you can.

BASE PAIRS There are four chemical building blocks known as nucleotides: adenine A, thymine T, guanine G, and cytosine C. These pair up to form base pairs. Adenine (A) pairs with thymine (T) to form a base pair. Cyanine (C) and guanine (G) pair with one another. The pairs are found on the rungs of the DNA helix ladder. A large pair of chromosomes, e.g. your pair of chromosomes number 1, has the most base pairs. (Chromosome 1 has 249 million base pairs).

CENTIMORGAN A unit of measurement for a DNA segment. The greater number of shared cM between two test takers, the more likely they are to be closely related, particularly if the segments are longer. In some instances two test takers may match each other with a large number of shared cM, but have no large segment – such a situation could be indicative of endogamy for instance. The number of cM shared between two test takers provides information using which a number of possible relationships may be identified. As the only exact sharing of DNA is between parents and children, then all other relationships are defined in a range of cMs shared and percentages.

CHAIN OF CUSTODY The steps taken to ensure that a DNA test hasn't been contaminated – particularly important when using DNA for police investigations.

CHROMOSOMES DNA wound up with proteins. Chromosomes contain varying numbers of base pairs and varying numbers of genes.

ENDOGAMY Endogamy is when groups of people marry within the same circles. It is not just one-off cousin marriage, but marriage choices that permeate the whole circle. Endogamy will have significant implications on the predicted amount of DNA you will share with relations. i.e. you will share much higher DNA than you might expect.

HALF COUSIN Shares one grandparent with you, rather than a pair of grandparents.

IBC Identical By Chance, also termed 'false segments' or 'frankensegments'! Often identified in the context of a DNA match with whom you share a very small amount of DNA.

IMPUTATION When the raw autosomal DNA test results are transferred from one DNA testing company and uploaded to another, imputation may be employed. This is to enable comparison between tests from different testing companies. Imputation can result in an inflated number of shared centiMorgans (cM) between matches.

MITOCHONDRIA Both eggs and sperm have mitochondria, but it is only the mother's that is passed on to her children, as the sperm contains much less, and on fertilisation of the egg the sperm mitochondria dies away. When you take an mtDNA test at FamilyTreeDNA, all 16,569 of the mtDNA base pairs are tested - i.e. this is a full sequence test of the entire mitochondria.

MONOSOMY The loss of one chromosome in a cell. For example, females with Turner syndrome have one X rather than a pair of X chromosomes.

PEDIGREE CHART A traditional family tree showing the direct lines of descent.

PEDIGREE COLLAPSE The situation in which there is intermarriage across branches of your family tree. This can mean, for instance, that you have 14 great-great-grandparents rather than the expected 16 – as one pair of your great-great-grandparents appears twice.

RUNS OF HOMOZYGOSITY Segments of DNA that are identical on your maternal and paternal chromosomes, and mean that your parents are related. This is possibly the case due to endogamy.

SECOND COUSINS Share one great-grandparental couple with you.

SNP Single Nucleotide Polymorphism. Pronounced 'snip'. When a new cell is replicated and an error occurs in the copying process, that error is called a snip. In a DNA test it is the SNPs that are tested. The SNPs are tested in autosomal testing. The SNPs are also a type of Y-DNA test, and they are particularly helpful for surname research and research over the past millennia due to the number of SNP markers that have been discovered.

STR Short Tandem Repeat. This sort of Y-DNA test is best for research focussed within the past 500 years.

TIMBER the Ancestry algorithm which tries to strip out Identical By Population segments of DNA and pile-up regions, so that the amount of DNA reported on as being shared with a DNA match is more helpful for genealogical DNA research.

W.G.S. Whole Genome Sequencing: analysis and reporting on your entire 3 billion base pairs. It is possible, but is much less popular among family historians as it is expensive.

X-DNA MATCHES A man will only need to look at six of his 32 x great-grandparents when examining his X matches. All his father's side, and his maternal grandfather's paternal line, can be ruled out. Women need to look at eight of their 32 3 x great-grandparents when trying to identify an X-DNA match. Currently only 23andMe and Family Tree DNA report on X-DNA and provide matches. Studying the X chromosome can reveal whether two women share the same father.